COUNTDOWN

PRESENTS

LORD HAVOK AND THE EXTREMISTS

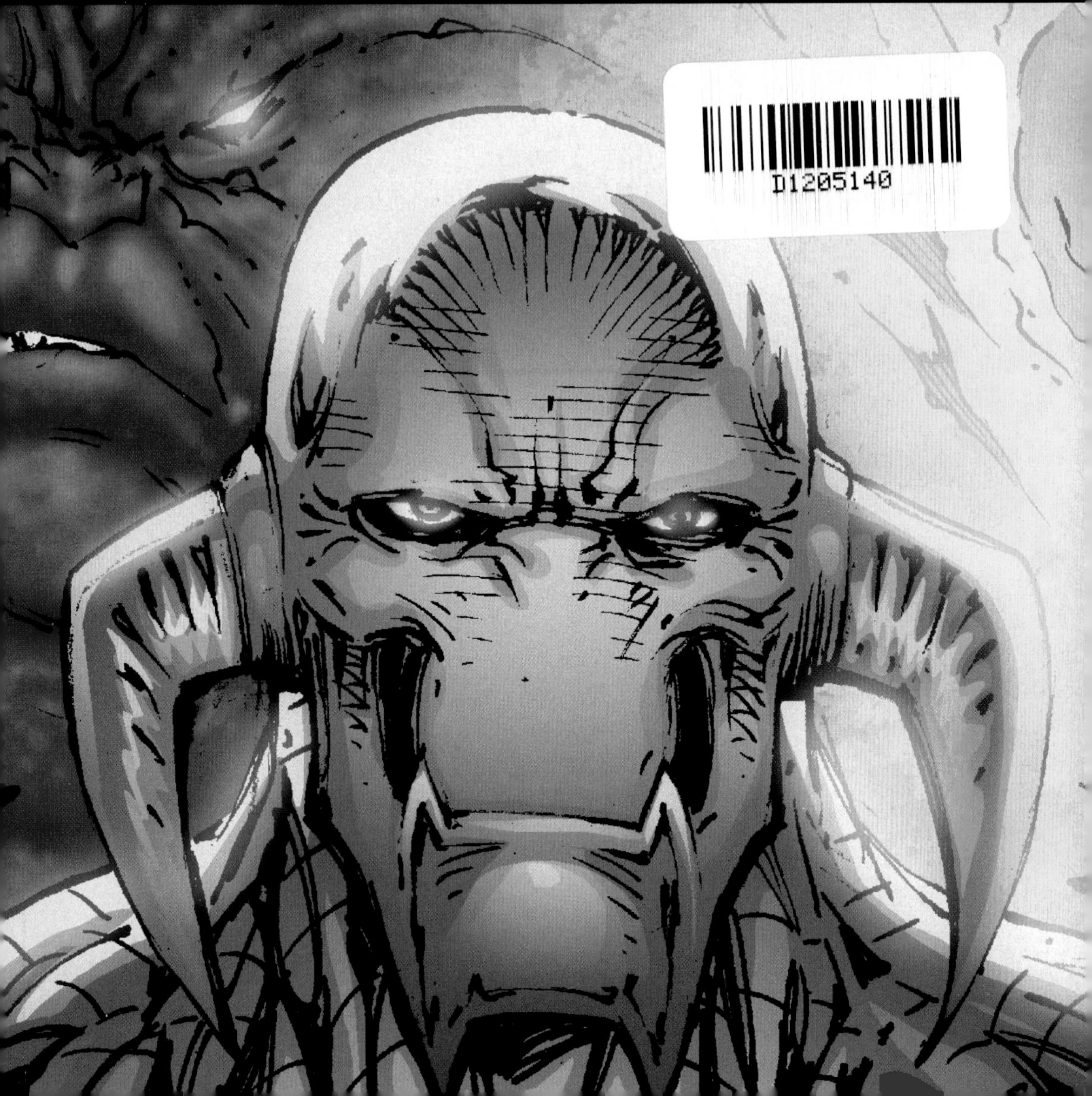

Frank Tieri
Writer

Liam Sharp
Mark Robinson
Pencillers

Rob Hunter
Mark McKenna
Mark Irwin
Mark Pennington
Sandu Florea
Liam Sharp
Inkers

Dave Baron
Kanila Tripp
Colorists

Pat Brosseau
John J. Hill
Rob Leigh
Swands
Travis Lanham
Letterers

COUNTDOWN PRESENTS

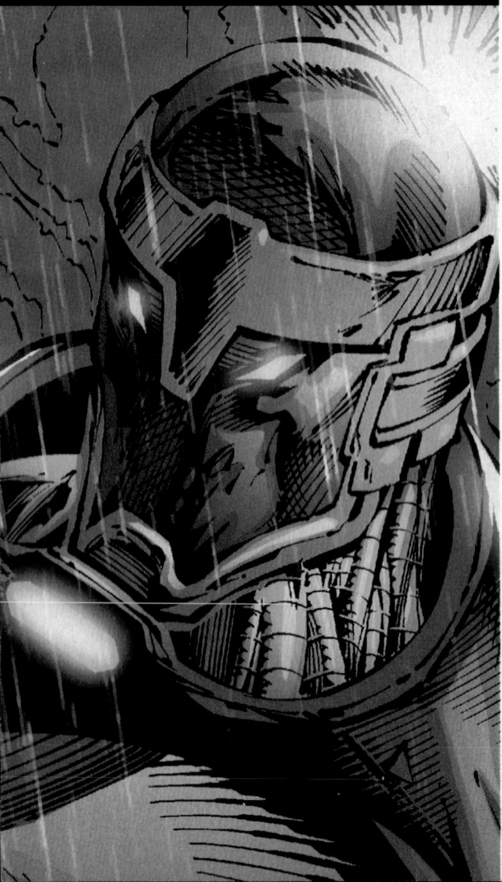

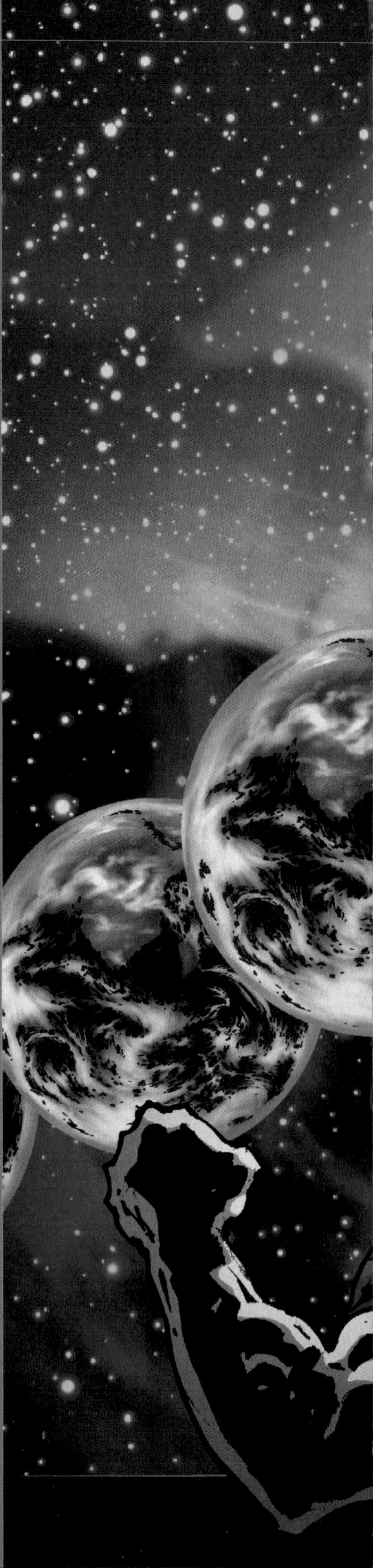

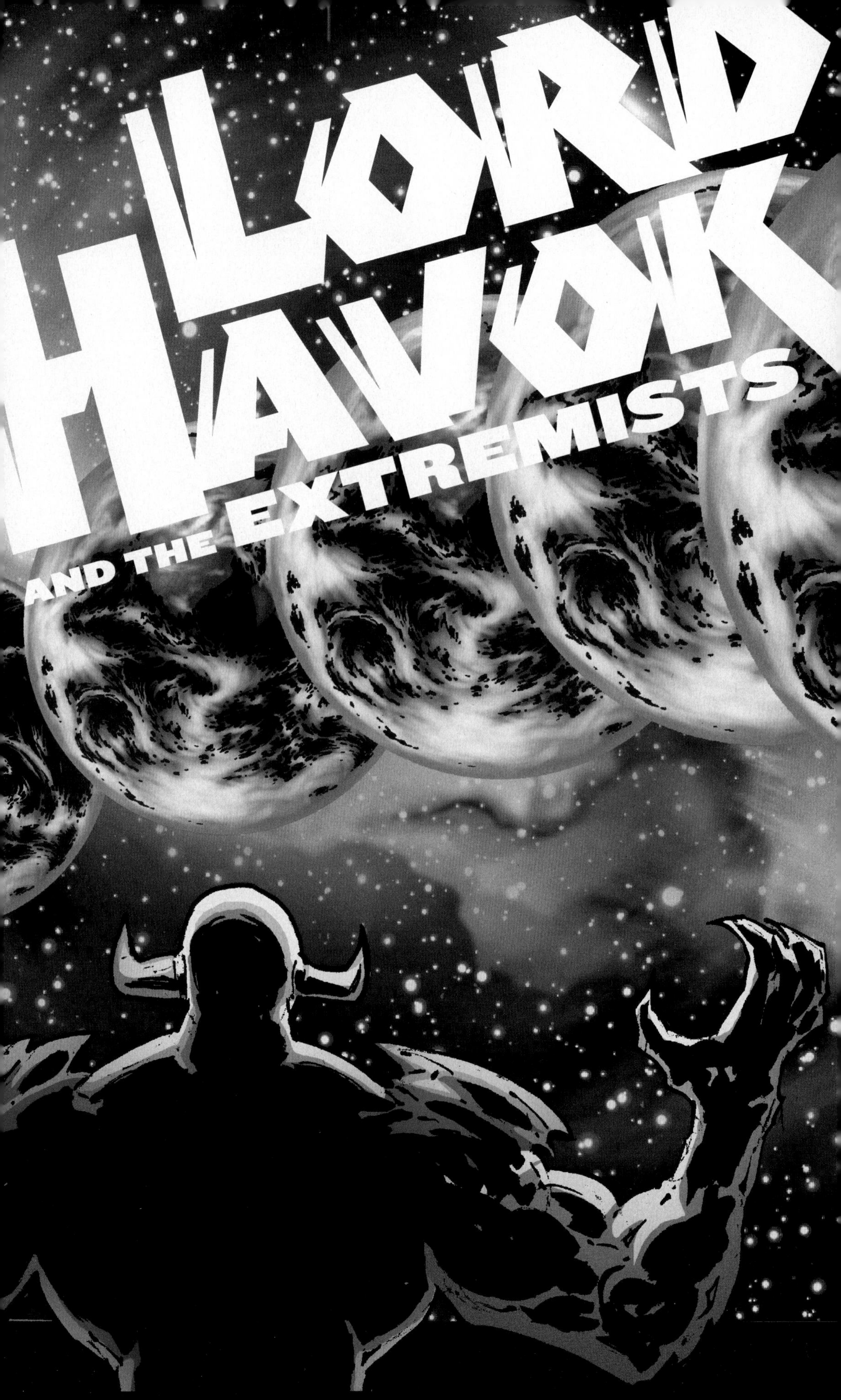
LORD HAVOK
AND THE EXTREMISTS

COUNTDOWN PRESENTS: LORD HAVOK AND THE EXTREMISTS
Published by DC Comics. Cover and compilation Copyright © 2008 DC
Comics. All Rights Reserved. Originally published in single magazine form
in COUNTDOWN PRESENTS: LORD HAVOK AND THE EXTREMISTS 1-6.
Copyright © 2007, 2008 DC Comics. All Rights Reserved. All characters,
their distinctive likenesses and related elements featured in this publica-
tion are trademarks of DC Comics. The stories, characters and incidents
featured in this publication are entirely fictional. DC Comics does not
read or accept unsolicited submissions of ideas, stories or artwork.
DC Comics, 1700 Broadway, New York, NY 10019
A Warner Bros. Entertainment Company
Printed in Canada. First Printing.
ISBN: 978-1-4012-1844-7

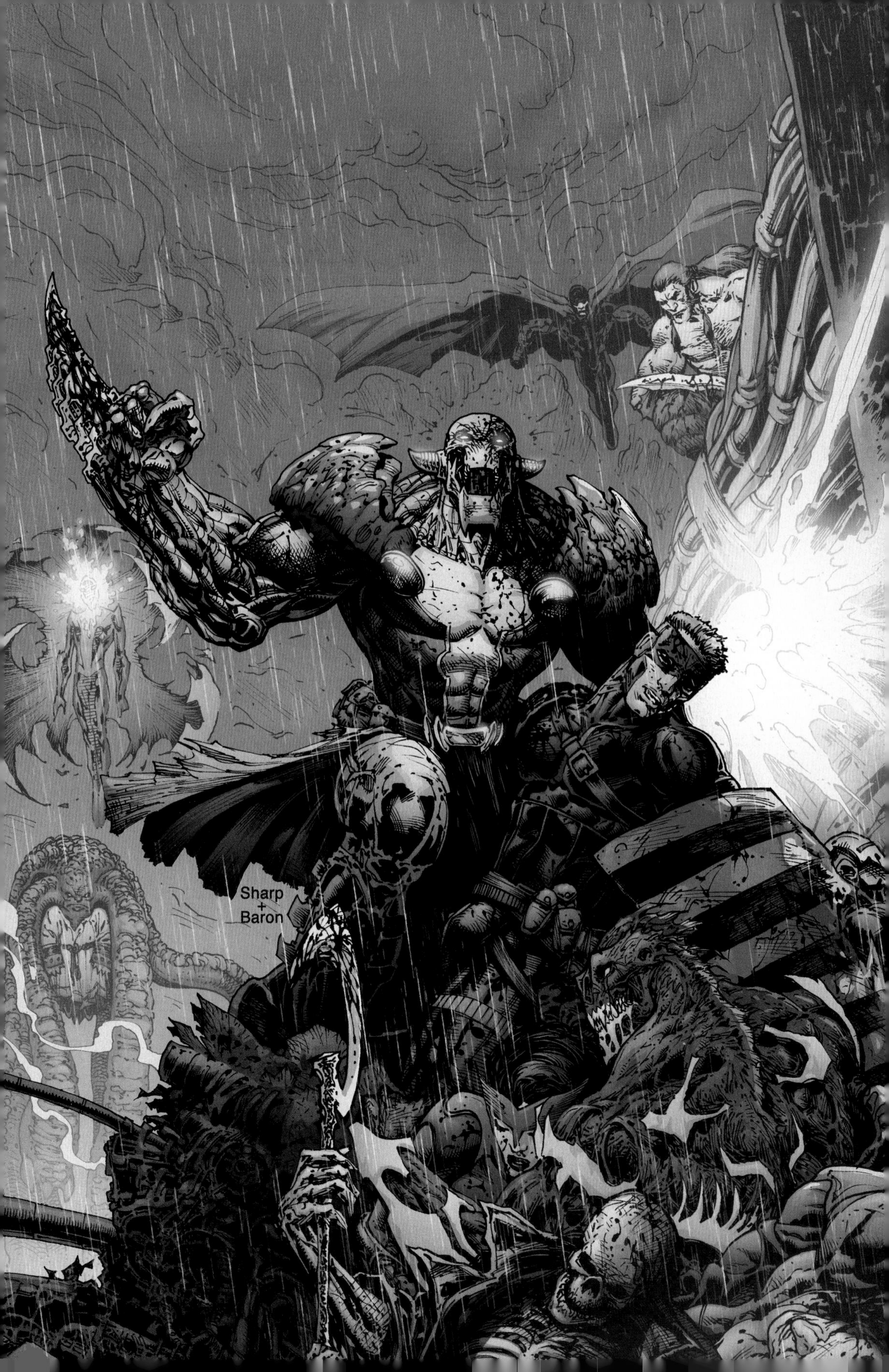
Sharp
+
Baron

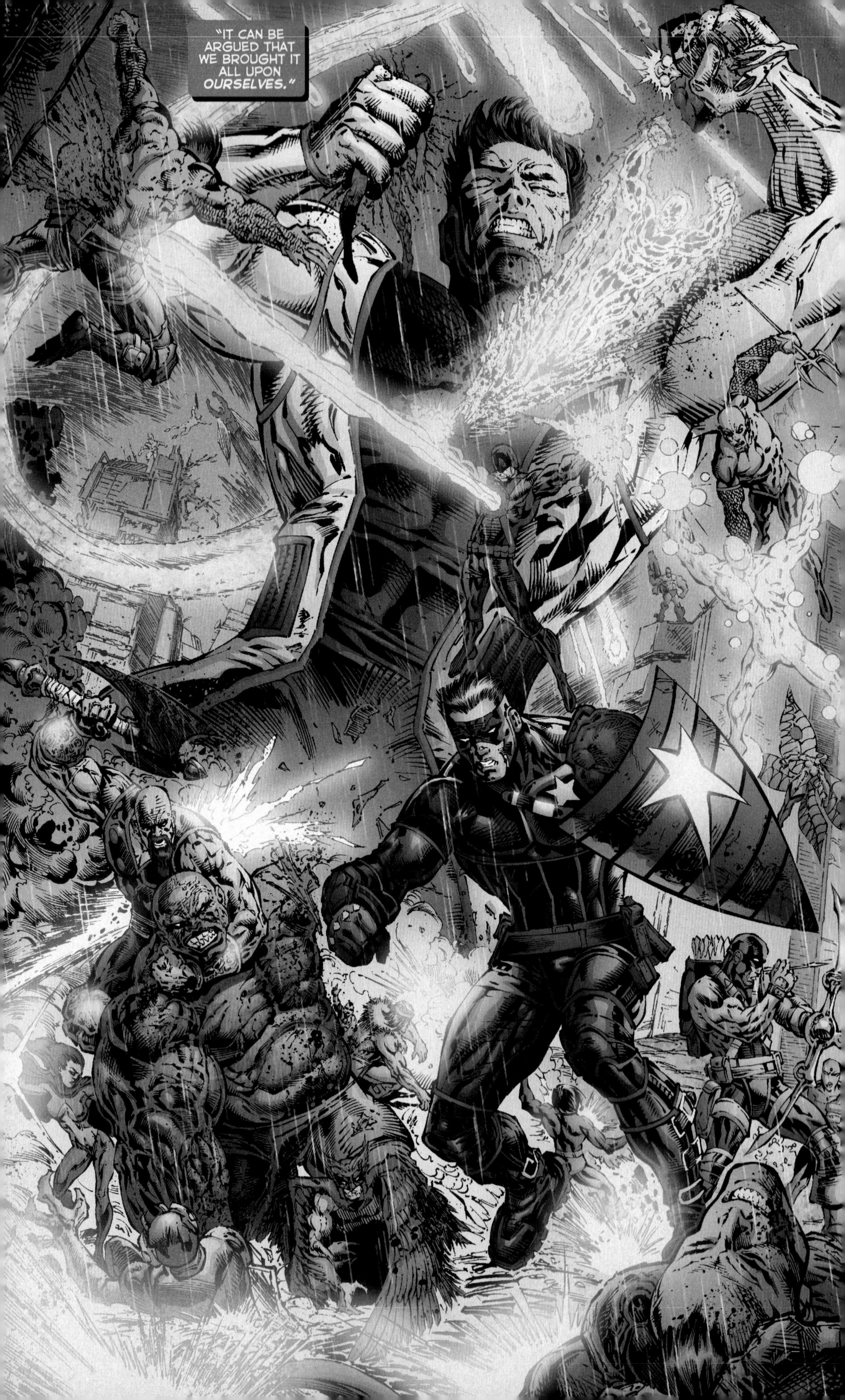
"IT CAN BE ARGUED THAT WE BROUGHT IT ALL UPON OURSELVES."

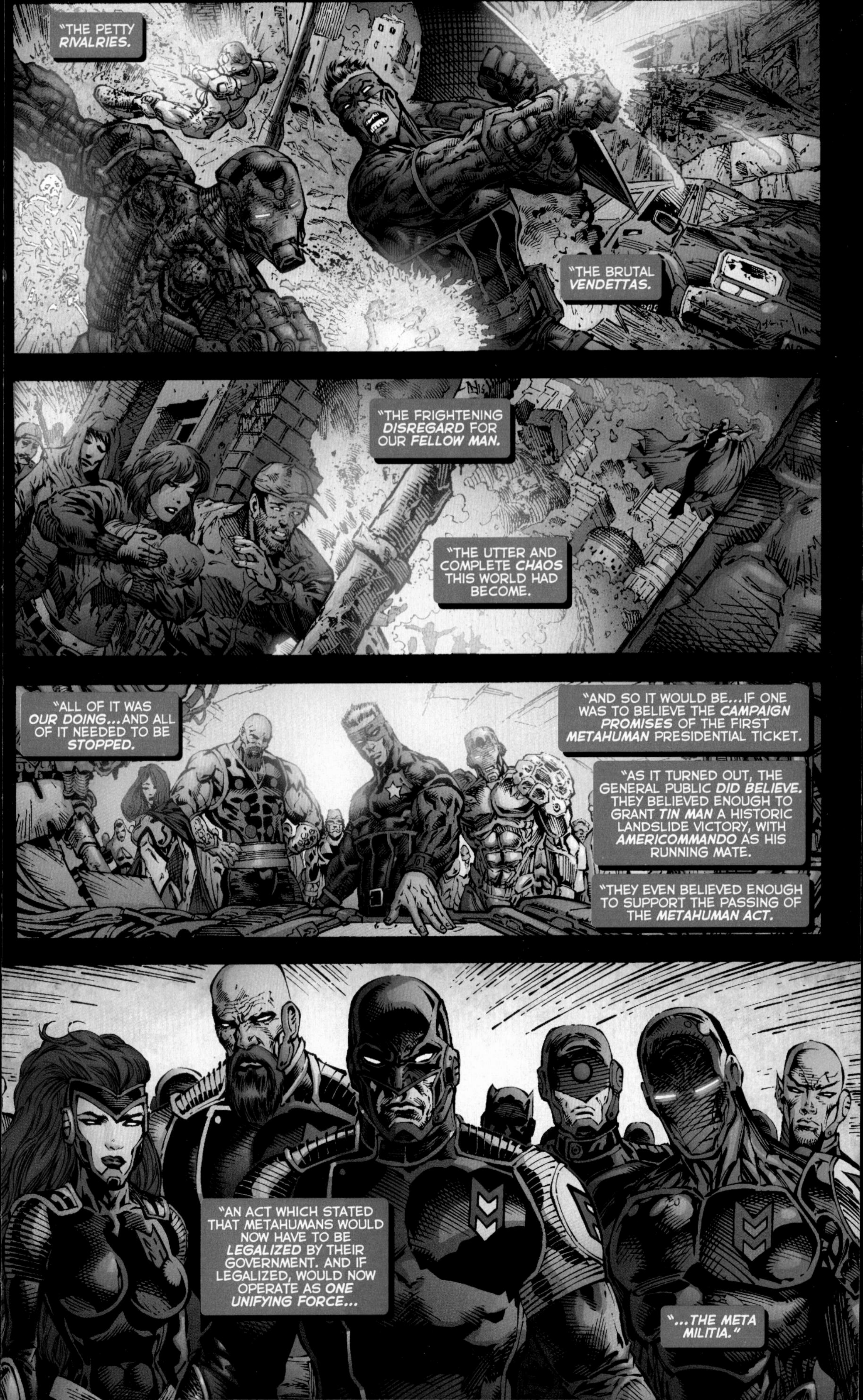
"THE PETTY RIVALRIES.
"THE BRUTAL VENDETTAS.
"THE FRIGHTENING DISREGARD FOR OUR FELLOW MAN.
"THE UTTER AND COMPLETE CHAOS THIS WORLD HAD BECOME.
"ALL OF IT WAS OUR DOING...AND ALL OF IT NEEDED TO BE STOPPED.
"AND SO IT WOULD BE...IF ONE WAS TO BELIEVE THE CAMPAIGN PROMISES OF THE FIRST METAHUMAN PRESIDENTIAL TICKET.
"AS IT TURNED OUT, THE GENERAL PUBLIC DID BELIEVE. THEY BELIEVED ENOUGH TO GRANT TIN MAN A HISTORIC LANDSLIDE VICTORY, WITH AMERICOMMANDO AS HIS RUNNING MATE.
"THEY EVEN BELIEVED ENOUGH TO SUPPORT THE PASSING OF THE METAHUMAN ACT.
"AN ACT WHICH STATED THAT METAHUMANS WOULD NOW HAVE TO BE LEGALIZED BY THEIR GOVERNMENT. AND IF LEGALIZED, WOULD NOW OPERATE AS ONE UNIFYING FORCE...
"...THE META MILITIA."

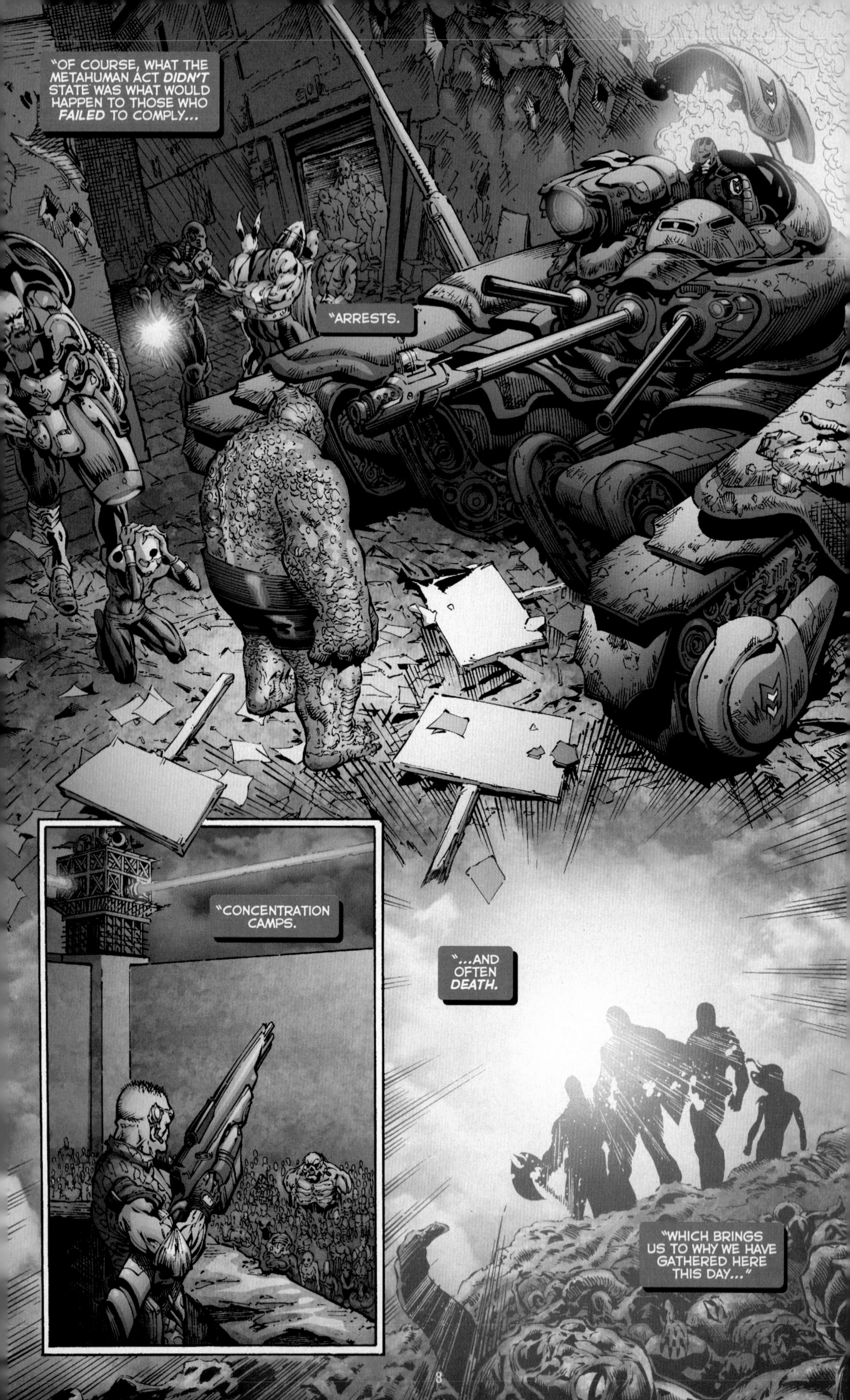
"OF COURSE, WHAT THE METAHUMAN ACT DIDN'T STATE WAS WHAT WOULD HAPPEN TO THOSE WHO FAILED TO COMPLY...
"ARRESTS.
"CONCENTRATION CAMPS.
"...AND OFTEN DEATH.
"WHICH BRINGS US TO WHY WE HAVE GATHERED HERE THIS DAY..."

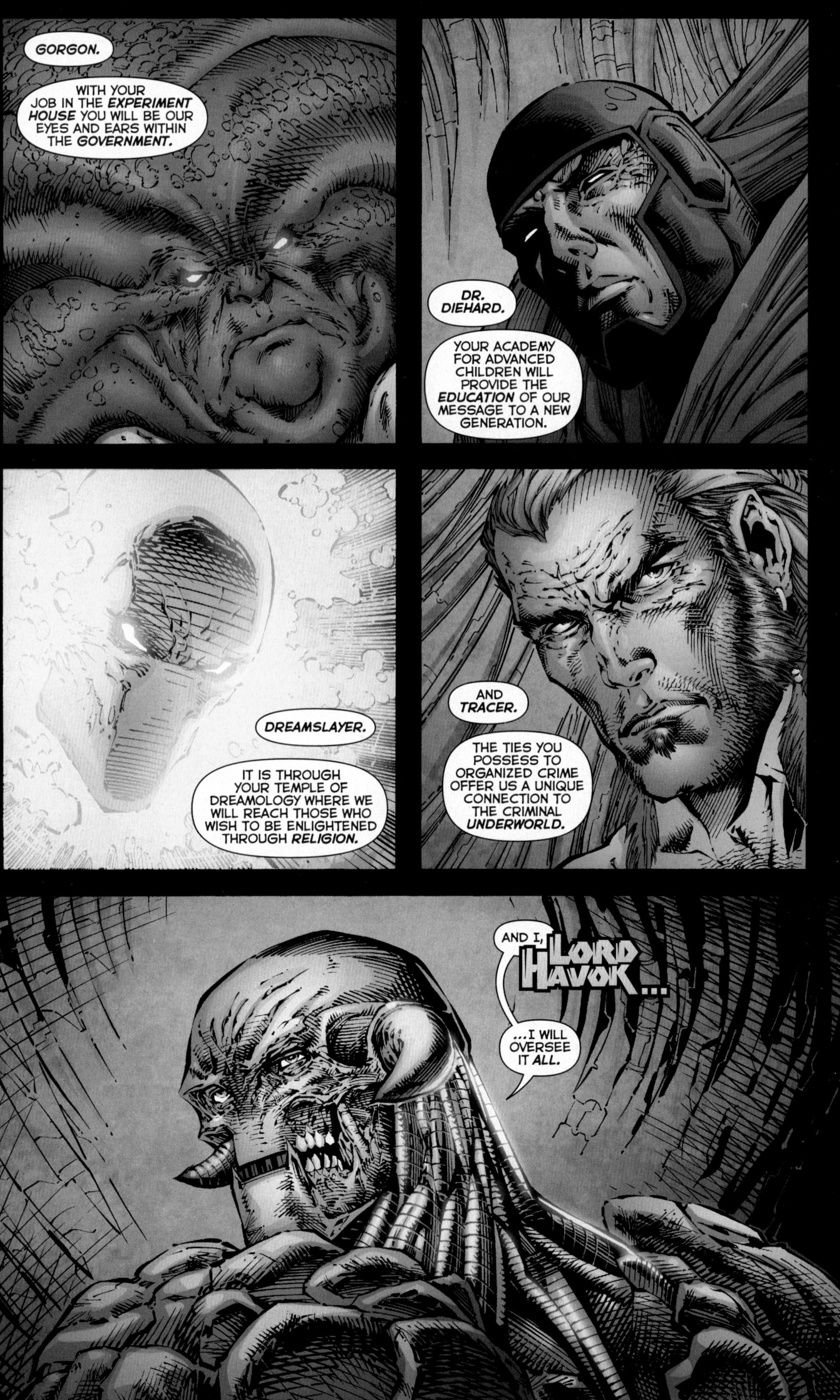
GORGON.
WITH YOUR JOB IN THE EXPERIMENT HOUSE YOU WILL BE OUR EYES AND EARS WITHIN THE GOVERNMENT.
DR. DIEHARD.
YOUR ACADEMY FOR ADVANCED CHILDREN WILL PROVIDE THE EDUCATION OF OUR MESSAGE TO A NEW GENERATION.
DREAMSLAYER.
IT IS THROUGH YOUR TEMPLE OF DREAMOLOGY WHERE WE WILL REACH THOSE WHO WISH TO BE ENLIGHTENED THROUGH RELIGION.
AND TRACER.
THE TIES YOU POSSESS TO ORGANIZED CRIME OFFER US A UNIQUE CONNECTION TO THE CRIMINAL UNDERWORLD.
AND I, LORD HAVOK...
...I WILL OVERSEE IT ALL.

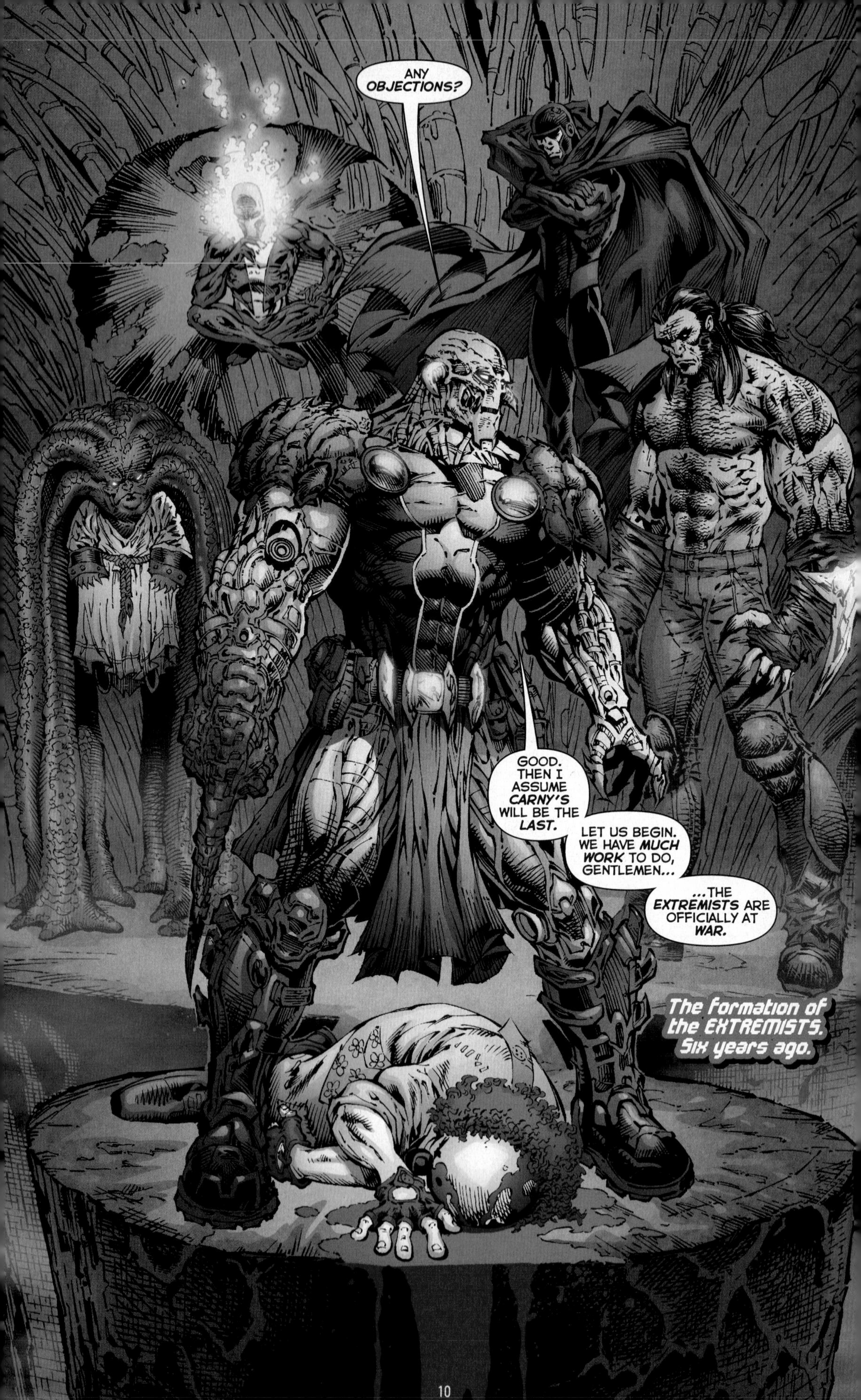

ANY OBJECTIONS?
GOOD. THEN I ASSUME CARNY'S WILL BE THE LAST.
LET US BEGIN. WE HAVE MUCH WORK TO DO, GENTLEMEN...
...THE EXTREMISTS ARE OFFICIALLY AT WAR.
The formation of the EXTREMISTS. Six years ago.

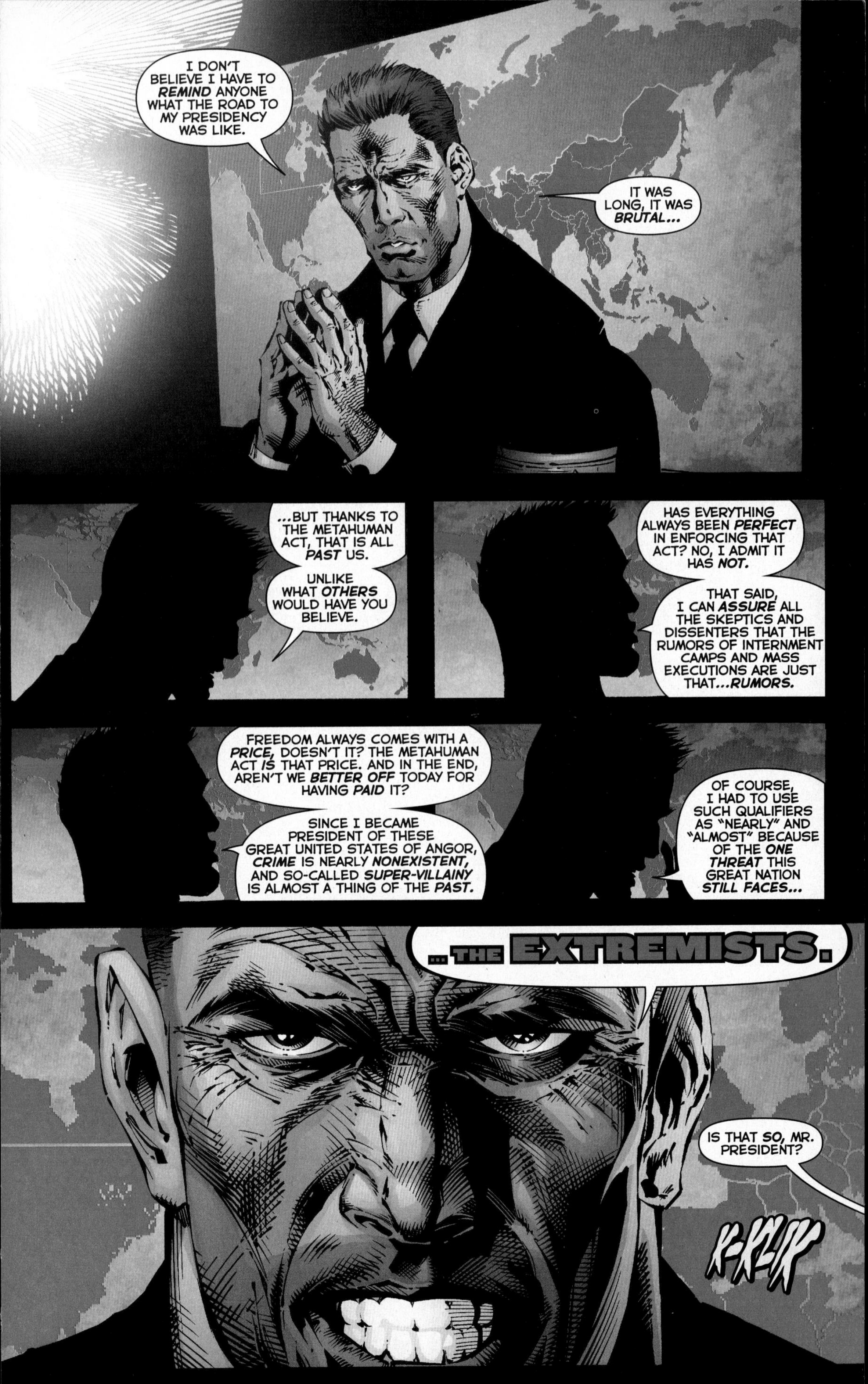
I DON'T BELIEVE I HAVE TO REMIND ANYONE WHAT THE ROAD TO MY PRESIDENCY WAS LIKE.
IT WAS LONG, IT WAS BRUTAL...
...BUT THANKS TO THE METAHUMAN ACT, THAT IS ALL PAST US.
UNLIKE WHAT OTHERS WOULD HAVE YOU BELIEVE.
HAS EVERYTHING ALWAYS BEEN PERFECT IN ENFORCING THAT ACT? NO, I ADMIT IT HAS NOT.
THAT SAID, I CAN ASSURE ALL THE SKEPTICS AND DISSENTERS THAT THE RUMORS OF INTERNMENT CAMPS AND MASS EXECUTIONS ARE JUST THAT...RUMORS.
FREEDOM ALWAYS COMES WITH A PRICE, DOESN'T IT? THE METAHUMAN ACT IS THAT PRICE. AND IN THE END, AREN'T WE BETTER OFF TODAY FOR HAVING PAID IT?
SINCE I BECAME PRESIDENT OF THESE GREAT UNITED STATES OF ANGOR, CRIME IS NEARLY NONEXISTENT, AND SO-CALLED SUPER-VILLAINY IS ALMOST A THING OF THE PAST.
OF COURSE, I HAD TO USE SUCH QUALIFIERS AS "NEARLY" AND "ALMOST" BECAUSE OF THE ONE THREAT THIS GREAT NATION STILL FACES...
...THE EXTREMISTS.
IS THAT SO, MR. PRESIDENT?
K-KLIK

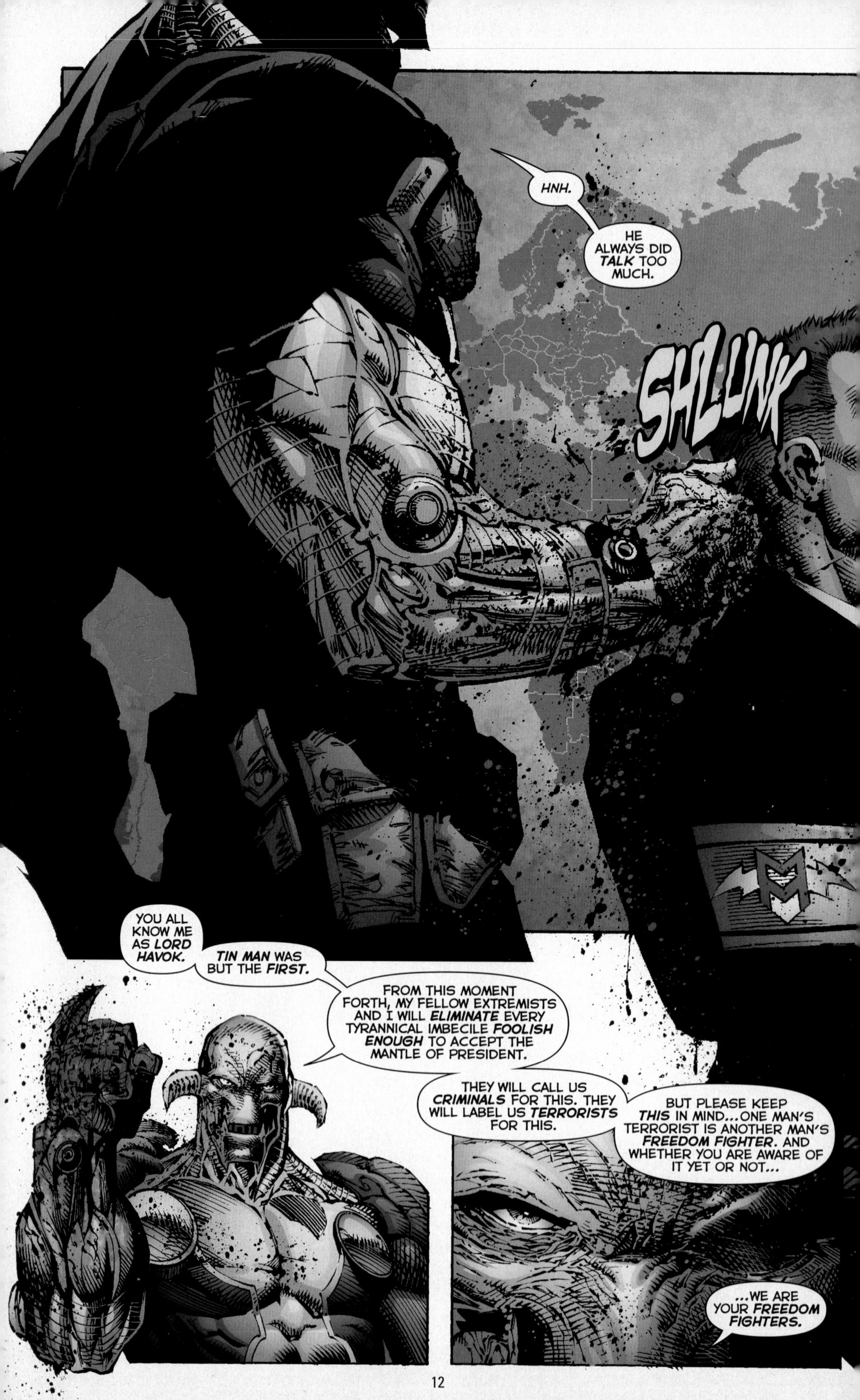
HNH.
HE ALWAYS DID TALK TOO MUCH.
SHLUNK
YOU ALL KNOW ME AS LORD HAVOK.
TIN MAN WAS BUT THE FIRST.
FROM THIS MOMENT FORTH, MY FELLOW EXTREMISTS AND I WILL ELIMINATE EVERY TYRANNICAL IMBECILE FOOLISH ENOUGH TO ACCEPT THE MANTLE OF PRESIDENT.
THEY WILL CALL US CRIMINALS FOR THIS. THEY WILL LABEL US TERRORISTS FOR THIS.
BUT PLEASE KEEP THIS IN MIND...ONE MAN'S TERRORIST IS ANOTHER MAN'S FREEDOM FIGHTER. AND WHETHER YOU ARE AWARE OF IT YET OR NOT...
...WE ARE YOUR FREEDOM FIGHTERS.

DINK!
OH YEAH?
Now. The Presidential White Tower. Philadelphia, Pennsylvania.
FOR ALL YOUR TALK, IT'S LIKE EIGHT MONTHS SINCE YOU TURNED THAT PAMPERED PRETTY-BOY'S HEAD INTO A CANOE--AND I'M STILL HERE, YOU MANIAC!
JIMMY, HOW MANY TIMES CAN YOU WATCH THAT? SHUT THAT STUPID TAPE OFF AND COME TO BED!
I TOLD YOU NOT TO CALL ME THAT. IT'S JIM. EVEN JAMES WILL DO.
JIMMY IS THE NAME OF A SOME SCHLEP WHO DRIVES YOU TO THE AIRPORT. OR THE GUY YOU CALL WHEN YOUR TOILET BACKS UP.
JIMMY'S NOT THE MOST DECORATED SOLDIER IN HISTORY. JIMMY'S NOT THE LEADER OF THE MOST POWERFUL COUNTRY ON THE PLANET!
AND HE'S NOT AMERICOMMANDO.
FINE. JAMES. AMERICOMMANDO. MR. PRESIDENT. OR WHATEVER THE HELL YOU WANT TO CALL YOURSELF...
...SHUT THE TAPE OFF, STOP DRINKING AND GET YOUR SWEET BUTT INTO BED.

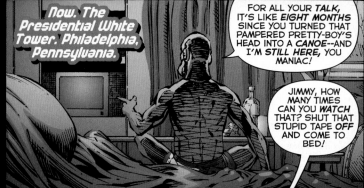

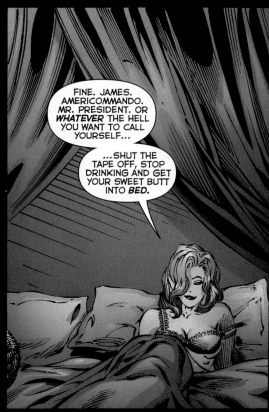

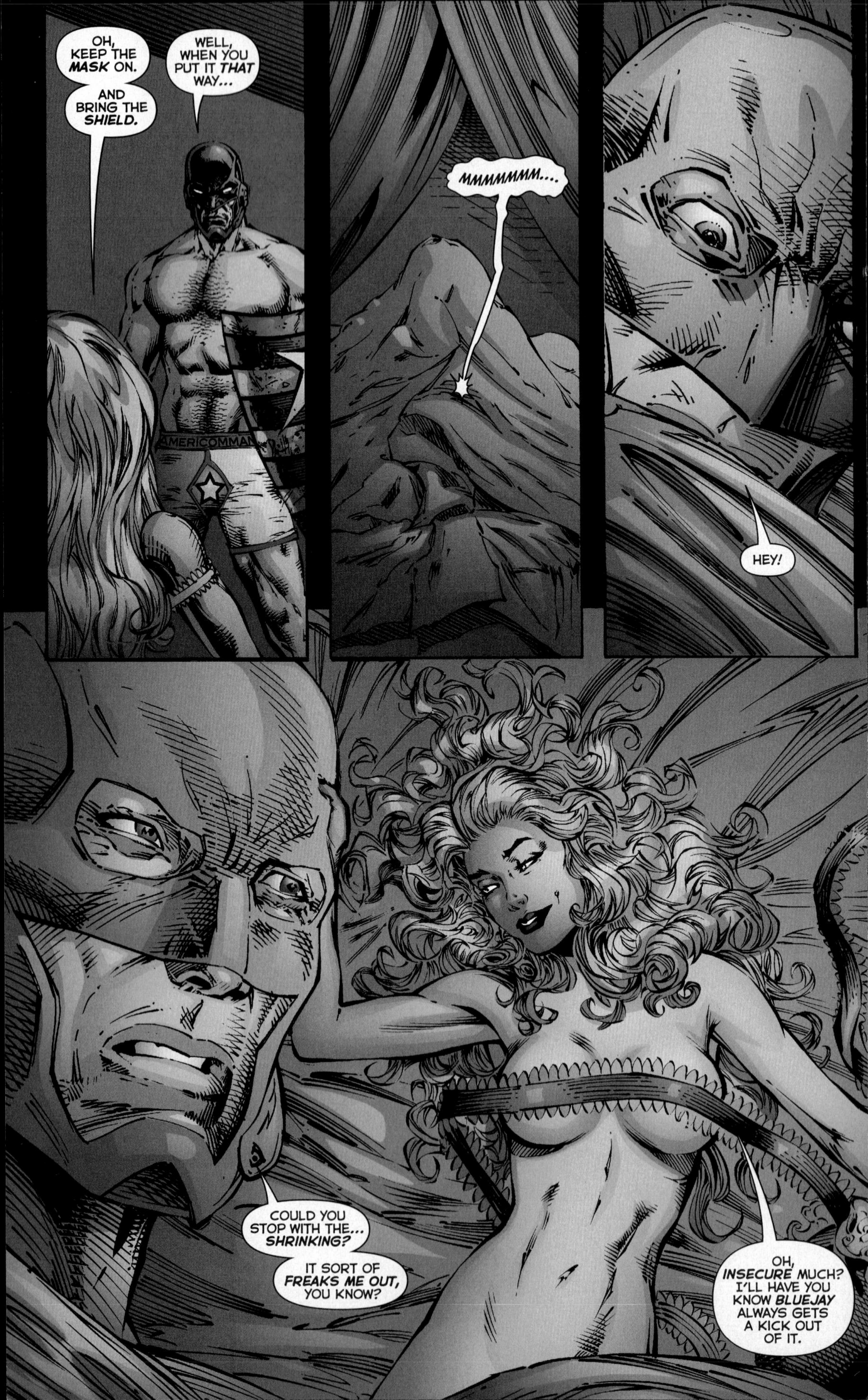
OH, KEEP THE MASK ON.
AND BRING THE SHIELD.
WELL, WHEN YOU PUT IT THAT WAY...
MMMMMMM....
HEY!
COULD YOU STOP WITH THE... SHRINKING?
IT SORT OF FREAKS ME OUT, YOU KNOW?
OH, INSECURE MUCH? I'LL HAVE YOU KNOW BLUEJAY ALWAYS GETS A KICK OUT OF IT.

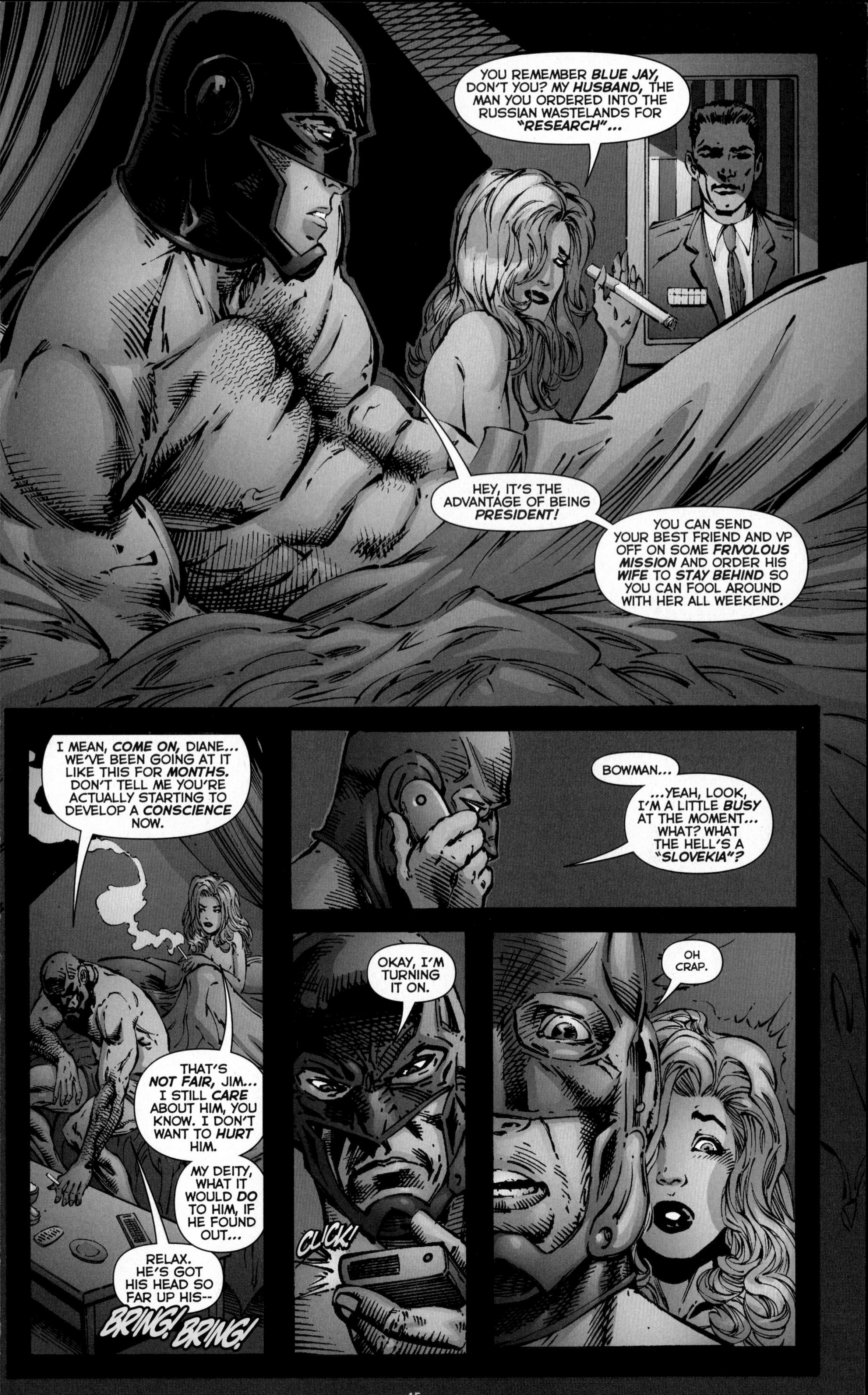

YOU REMEMBER BLUE JAY, DON'T YOU? MY HUSBAND, THE MAN YOU ORDERED INTO THE RUSSIAN WASTELANDS FOR "RESEARCH"...
HEY, IT'S THE ADVANTAGE OF BEING PRESIDENT!
YOU CAN SEND YOUR BEST FRIEND AND VP OFF ON SOME FRIVOLOUS MISSION AND ORDER HIS WIFE TO STAY BEHIND SO YOU CAN FOOL AROUND WITH HER ALL WEEKEND.
I MEAN, COME ON, DIANE... WE'VE BEEN GOING AT IT LIKE THIS FOR MONTHS. DON'T TELL ME YOU'RE ACTUALLY STARTING TO DEVELOP A CONSCIENCE NOW.
THAT'S NOT FAIR, JIM... I STILL CARE ABOUT HIM, YOU KNOW. I DON'T WANT TO HURT HIM.
MY DEITY, WHAT IT WOULD DO TO HIM, IF HE FOUND OUT...
RELAX. HE'S GOT HIS HEAD SO FAR UP HIS--
BRING! BRING!
BOWMAN...
...YEAH, LOOK, I'M A LITTLE BUSY AT THE MOMENT... WHAT? WHAT THE HELL'S A "SLOVEKIA"?
OKAY, I'M TURNING IT ON.
CLICK!
OH CRAP.

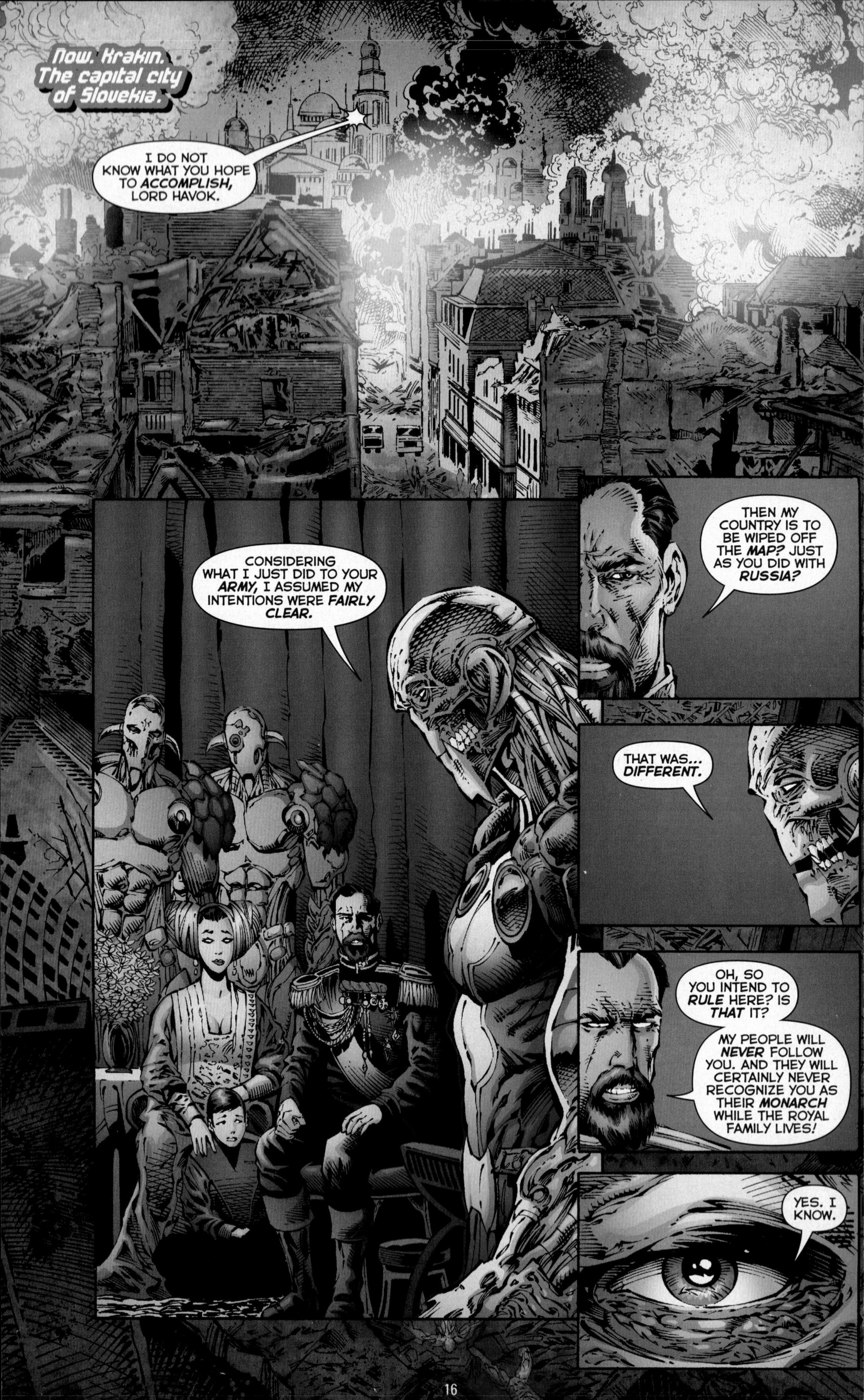
Now. Krakin. The capital city of Slovekia.
I DO NOT KNOW WHAT YOU HOPE TO ACCOMPLISH, LORD HAVOK.
CONSIDERING WHAT I JUST DID TO YOUR ARMY, I ASSUMED MY INTENTIONS WERE FAIRLY CLEAR.
THEN MY COUNTRY IS TO BE WIPED OFF THE MAP? JUST AS YOU DID WITH RUSSIA?
THAT WAS... DIFFERENT.
OH, SO YOU INTEND TO RULE HERE? IS THAT IT?
MY PEOPLE WILL NEVER FOLLOW YOU. AND THEY WILL CERTAINLY NEVER RECOGNIZE YOU AS THEIR MONARCH WHILE THE ROYAL FAMILY LIVES!
YES. I KNOW.

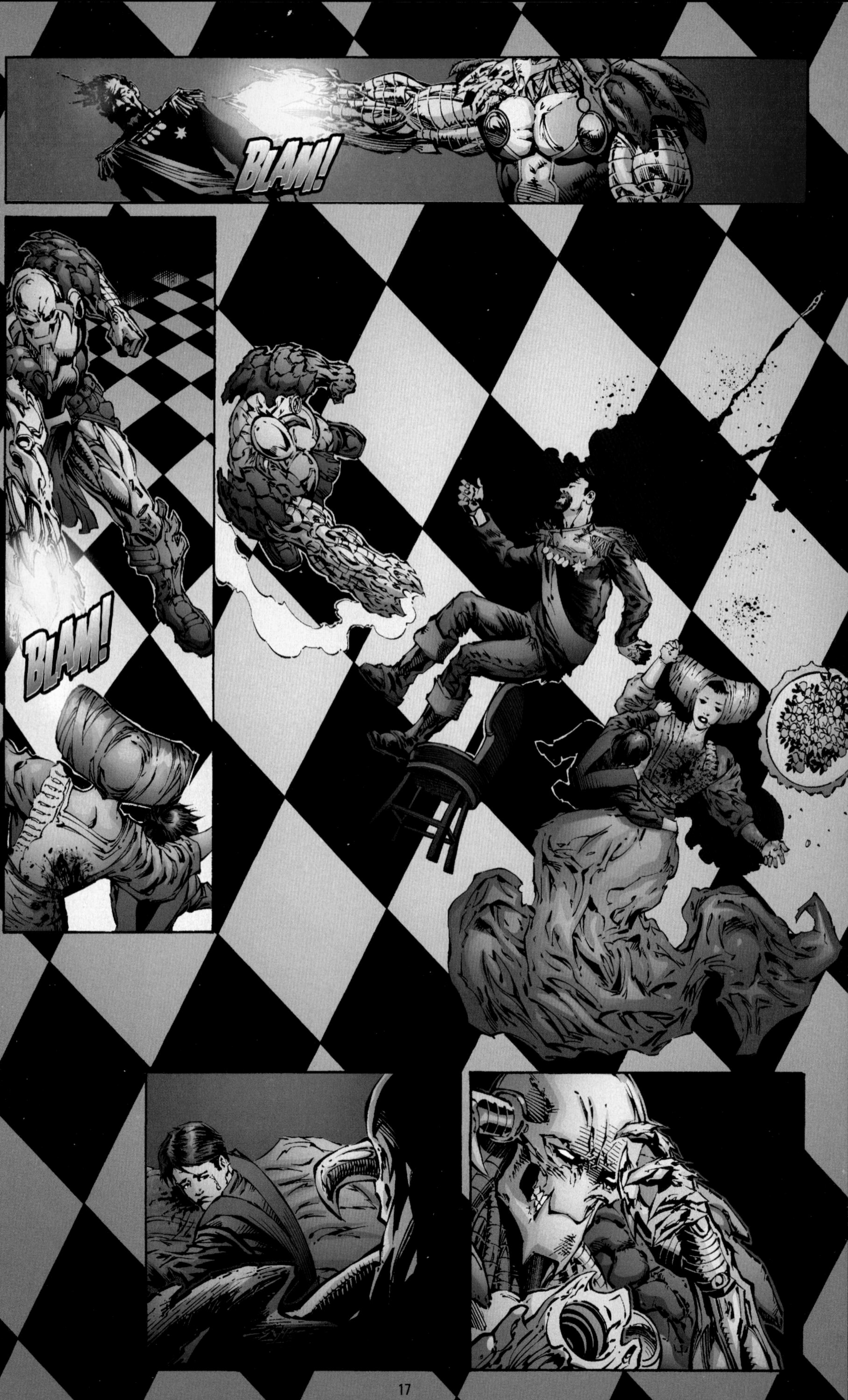
BLAM!
BLAM!

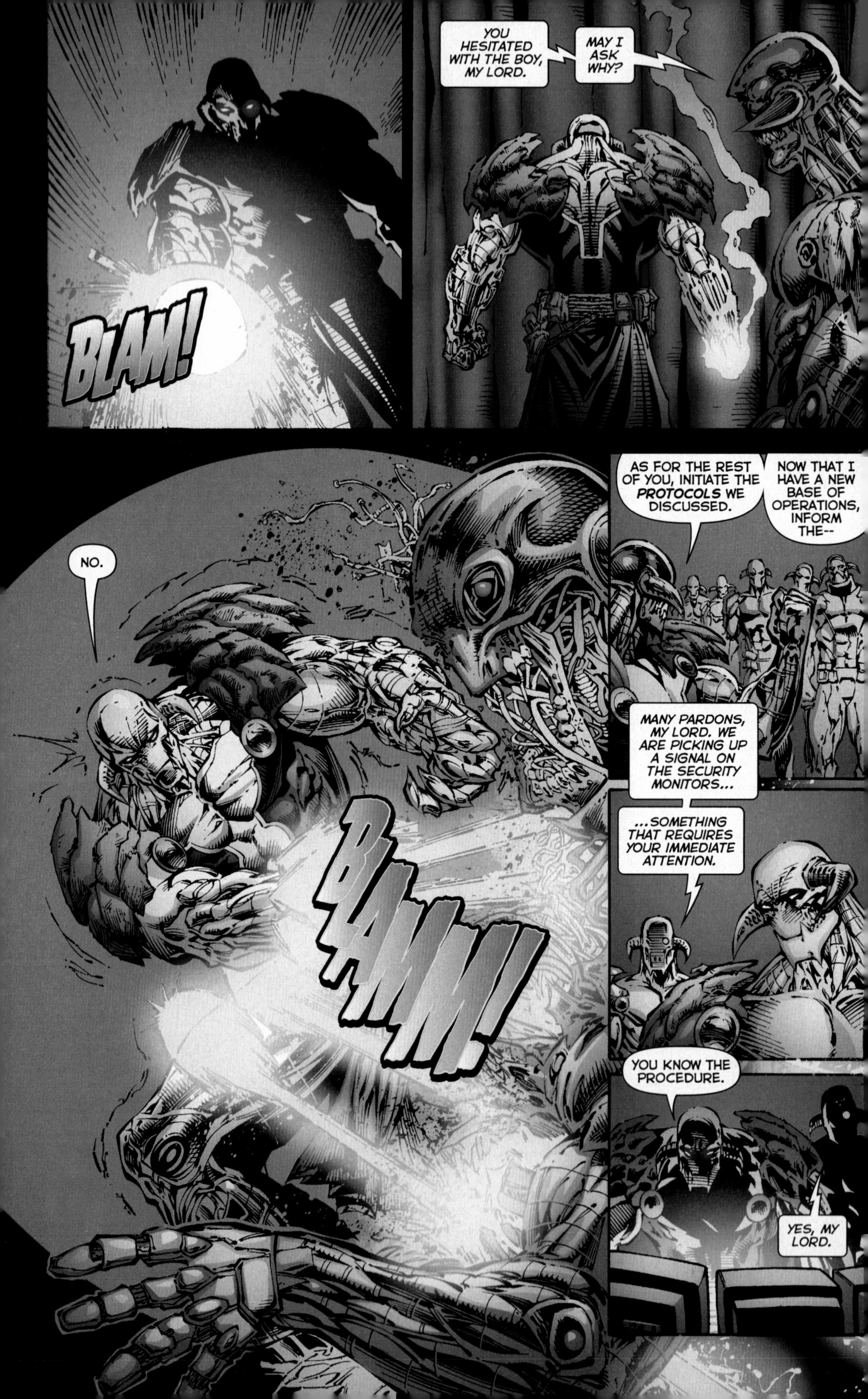
BLAM!
YOU HESITATED WITH THE BOY, MY LORD.
MAY I ASK WHY?
NO.
BLAMM!
AS FOR THE REST OF YOU, INITIATE THE PROTOCOLS WE DISCUSSED.
NOW THAT I HAVE A NEW BASE OF OPERATIONS, INFORM THE--
MANY PARDONS, MY LORD. WE ARE PICKING UP A SIGNAL ON THE SECURITY MONITORS...
...SOMETHING THAT REQUIRES YOUR IMMEDIATE ATTENTION.
YOU KNOW THE PROCEDURE.
YES, MY LORD.

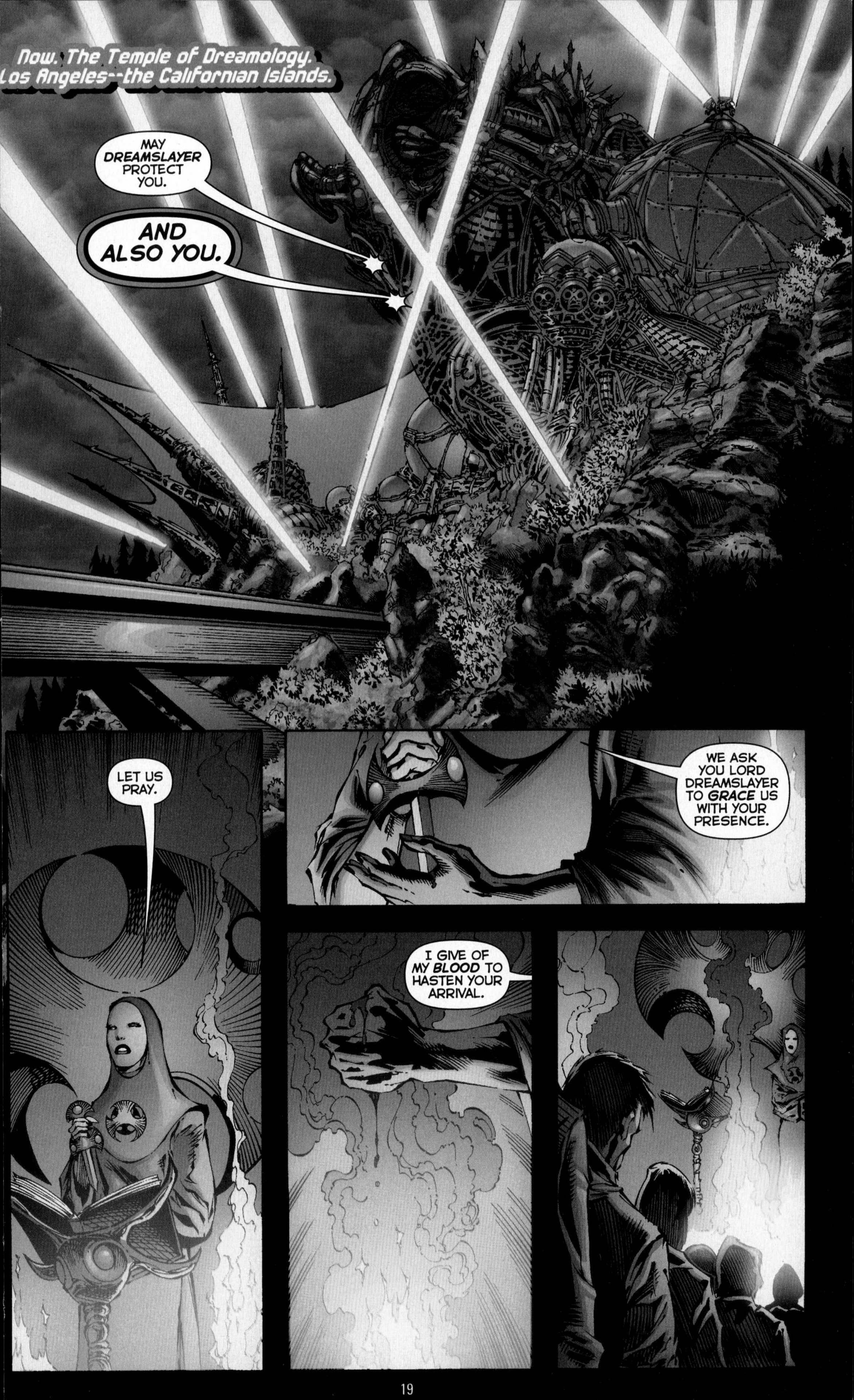
Now. The Temple of Dreamology. Los Angeles--the Californian Islands.
MAY DREAMSLAYER PROTECT YOU.
AND ALSO YOU.
LET US PRAY.
WE ASK YOU LORD DREAMSLAYER TO GRACE US WITH YOUR PRESENCE.
I GIVE OF MY BLOOD TO HASTEN YOUR ARRIVAL.

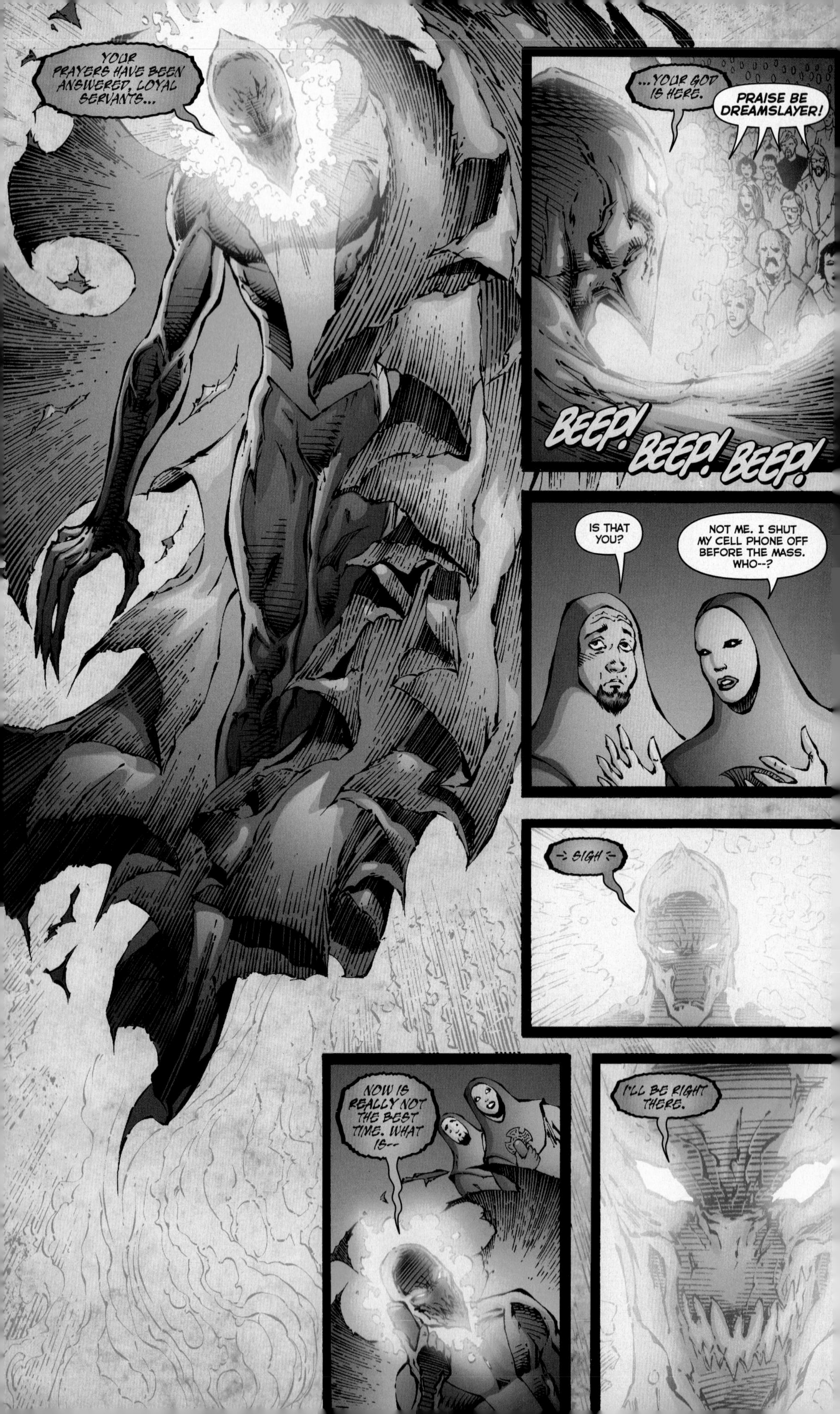
YOUR PRAYERS HAVE BEEN ANSWERED, LOYAL SERVANTS...
...YOUR GOD IS HERE.
PRAISE BE DREAMSLAYER!
BEEP! BEEP! BEEP!
IS THAT YOU?
NOT ME. I SHUT MY CELL PHONE OFF BEFORE THE MASS. WHO--?
-: SIGH :-
NOW IS REALLY NOT THE BEST TIME. WHAT IS--
I'LL BE RIGHT THERE.

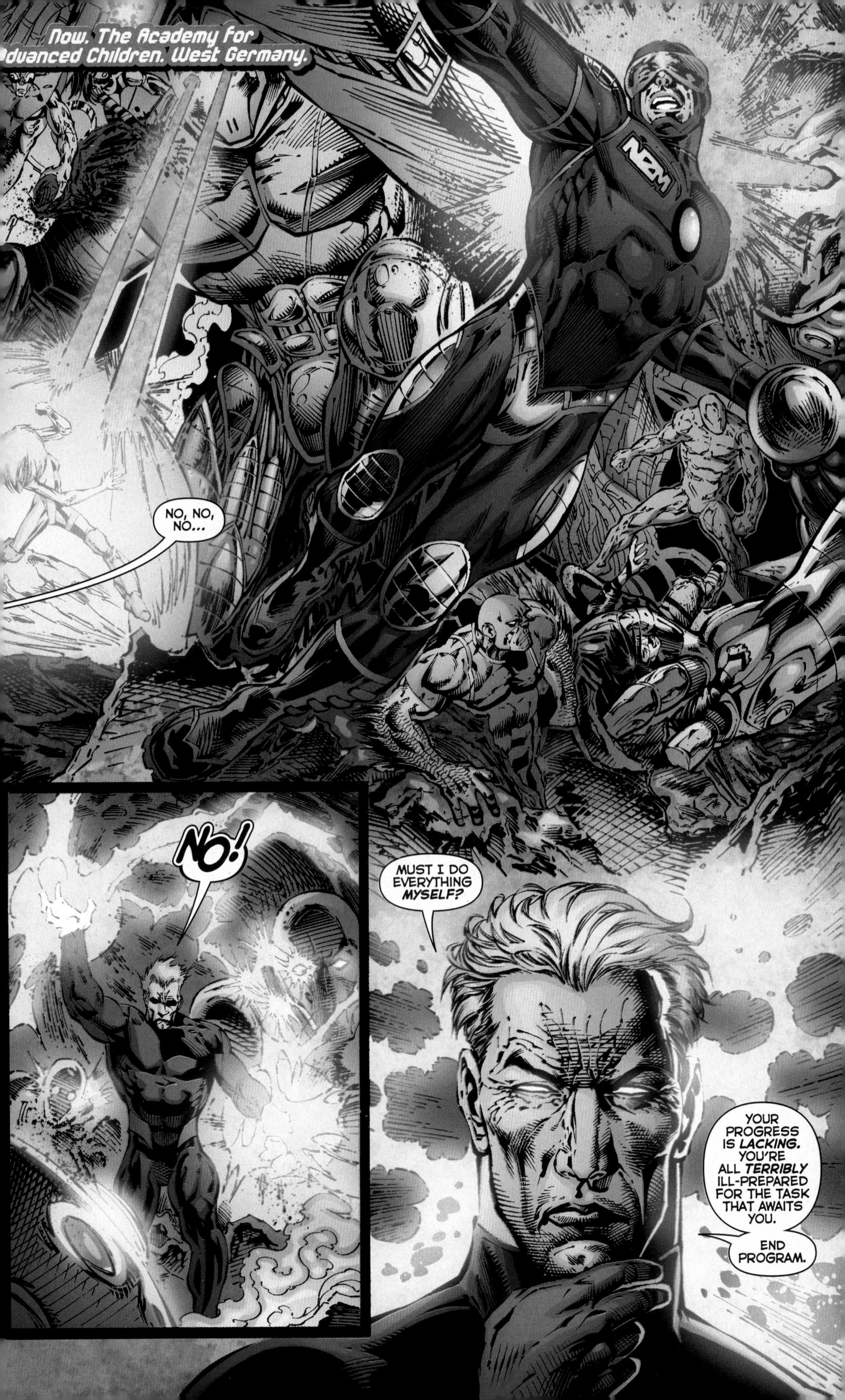
Now. The Academy for Advanced Children. West Germany.
NO, NO, NO...
NO!
MUST I DO EVERYTHING MYSELF?
YOUR PROGRESS IS LACKING. YOU'RE ALL TERRIBLY ILL-PREPARED FOR THE TASK THAT AWAITS YOU.
END PROGRAM.

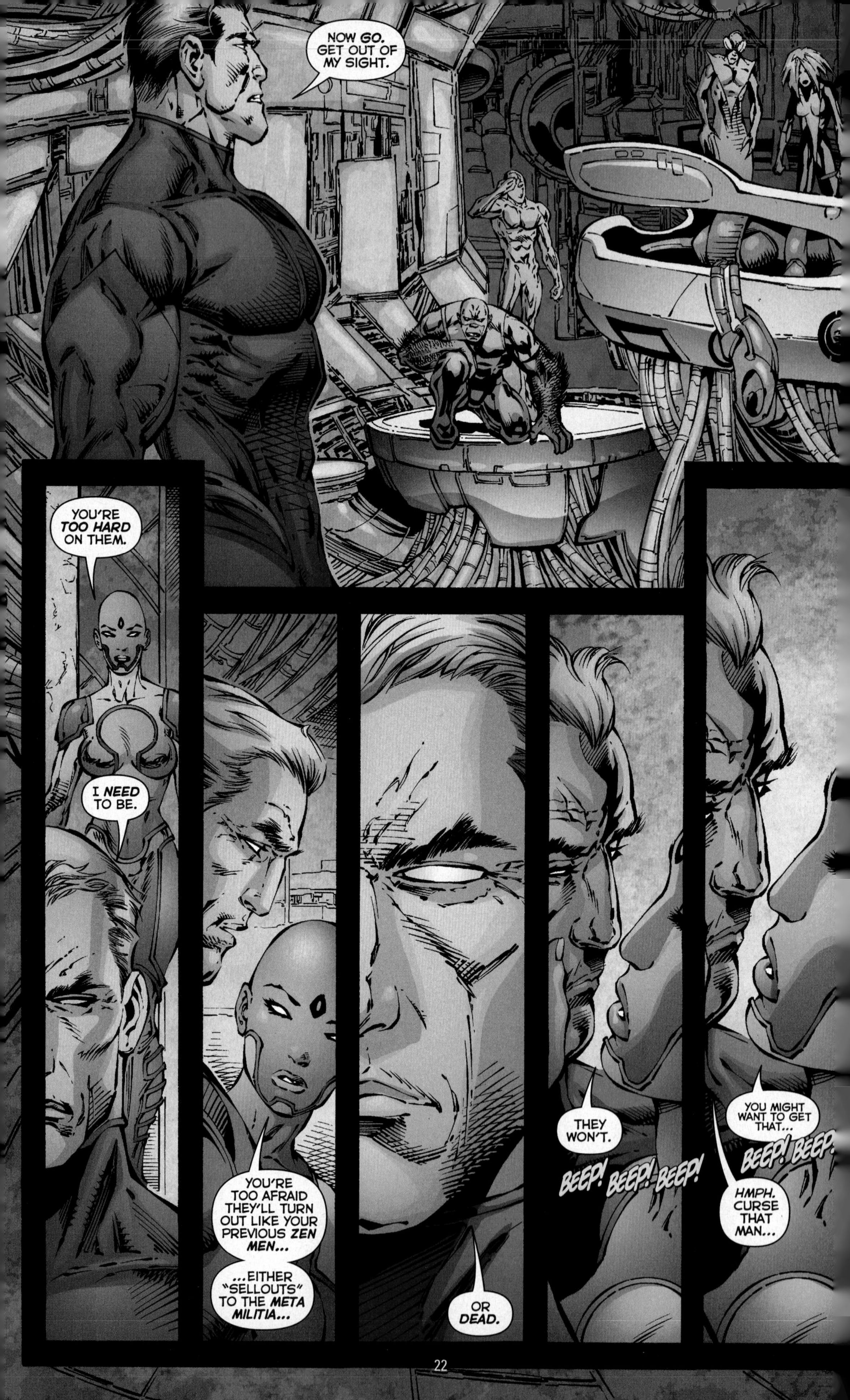
NOW GO. GET OUT OF MY SIGHT.
YOU'RE TOO HARD ON THEM.
I NEED TO BE.
YOU'RE TOO AFRAID THEY'LL TURN OUT LIKE YOUR PREVIOUS ZEN MEN...
...EITHER "SELLOUTS" TO THE META MILITIA...
OR DEAD.
THEY WON'T.
BEEP! BEEP! BEEP!
YOU MIGHT WANT TO GET THAT...
BEEP! BEEP!
HMPH. CURSE THAT MAN...

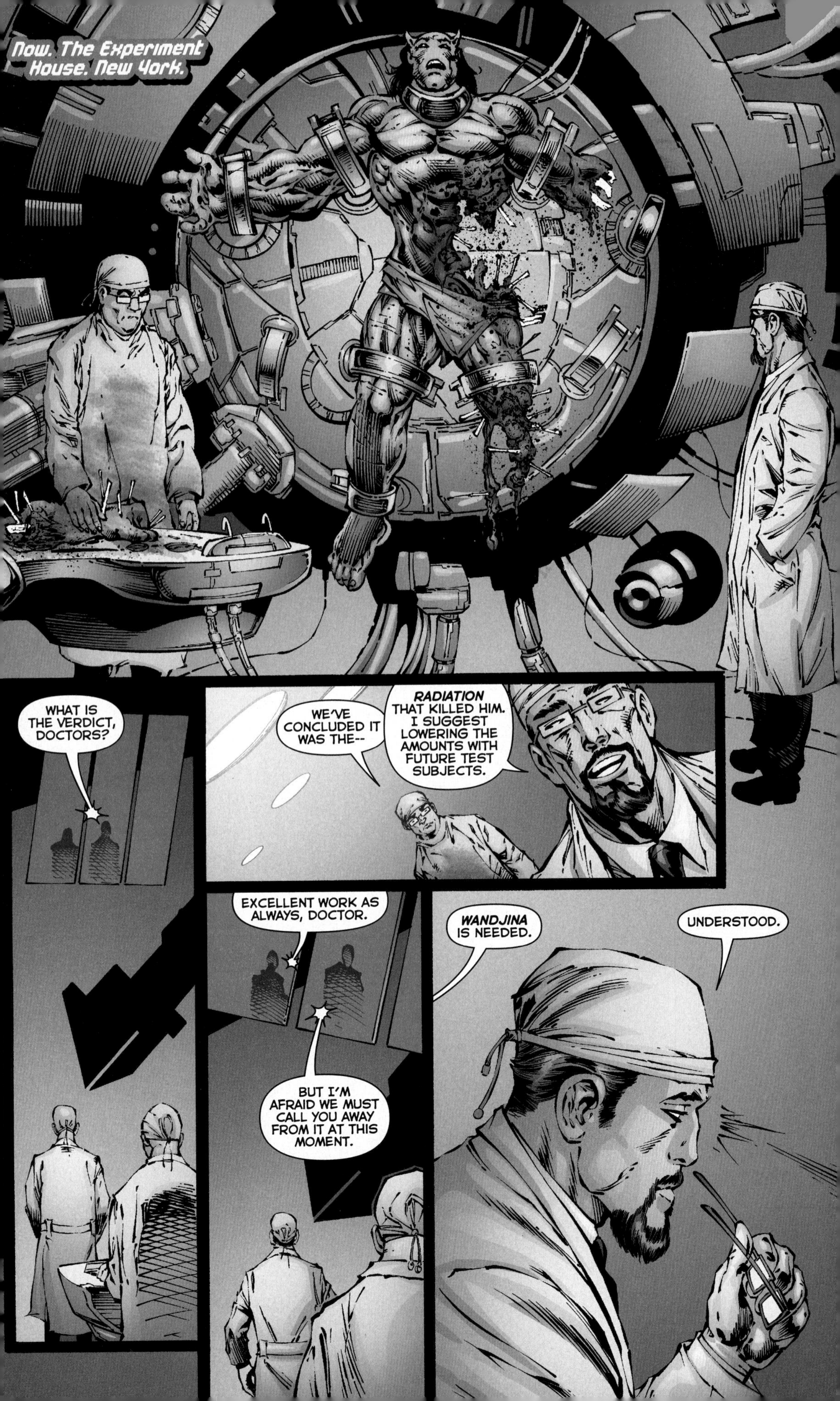

Now. The Experiment House. New York.
WHAT IS THE VERDICT, DOCTORS?
WE'VE CONCLUDED IT WAS THE--
RADIATION THAT KILLED HIM. I SUGGEST LOWERING THE AMOUNTS WITH FUTURE TEST SUBJECTS.
EXCELLENT WORK AS ALWAYS, DOCTOR.
BUT I'M AFRAID WE MUST CALL YOU AWAY FROM IT AT THIS MOMENT.
WANDJINA IS NEEDED.
UNDERSTOOD.

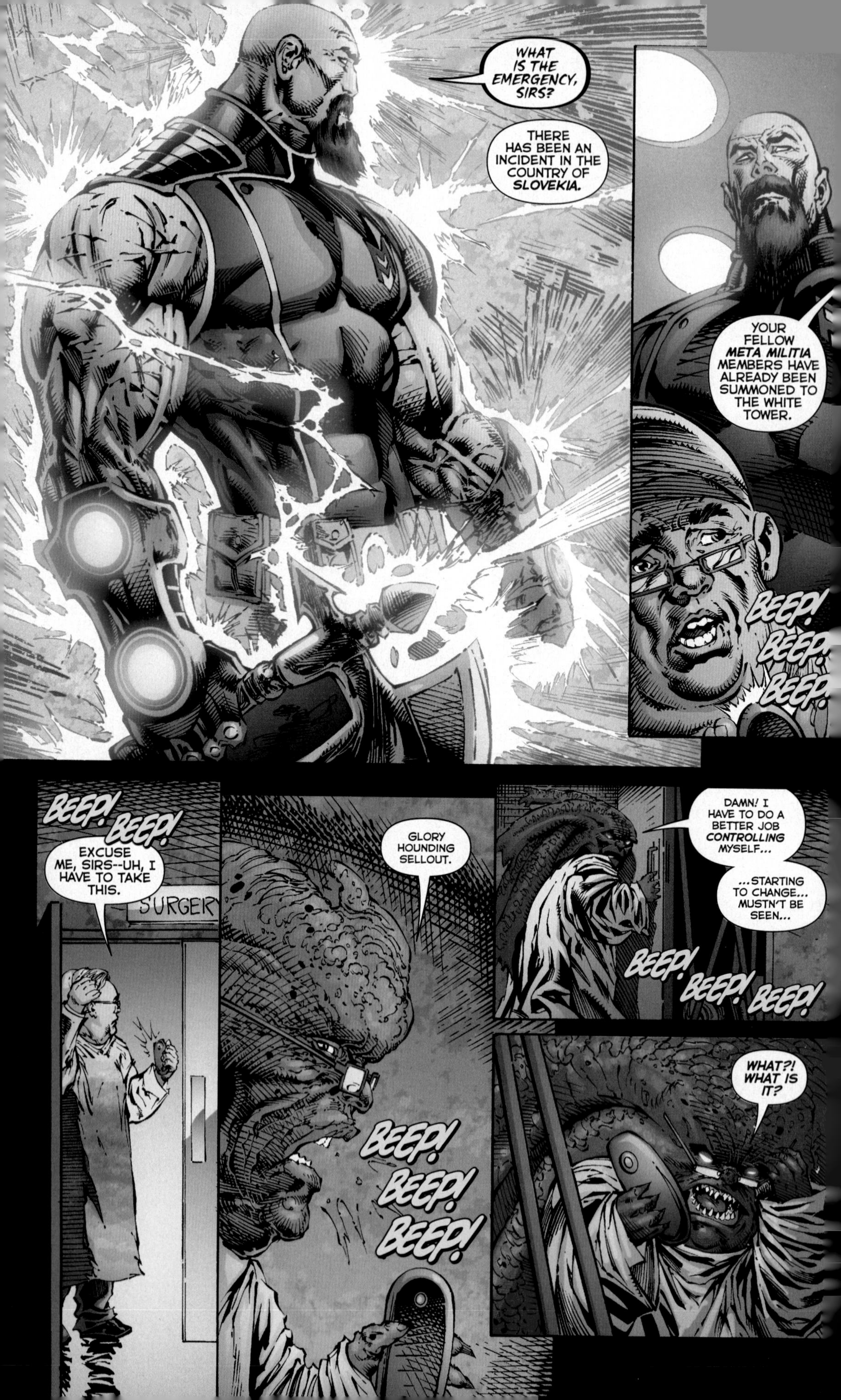
WHAT IS THE EMERGENCY, SIRS?
THERE HAS BEEN AN INCIDENT IN THE COUNTRY OF SLOVEKIA.
YOUR FELLOW META MILITIA MEMBERS HAVE ALREADY BEEN SUMMONED TO THE WHITE TOWER.
BEEP! BEEP! BEEP!
BEEP! BEEP!
EXCUSE ME, SIRS--UH, I HAVE TO TAKE THIS.
SURGERY
GLORY HOUNDING SELLOUT.
BEEP! BEEP! BEEP!
DAMN! I HAVE TO DO A BETTER JOB CONTROLLING MYSELF...
...STARTING TO CHANGE... MUSTN'T BE SEEN...
BEEP! BEEP! BEEP!
WHAT?! WHAT IS IT?

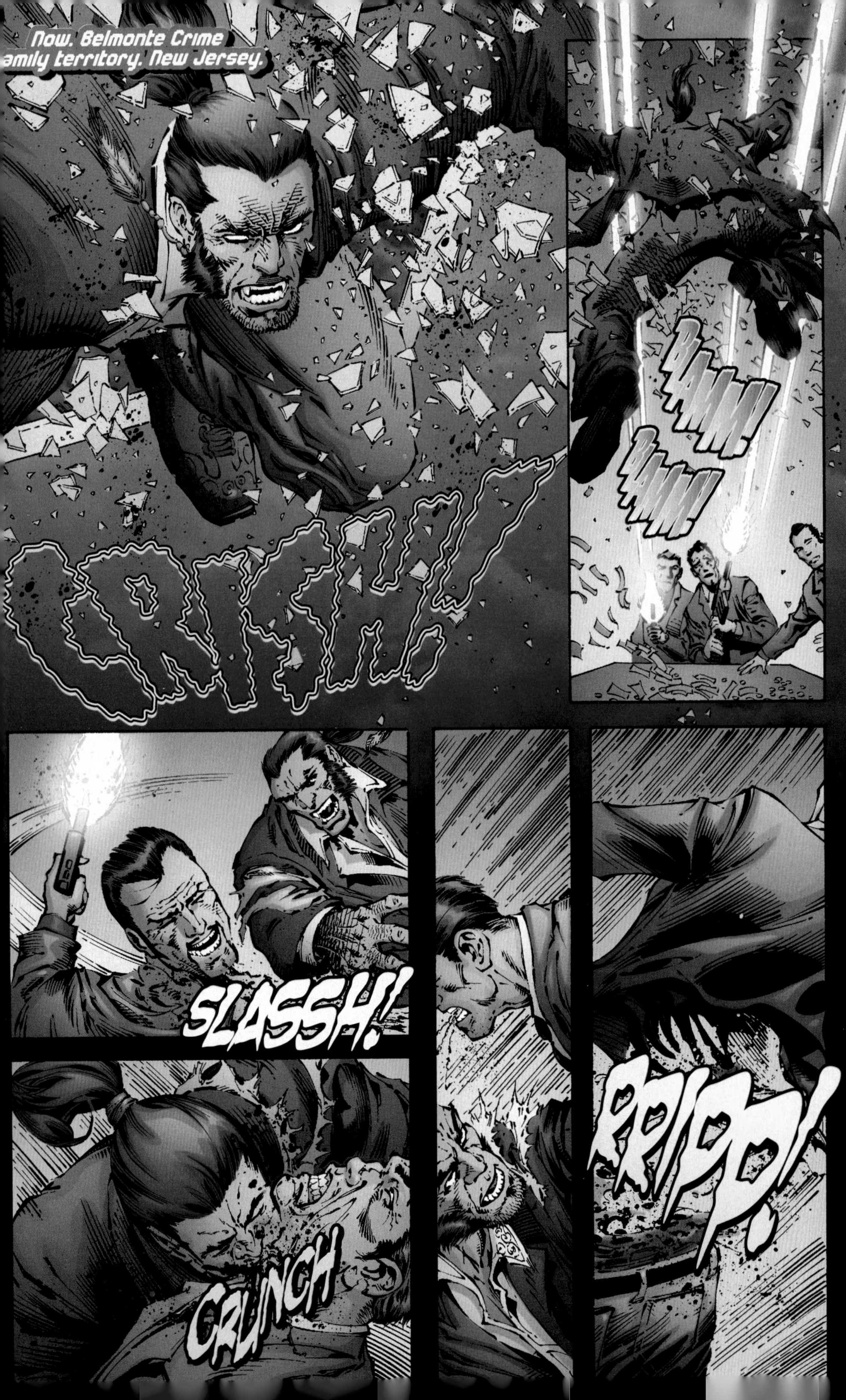
Now. Belmonte Crime
amily territory. New Jersey.
CRASH!
BLAMM!
BLAMM!
SLASSH!
CRUNCH
RRIPP!

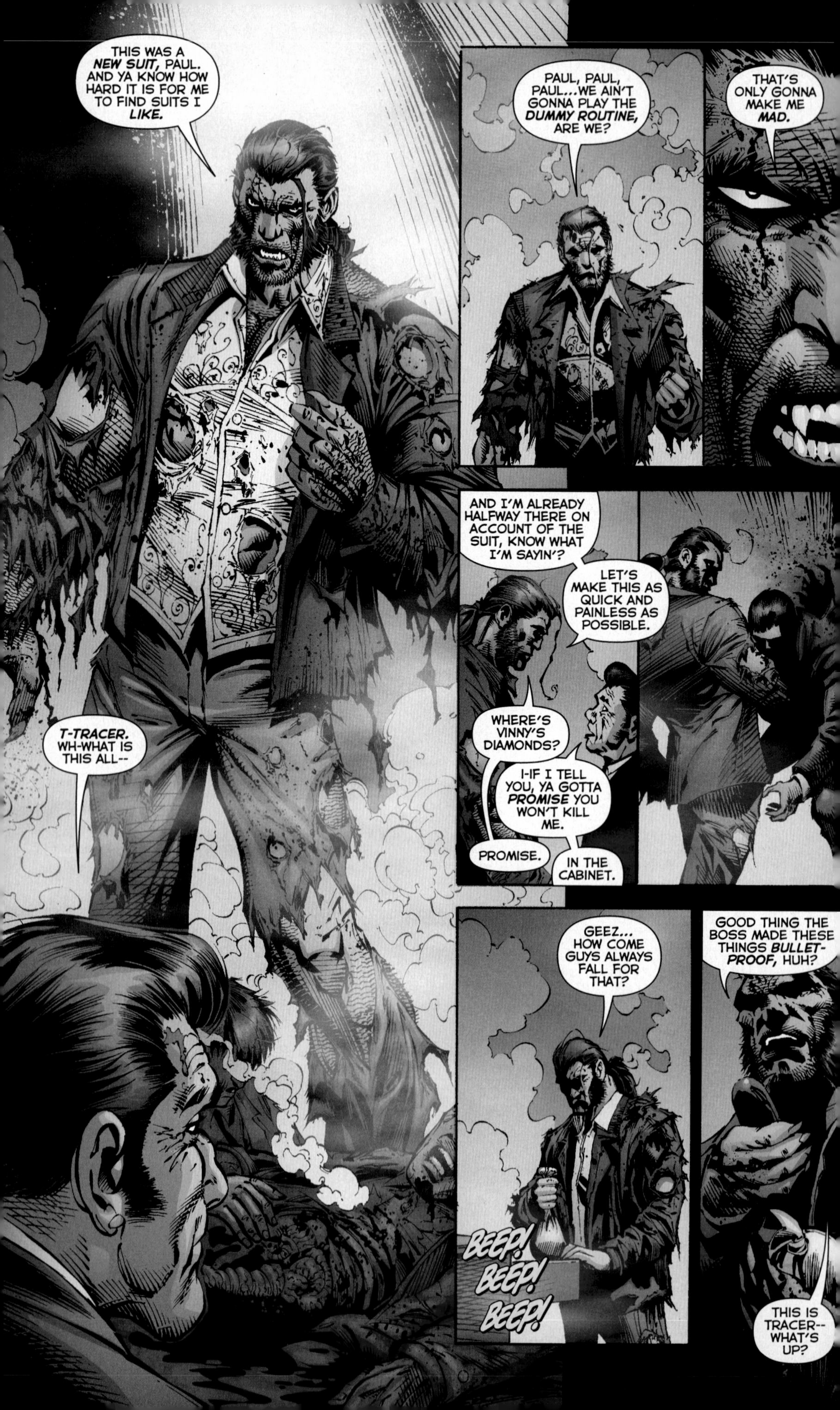
THIS WAS A NEW SUIT, PAUL. AND YA KNOW HOW HARD IT IS FOR ME TO FIND SUITS I LIKE.
T-TRACER. WH-WHAT IS THIS ALL--
PAUL, PAUL, PAUL...WE AIN'T GONNA PLAY THE DUMMY ROUTINE, ARE WE?
THAT'S ONLY GONNA MAKE ME MAD.
AND I'M ALREADY HALFWAY THERE ON ACCOUNT OF THE SUIT, KNOW WHAT I'M SAYIN'?
LET'S MAKE THIS AS QUICK AND PAINLESS AS POSSIBLE.
WHERE'S VINNY'S DIAMONDS?
I-IF I TELL YOU, YA GOTTA PROMISE YOU WON'T KILL ME.
PROMISE.
IN THE CABINET.
GEEZ... HOW COME GUYS ALWAYS FALL FOR THAT?
BEEP! BEEP! BEEP!
GOOD THING THE BOSS MADE THESE THINGS BULLET-PROOF, HUH?
THIS IS TRACER-- WHAT'S UP?

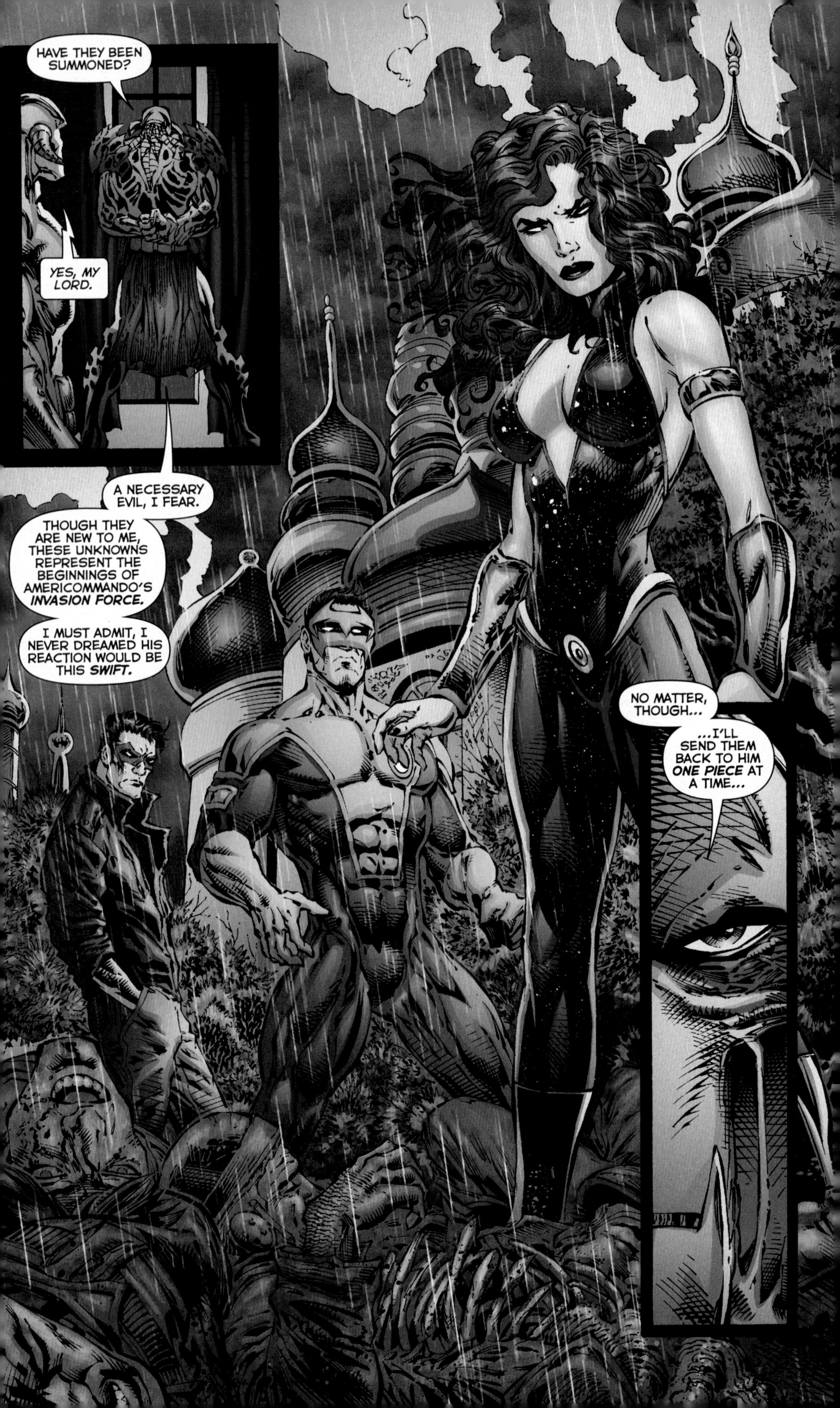

HAVE THEY BEEN SUMMONED?
YES, MY LORD.
A NECESSARY EVIL, I FEAR.
THOUGH THEY ARE NEW TO ME, THESE UNKNOWNS REPRESENT THE BEGINNINGS OF AMERICOMMANDO'S *INVASION FORCE.*
I MUST ADMIT, I NEVER DREAMED HIS REACTION WOULD BE THIS *SWIFT.*
NO MATTER, THOUGH...
...I'LL SEND THEM BACK TO HIM *ONE PIECE* AT A TIME...

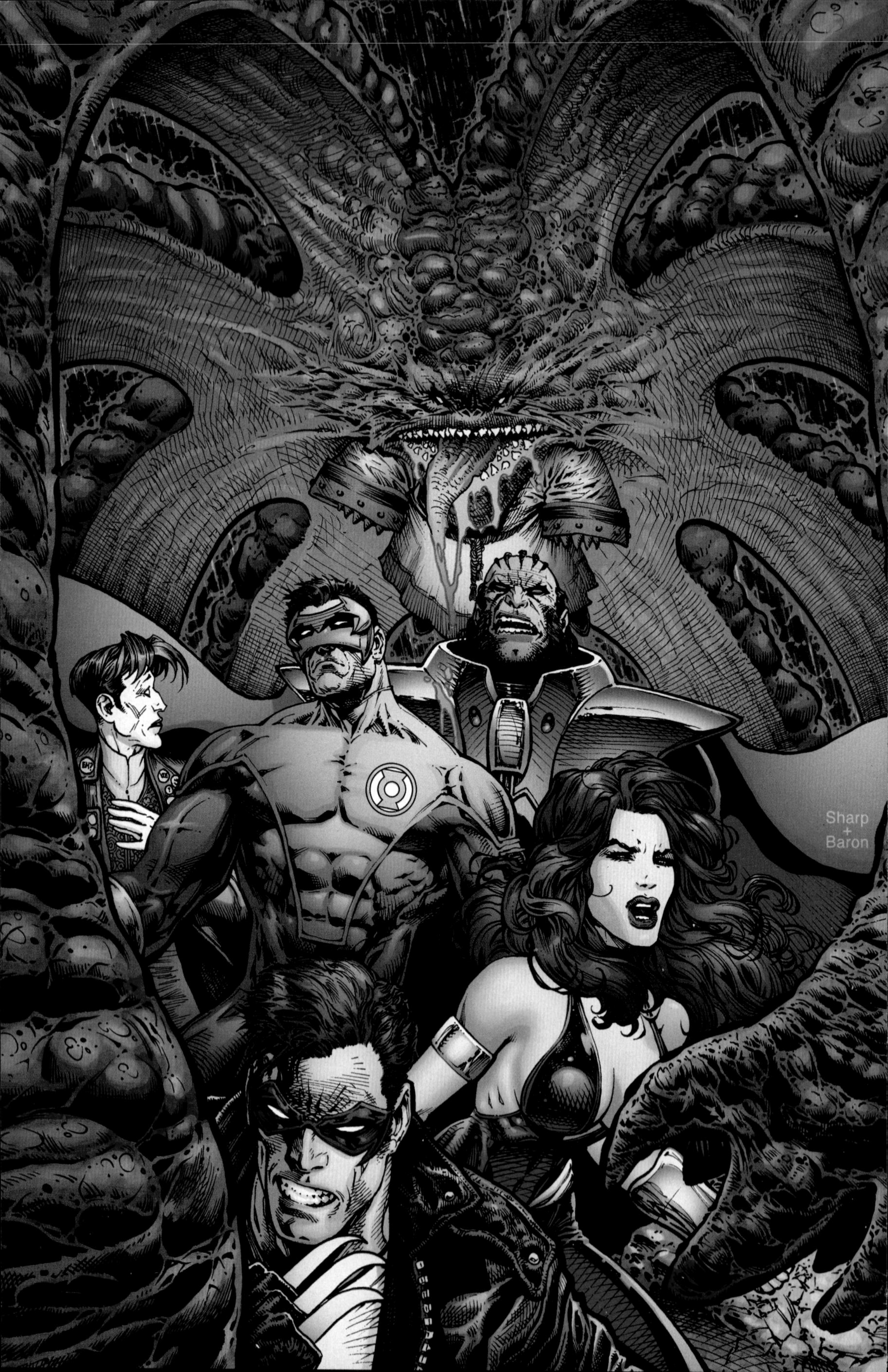
Sharp
+
Baron

Part 2: The Last Days of the Extremists

Chapter pencilled by Liam Sharp   Chapter inked by Rob Hunter   Cover art by Liam Sharp & Dave Baron

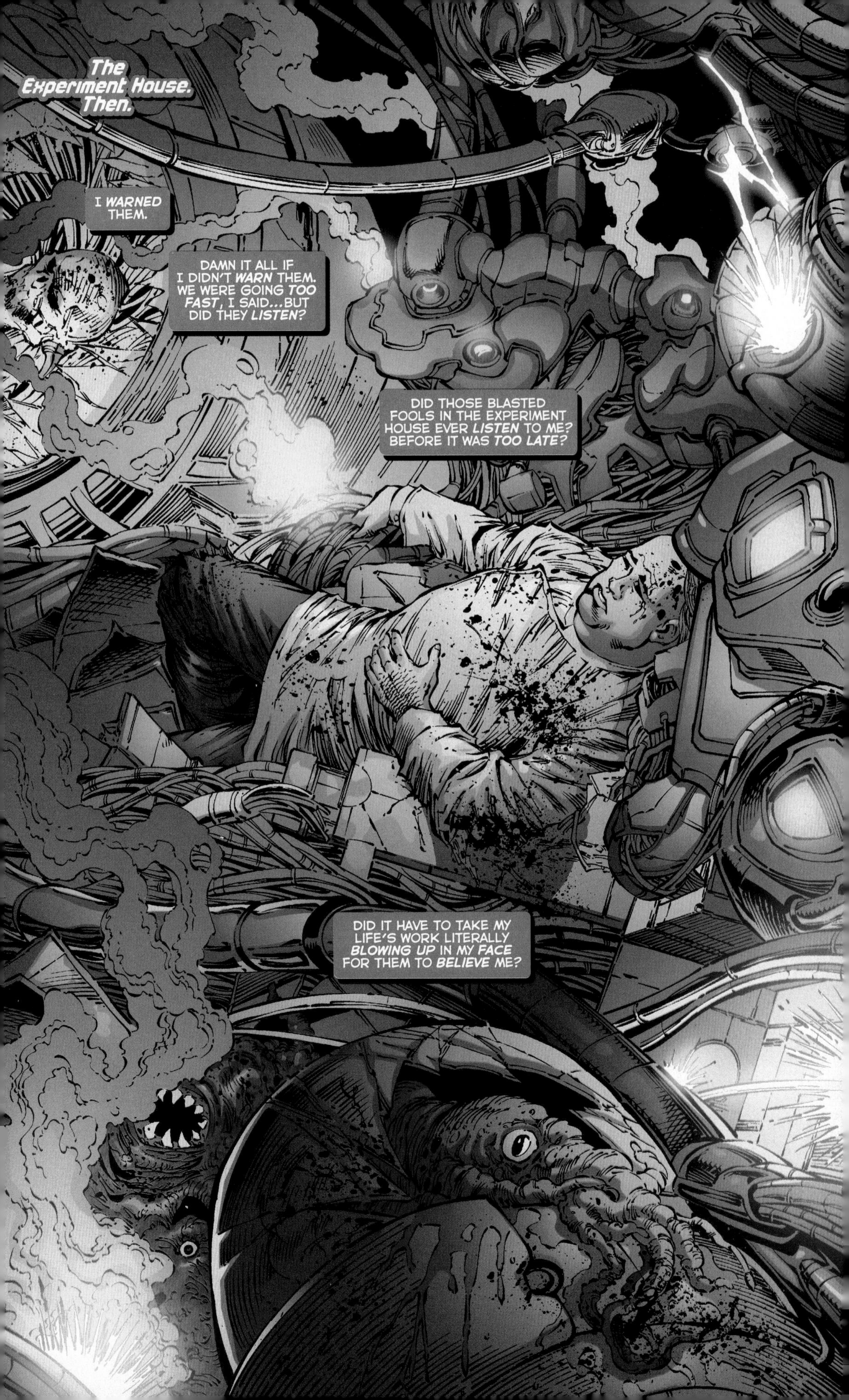
The Experiment House. Then.
I *WARNED* THEM.
DAMN IT ALL IF I DIDN'T *WARN* THEM. WE WERE GOING *TOO FAST*, I SAID...BUT DID THEY *LISTEN*?
DID THOSE BLASTED FOOLS IN THE EXPERIMENT HOUSE EVER *LISTEN* TO ME? BEFORE IT WAS *TOO LATE*?
DID IT HAVE TO TAKE MY LIFE'S WORK LITERALLY *BLOWING UP* IN MY *FACE* FOR THEM TO *BELIEVE* ME?

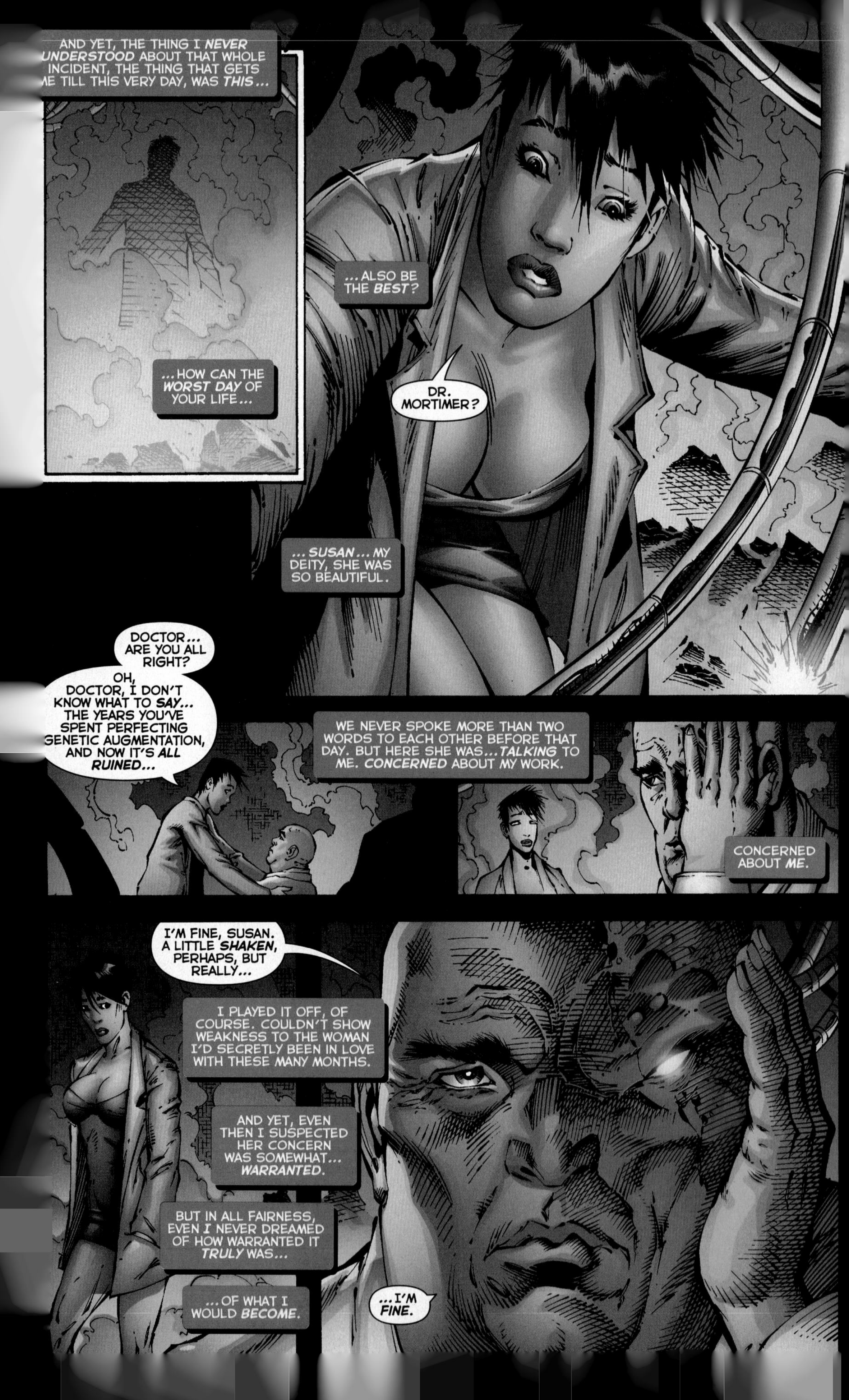
AND YET, THE THING I NEVER UNDERSTOOD ABOUT THAT WHOLE INCIDENT, THE THING THAT GETS ME TILL THIS VERY DAY, WAS THIS...
...HOW CAN THE WORST DAY OF YOUR LIFE...
...ALSO BE THE BEST?
DR. MORTIMER?
...SUSAN... MY DEITY, SHE WAS SO BEAUTIFUL.
DOCTOR... ARE YOU ALL RIGHT?
OH, DOCTOR, I DON'T KNOW WHAT TO SAY... THE YEARS YOU'VE SPENT PERFECTING GENETIC AUGMENTATION, AND NOW IT'S ALL RUINED...
WE NEVER SPOKE MORE THAN TWO WORDS TO EACH OTHER BEFORE THAT DAY. BUT HERE SHE WAS...TALKING TO ME. CONCERNED ABOUT MY WORK.
CONCERNED ABOUT ME.
I'M FINE, SUSAN. A LITTLE SHAKEN, PERHAPS, BUT REALLY...
I PLAYED IT OFF, OF COURSE. COULDN'T SHOW WEAKNESS TO THE WOMAN I'D SECRETLY BEEN IN LOVE WITH THESE MANY MONTHS.
AND YET, EVEN THEN I SUSPECTED HER CONCERN WAS SOMEWHAT... WARRANTED.
BUT IN ALL FAIRNESS, EVEN I NEVER DREAMED OF HOW WARRANTED IT TRULY WAS...
...OF WHAT I WOULD BECOME.
...I'M FINE.

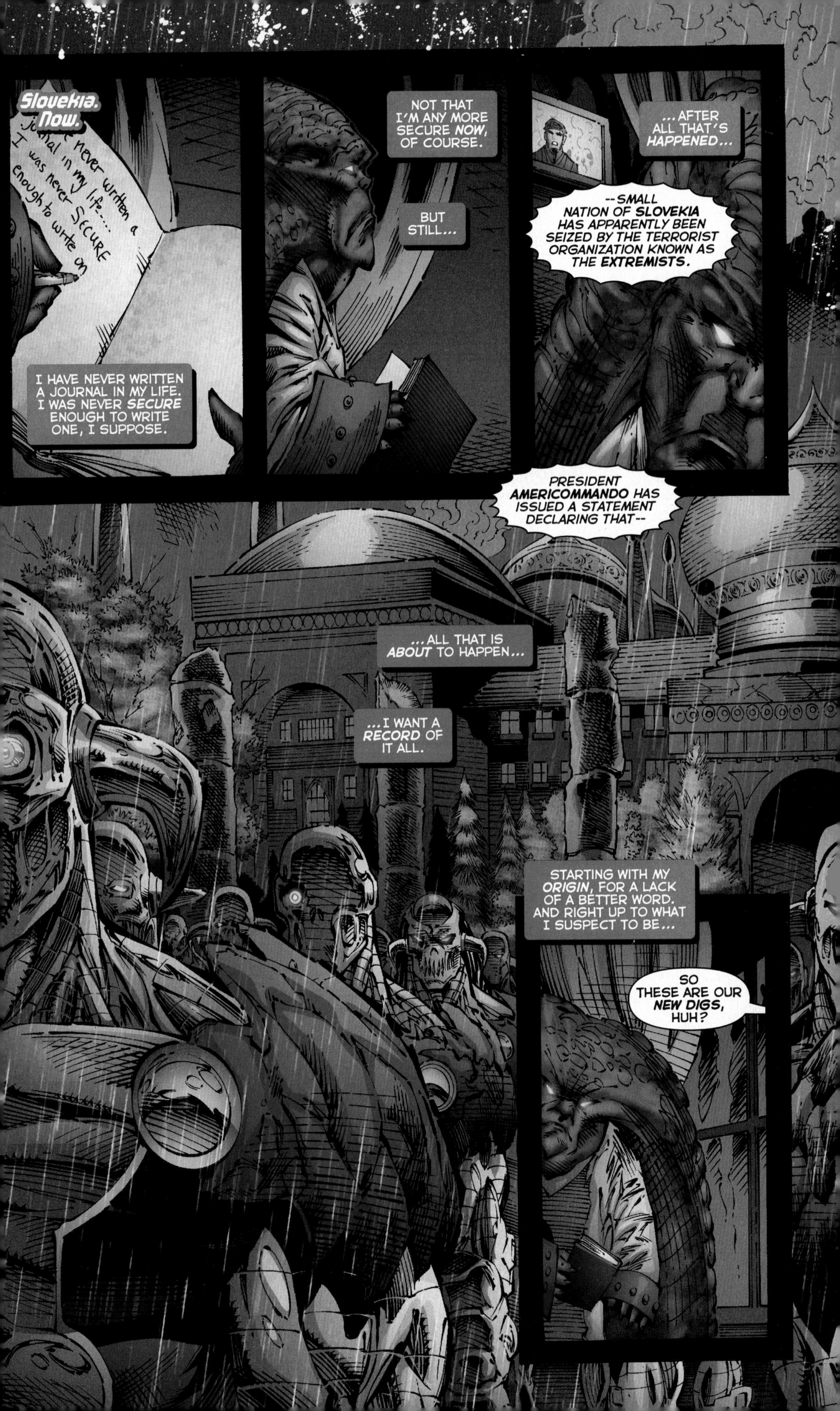

Slovekia. Now.
I have never written a journal in my life.... I was never SECURE enough to write one
I HAVE NEVER WRITTEN A JOURNAL IN MY LIFE. I WAS NEVER SECURE ENOUGH TO WRITE ONE, I SUPPOSE.
NOT THAT I'M ANY MORE SECURE NOW, OF COURSE.
BUT STILL...
...AFTER ALL THAT'S HAPPENED...
--SMALL NATION OF SLOVEKIA HAS APPARENTLY BEEN SEIZED BY THE TERRORIST ORGANIZATION KNOWN AS THE EXTREMISTS.
PRESIDENT AMERICOMMANDO HAS ISSUED A STATEMENT DECLARING THAT--
...ALL THAT IS ABOUT TO HAPPEN...
...I WANT A RECORD OF IT ALL.
STARTING WITH MY ORIGIN, FOR A LACK OF A BETTER WORD. AND RIGHT UP TO WHAT I SUSPECT TO BE...
SO THESE ARE OUR NEW DIGS, HUH?

...THE LAST DAYS OF
THE EXTREMISTS
QUAINT, HUH?
A MISTAKE IS MORE LIKE IT, TRACER.
THE ADVANTAGE OF HAVING OUR OWN COUNTRY AS A BASE OF OPERATIONS IS FAR OUTWEIGHED BY THE UPROAR IT'S CREATED IN THE INTERNATIONAL COMMUNITY.
ESPECIALLY JUST MONTHS AFTER OUR ASSASSINATION OF PRESIDENT TIN MAN.
I'M FAIRLY CERTAIN AMERICOMMANDO'S NEXT MOVE WILL BE TO APPROACH THE INTERNATIONAL COUNCIL WITH A DECLARATION OF WAR... ONE THEY'LL BE ALL TOO HAPPY TO GRANT HIM.
I DUNNO, DOC. IF THE BOSSMAN THINKS IT'S ALL A GOOD IDEA, THEN I GUESS IT'S A GOOD IDEA.
HE AIN'T NEVER LET US DOWN BEFORE.
HIS EGO HAS GROWN TO UNMANAGEABLE PROPORTIONS. AFTER ALL, WHY WERE WE NOT CONSULTED ON THIS?
TELL ME THAT'S NOT THE TRUE REASON BEHIND ALL YOUR BLATHERING, DIEHARD. THAT YOUR OWN FRAGILE EGO HAS BEEN BRUISED?
DON'T BE RIDICULOUS, DREAMSLAYER. ANY MAN WITH AN IOTA OF INTELLIGENCE CAN SEE I'M RIGHT.
SURELY YOU OF ALL PEOPLE MUST SEE IT MY WAY, GORGON?
ME? I...I...
NOW'S YOUR CHANCE TO SAY SOMETHING, YOU SPINELESS COWARD! SPEAK UP! YOU KNOW DIEHARD IS RIGHT.
...I DON'T HAVE AN OPINION ONE WAY OR THE OTHER.
PATHETIC, MORTIMER. TRULY PATHETIC.
AND DIEHARD SEEMS TO HAVE FAR TOO MANY OPINIONS THESE DAYS...

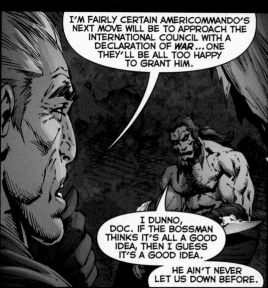

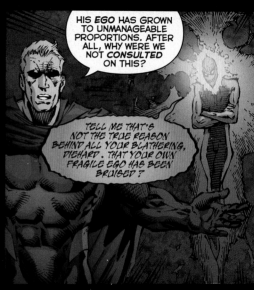

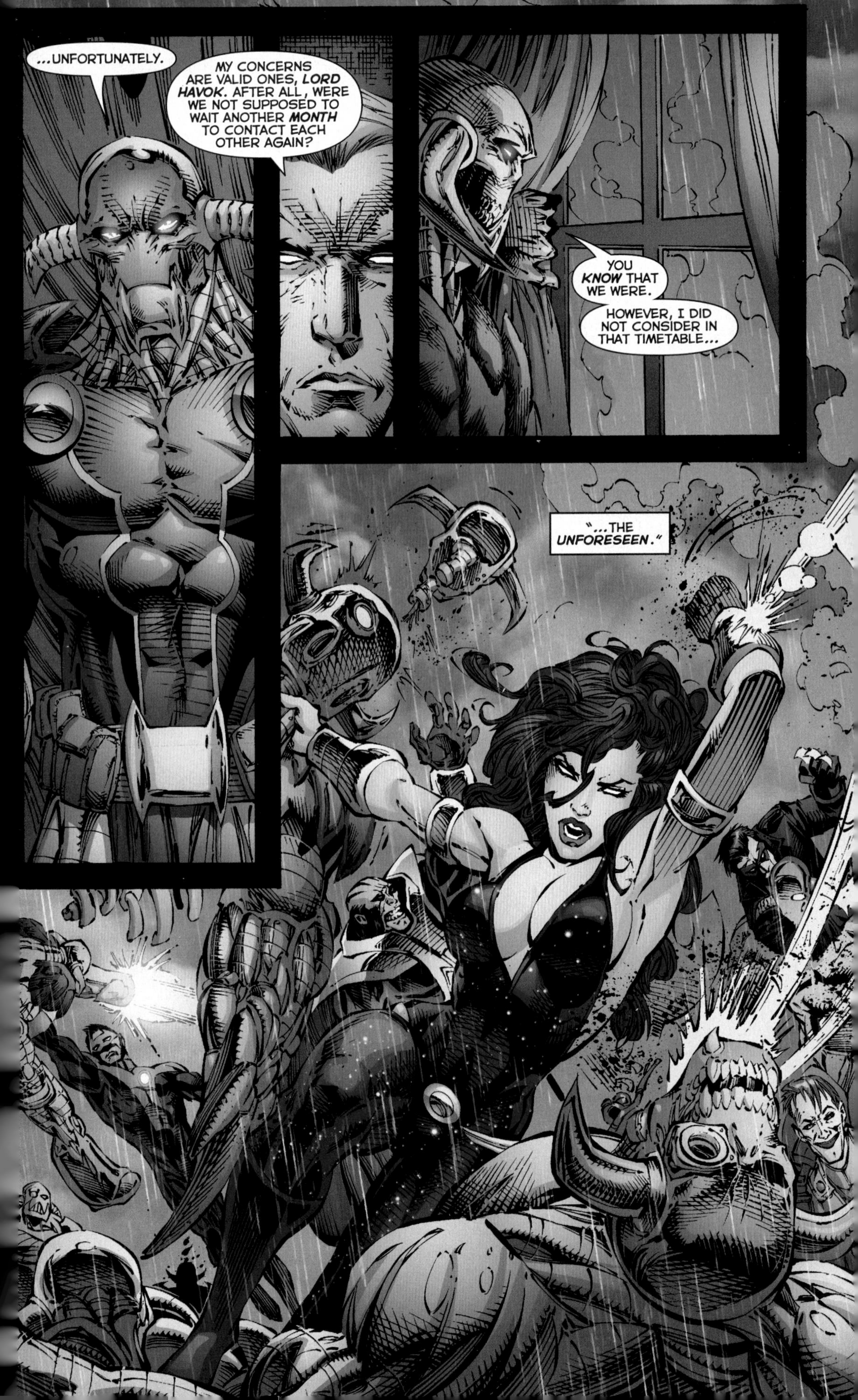
...UNFORTUNATELY.
MY CONCERNS ARE VALID ONES, LORD HAVOK. AFTER ALL, WERE WE NOT SUPPOSED TO WAIT ANOTHER MONTH TO CONTACT EACH OTHER AGAIN?
YOU KNOW THAT WE WERE.
HOWEVER, I DID NOT CONSIDER IN THAT TIMETABLE...
"...THE UNFORESEEN."

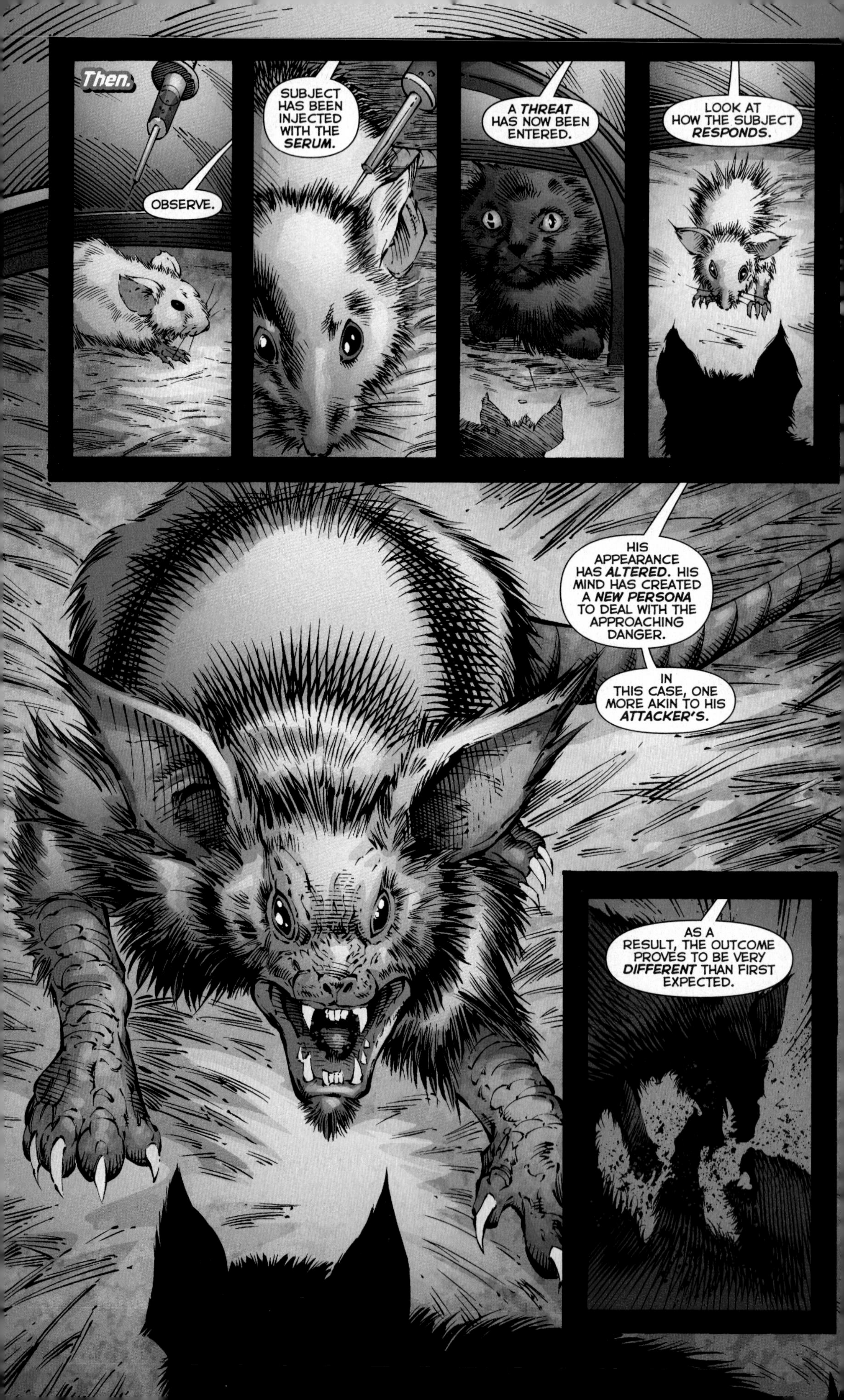
Then.
OBSERVE.
SUBJECT HAS BEEN INJECTED WITH THE SERUM.
A THREAT HAS NOW BEEN ENTERED.
LOOK AT HOW THE SUBJECT RESPONDS.
HIS APPEARANCE HAS ALTERED. HIS MIND HAS CREATED A NEW PERSONA TO DEAL WITH THE APPROACHING DANGER.
IN THIS CASE, ONE MORE AKIN TO HIS ATTACKER'S.
AS A RESULT, THE OUTCOME PROVES TO BE VERY DIFFERENT THAN FIRST EXPECTED.

GOOD WORK, DOCTOR.

I SAY WE BEGIN TESTING WITHIN THE MONTH.

WHY WAIT? BEGIN NOW. THE MORE SUPER FREAKS AT OUR DISPOSAL, THE BETTER.

WORK WAS *NEVER BETTER.* I WAS FINALLY STARTING TO GET THE RECOGNITION I *DESERVED.*

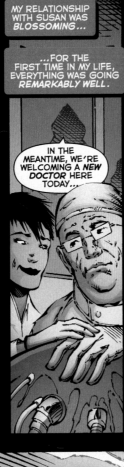

MY RELATIONSHIP WITH SUSAN WAS *BLOSSOMING...*

...FOR THE FIRST TIME IN MY LIFE, EVERYTHING WAS GOING *REMARKABLY WELL.*

IN THE MEANTIME, WE'RE WELCOMING A *NEW* DOCTOR HERE TODAY...

THAT IS UNTIL *HE* SHOWED UP.

...DR. *LEONARD GRANT.*

"LEN." PLEASE. LOOKING FORWARD TO WORKING WITH YOU.

ER... YES. YES, OF COURSE.

OF COURSE.

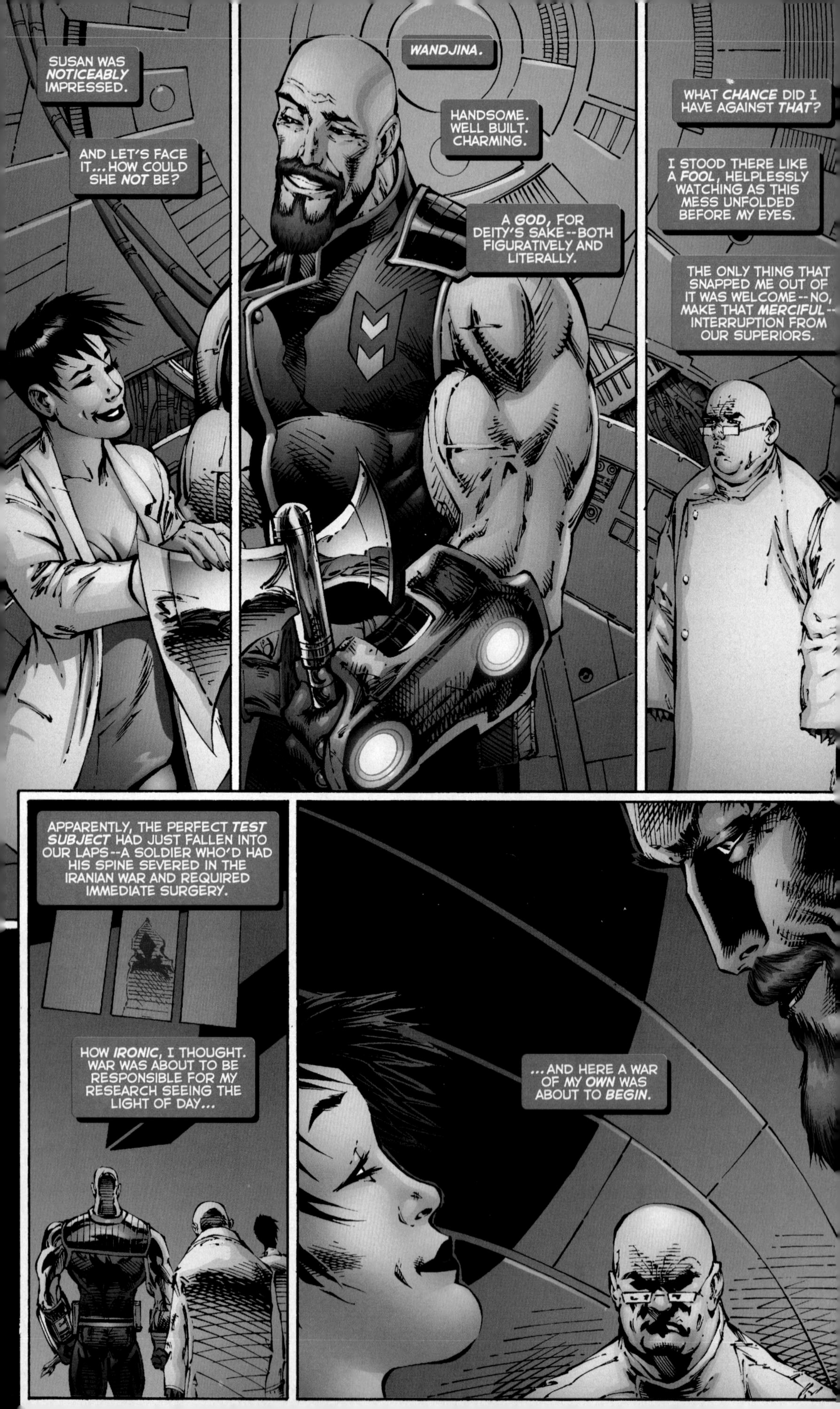

SUSAN WAS NOTICEABLY IMPRESSED.
AND LET'S FACE IT...HOW COULD SHE NOT BE?
WANDJINA.
HANDSOME. WELL BUILT. CHARMING.
A GOD, FOR DEITY'S SAKE--BOTH FIGURATIVELY AND LITERALLY.
WHAT CHANCE DID I HAVE AGAINST THAT?
I STOOD THERE LIKE A FOOL, HELPLESSLY WATCHING AS THIS MESS UNFOLDED BEFORE MY EYES.
THE ONLY THING THAT SNAPPED ME OUT OF IT WAS WELCOME--NO, MAKE THAT MERCIFUL--INTERRUPTION FROM OUR SUPERIORS.
APPARENTLY, THE PERFECT TEST SUBJECT HAD JUST FALLEN INTO OUR LAPS--A SOLDIER WHO'D HAD HIS SPINE SEVERED IN THE IRANIAN WAR AND REQUIRED IMMEDIATE SURGERY.
HOW IRONIC, I THOUGHT. WAR WAS ABOUT TO BE RESPONSIBLE FOR MY RESEARCH SEEING THE LIGHT OF DAY...
...AND HERE A WAR OF MY OWN WAS ABOUT TO BEGIN.

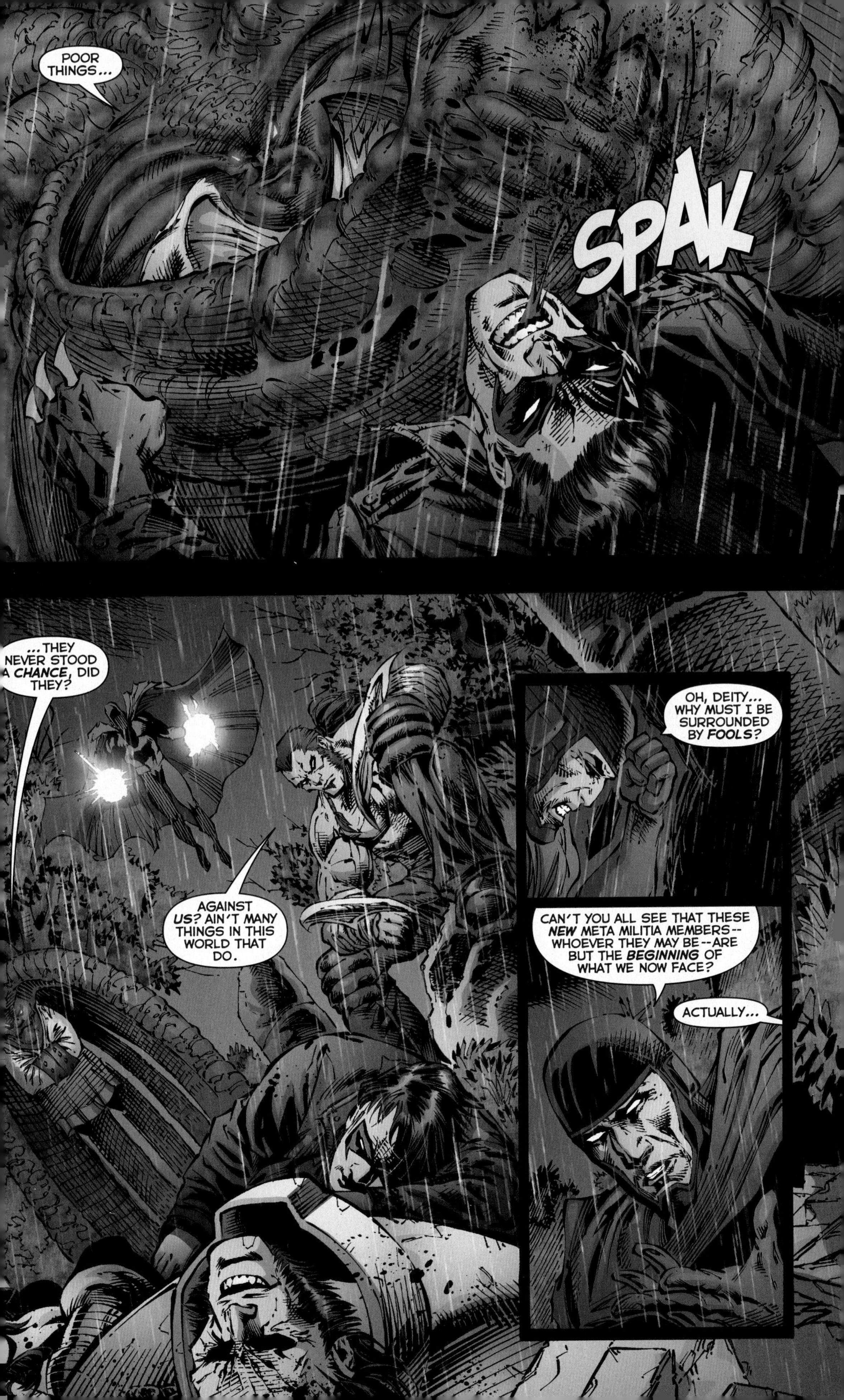
POOR THINGS...
SPAK
...THEY NEVER STOOD A CHANCE, DID THEY?
AGAINST US? AIN'T MANY THINGS IN THIS WORLD THAT DO.
OH, DEITY... WHY MUST I BE SURROUNDED BY FOOLS?
CAN'T YOU ALL SEE THAT THESE NEW META MILITIA MEMBERS-- WHOEVER THEY MAY BE--ARE BUT THE BEGINNING OF WHAT WE NOW FACE?
ACTUALLY...

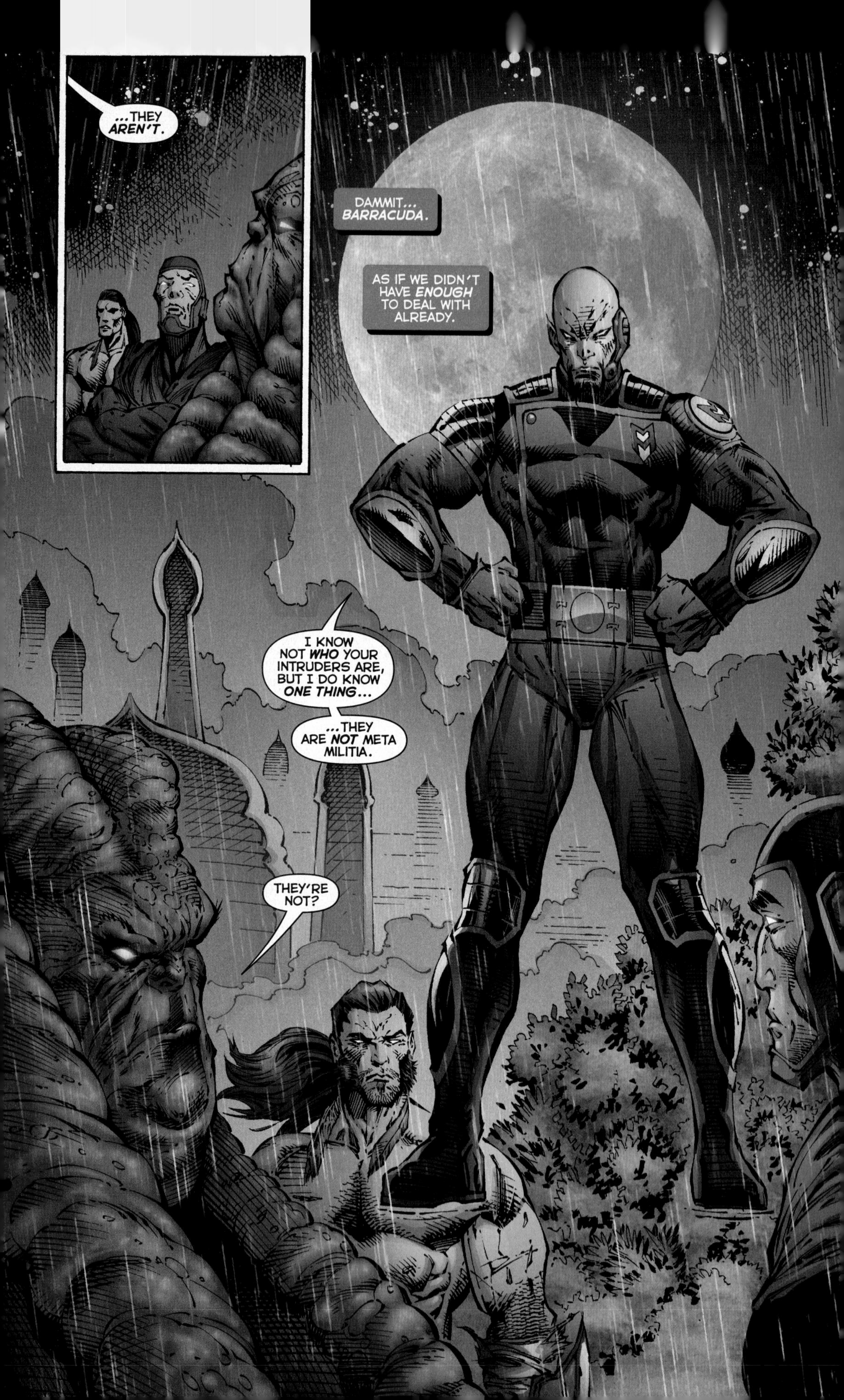

...THEY AREN'T.
DAMMIT... BARRACUDA.
AS IF WE DIDN'T HAVE ENOUGH TO DEAL WITH ALREADY.
I KNOW NOT WHO YOUR INTRUDERS ARE, BUT I DO KNOW ONE THING...
...THEY ARE NOT META MILITIA.
THEY'RE NOT?

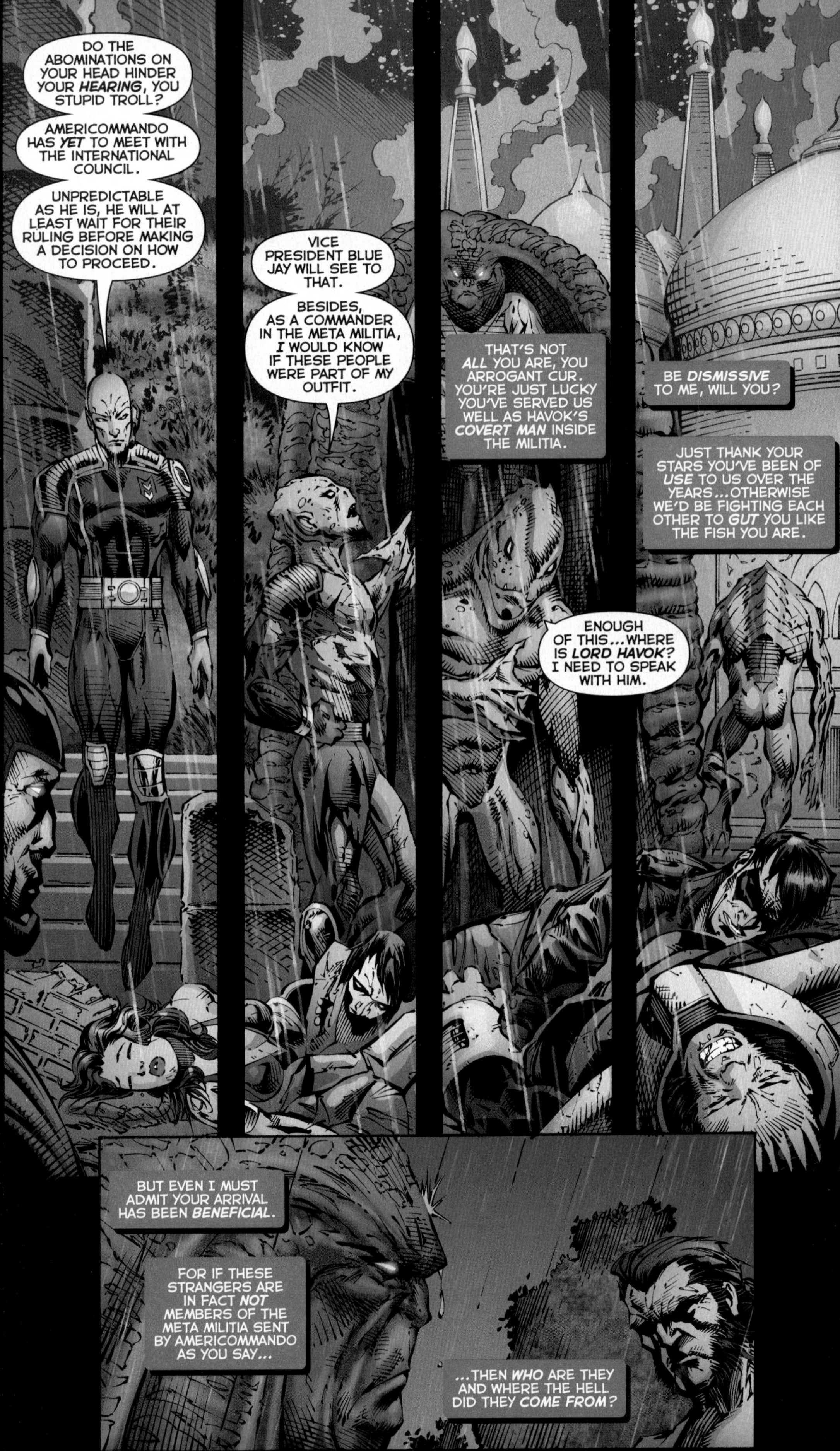
DO THE ABOMINATIONS ON YOUR HEAD HINDER YOUR *HEARING*, YOU STUPID TROLL?
AMERICOMMANDO HAS *YET* TO MEET WITH THE INTERNATIONAL COUNCIL.
UNPREDICTABLE AS HE IS, HE WILL AT LEAST WAIT FOR THEIR RULING BEFORE MAKING A DECISION ON HOW TO PROCEED.
VICE PRESIDENT BLUE JAY WILL SEE TO THAT.
BESIDES, AS A COMMANDER IN THE META MILITIA, *I* WOULD KNOW IF THESE PEOPLE WERE PART OF MY OUTFIT.
THAT'S NOT *ALL* YOU ARE, YOU ARROGANT CUR. YOU'RE JUST LUCKY YOU'VE SERVED US WELL AS HAVOK'S *COVERT MAN* INSIDE THE MILITIA.
ENOUGH OF THIS... WHERE IS *LORD HAVOK*? I NEED TO SPEAK WITH HIM.
BE *DISMISSIVE* TO ME, WILL YOU?
JUST THANK YOUR STARS YOU'VE BEEN OF *USE* TO US OVER THE YEARS... OTHERWISE WE'D BE FIGHTING EACH OTHER TO *GUT* YOU LIKE THE FISH YOU ARE.
BUT EVEN I MUST ADMIT YOUR ARRIVAL HAS BEEN *BENEFICIAL*.
FOR IF THESE STRANGERS ARE IN FACT *NOT* MEMBERS OF THE META MILITIA SENT BY AMERICOMMANDO AS YOU SAY...
...THEN *WHO* ARE THEY AND WHERE THE HELL DID THEY *COME FROM*?

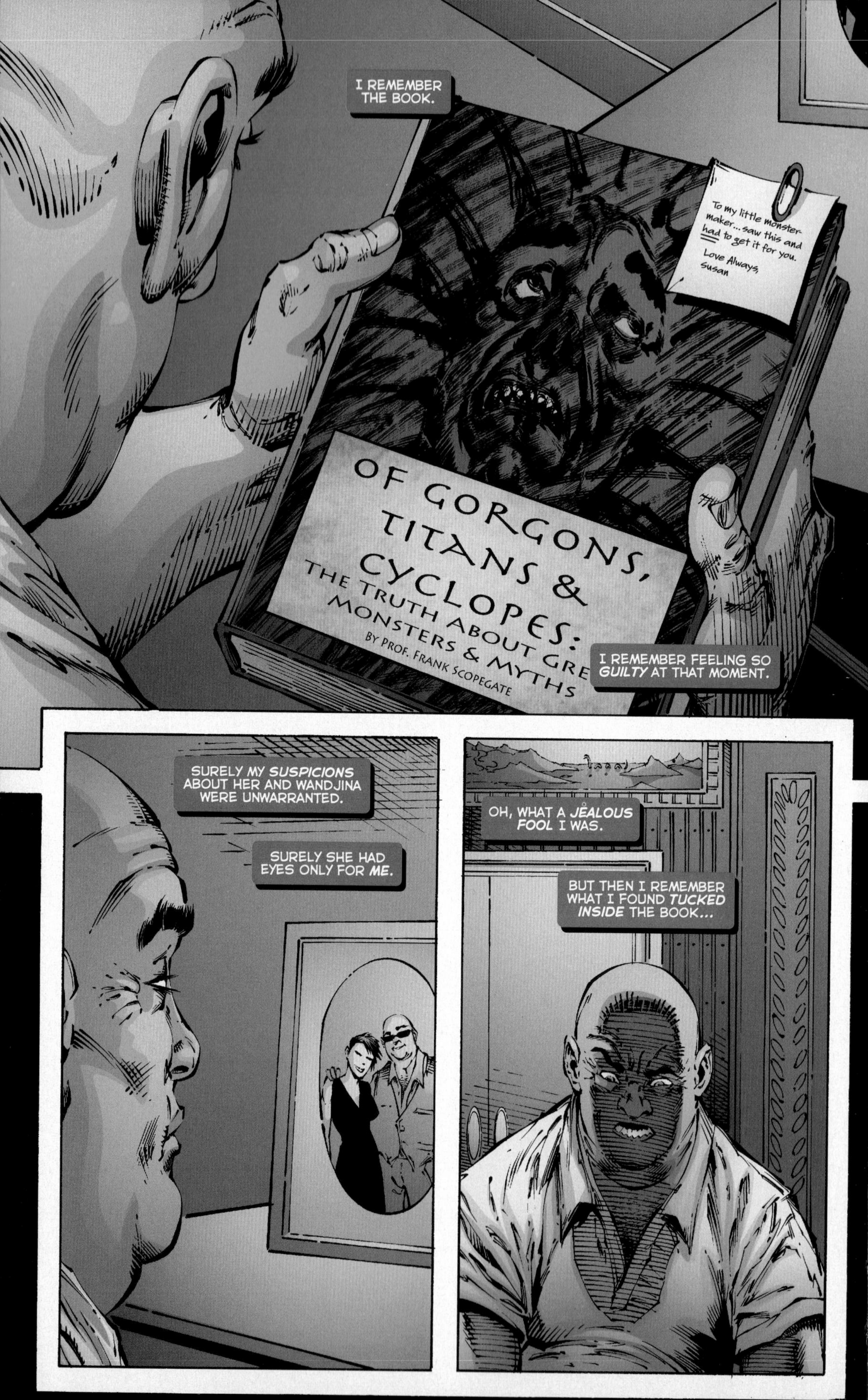
I REMEMBER THE BOOK.
To my little monster-maker... saw this and had to get it for you.
Love Always,
Susan
OF GORGONS, TITANS & CYCLOPES:
THE TRUTH ABOUT GRE
MONSTERS & MYTHS
BY PROF. FRANK SCOPEGATE
I REMEMBER FEELING SO GUILTY AT THAT MOMENT.
SURELY MY SUSPICIONS ABOUT HER AND WANDJINA WERE UNWARRANTED.
SURELY SHE HAD EYES ONLY FOR ME.
OH, WHAT A JEALOUS FOOL I WAS.
BUT THEN I REMEMBER WHAT I FOUND TUCKED INSIDE THE BOOK...

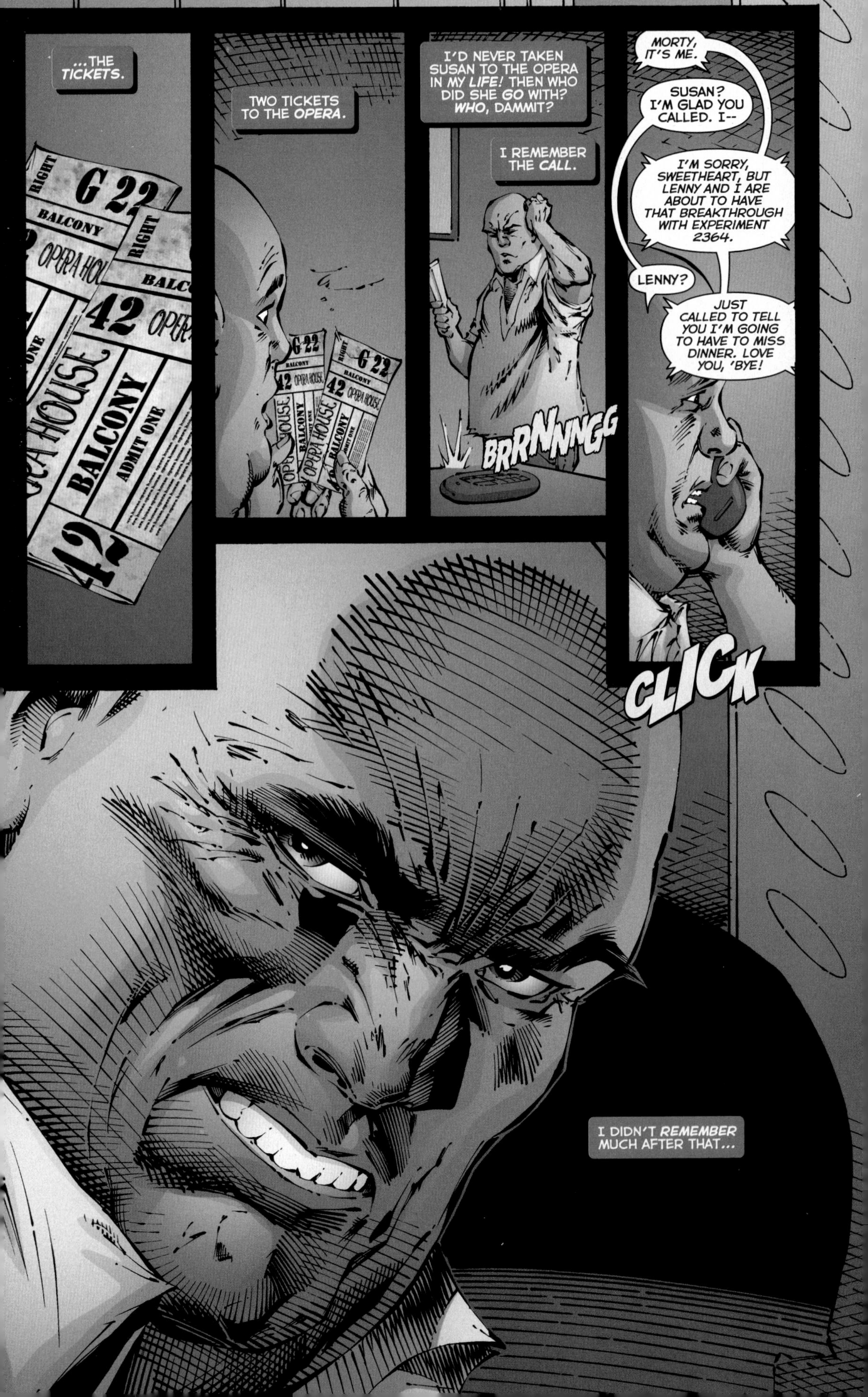
...THE TICKETS.
RIGHT G 22 BALCONY OPERA HOUSE
RIGHT BALCONY 42 OPERA HOUSE BALCONY ADMIT ONE
TWO TICKETS TO THE OPERA.
I'D NEVER TAKEN SUSAN TO THE OPERA IN MY LIFE! THEN WHO DID SHE GO WITH? WHO, DAMMIT?
I REMEMBER THE CALL.
BRRNNNGG
MORTY, IT'S ME.
SUSAN? I'M GLAD YOU CALLED. I--
I'M SORRY, SWEETHEART, BUT LENNY AND I ARE ABOUT TO HAVE THAT BREAKTHROUGH WITH EXPERIMENT 2364.
LENNY?
JUST CALLED TO TELL YOU I'M GOING TO HAVE TO MISS DINNER. LOVE YOU, 'BYE!
CLICK
I DIDN'T REMEMBER MUCH AFTER THAT...

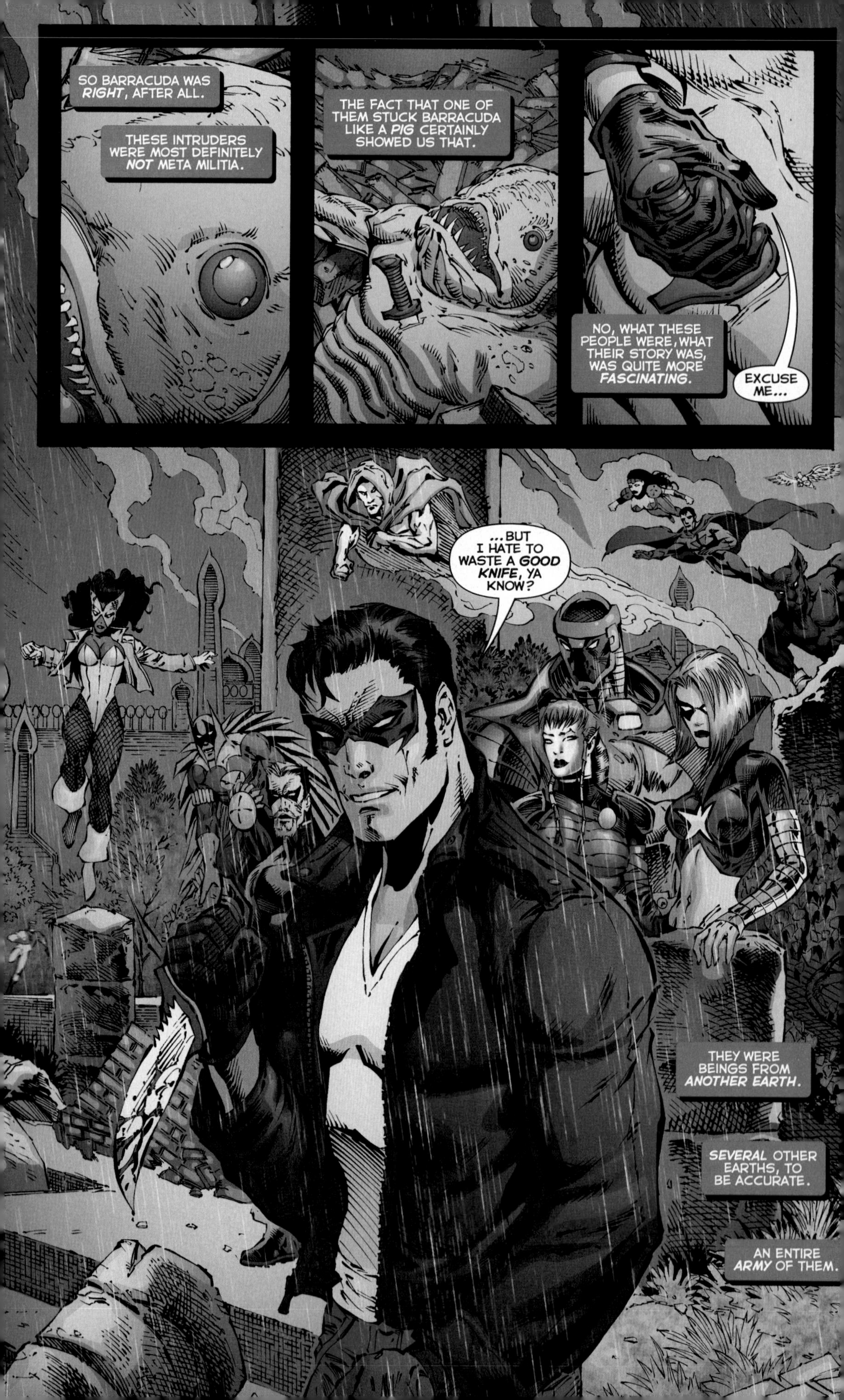
SO BARRACUDA WAS *RIGHT*, AFTER ALL.
THESE INTRUDERS WERE MOST DEFINITELY *NOT* META MILITIA.
THE FACT THAT ONE OF THEM STUCK BARRACUDA LIKE A *PIG* CERTAINLY SHOWED US THAT.
NO, WHAT THESE PEOPLE WERE, WHAT THEIR STORY WAS, WAS QUITE MORE *FASCINATING*.
EXCUSE ME...
...BUT I HATE TO WASTE A *GOOD KNIFE*, YA KNOW?
THEY WERE BEINGS FROM *ANOTHER EARTH*.
SEVERAL OTHER EARTHS, TO BE ACCURATE.
AN ENTIRE *ARMY* OF THEM.

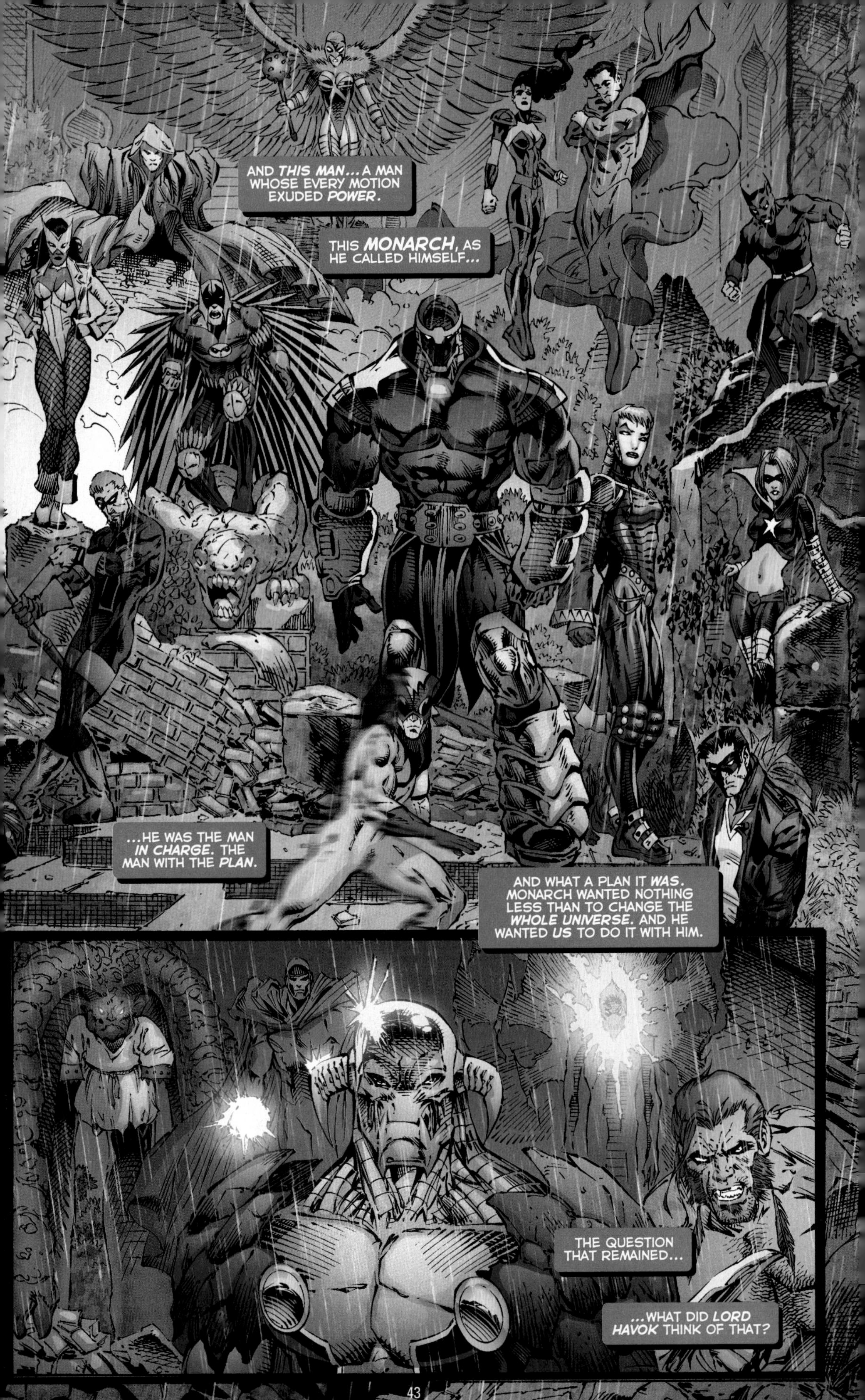
AND *THIS MAN*... A MAN WHOSE EVERY MOTION EXUDED *POWER*.
THIS ***MONARCH***, AS HE CALLED HIMSELF...
...HE WAS THE MAN *IN CHARGE*. THE MAN WITH THE *PLAN*.
AND WHAT A PLAN IT *WAS*. MONARCH WANTED NOTHING LESS THAN TO CHANGE THE *WHOLE UNIVERSE*. AND HE WANTED *US* TO DO IT WITH HIM.
THE QUESTION THAT REMAINED...
...WHAT DID *LORD HAVOK* THINK OF THAT?

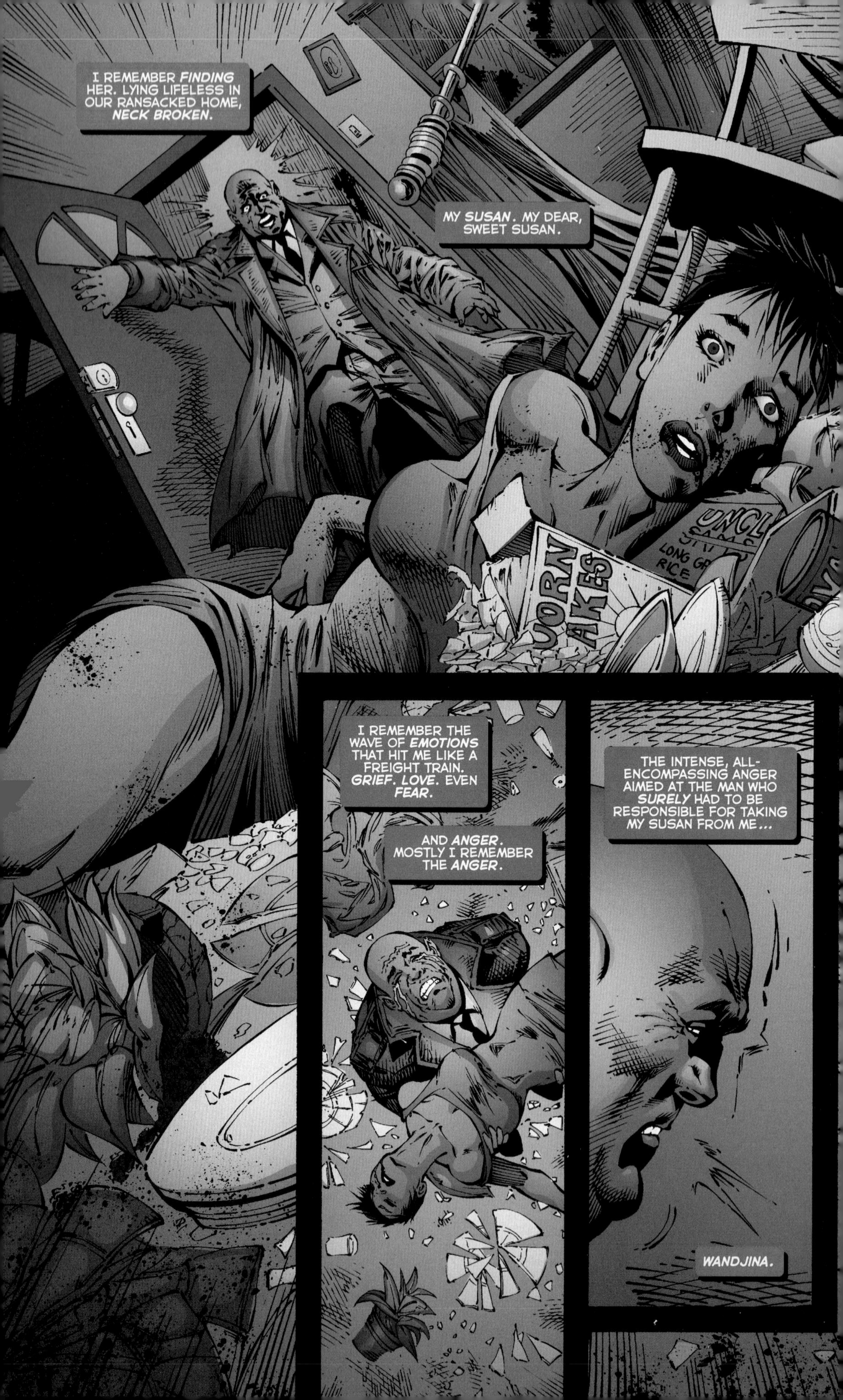
I REMEMBER *FINDING* HER. LYING LIFELESS IN OUR RANSACKED HOME, ***NECK BROKEN***.
MY *SUSAN*. MY DEAR, SWEET SUSAN.
UNCL
LONG GR
RICE
ORN
AKES
I REMEMBER THE WAVE OF *EMOTIONS* THAT HIT ME LIKE A FREIGHT TRAIN. ***GRIEF. LOVE.*** EVEN ***FEAR***.
AND *ANGER*. MOSTLY I REMEMBER THE *ANGER*.
THE INTENSE, ALL-ENCOMPASSING ANGER AIMED AT THE MAN WHO *SURELY* HAD TO BE RESPONSIBLE FOR TAKING MY SUSAN FROM ME...
WANDJINA.

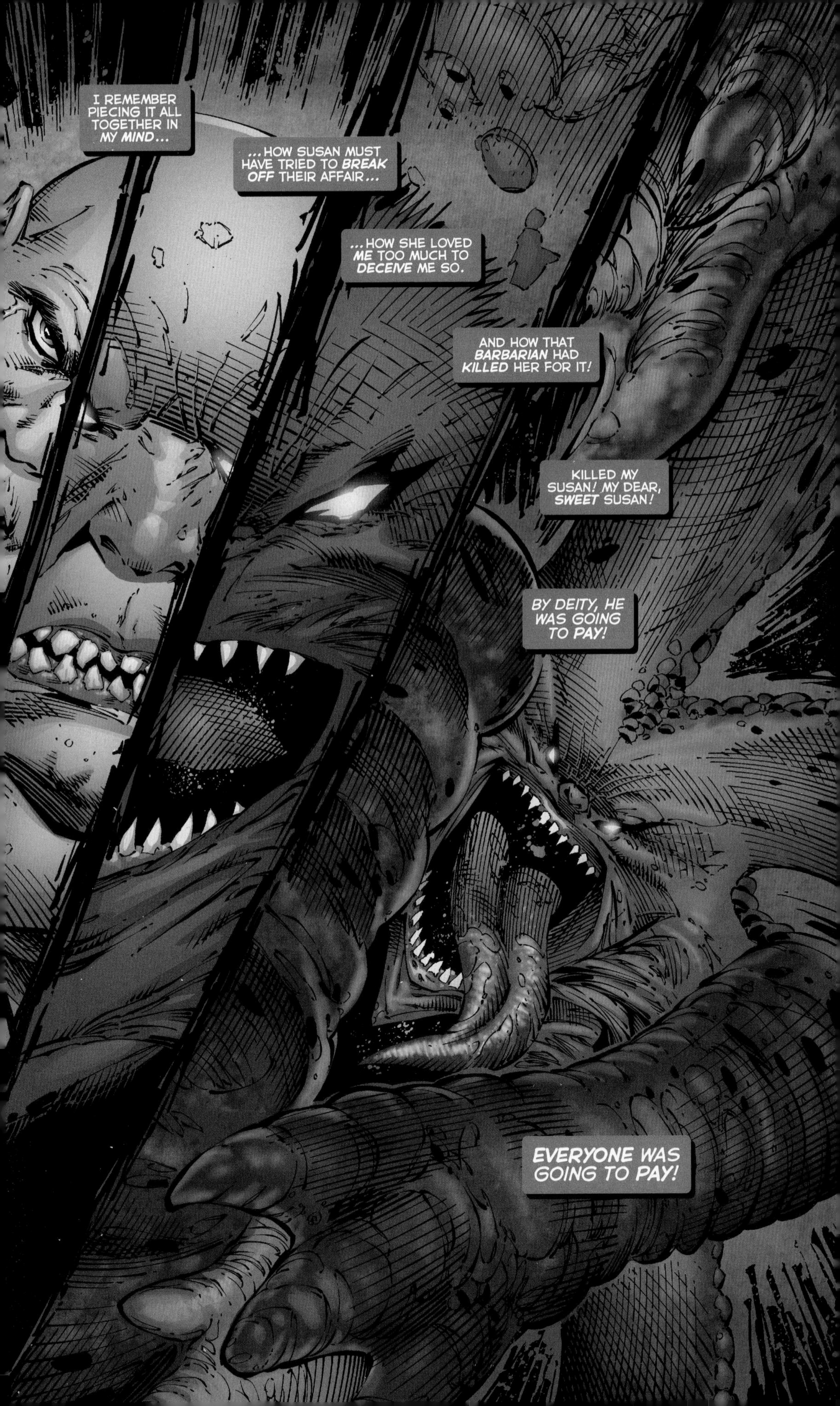
I REMEMBER PIECING IT ALL TOGETHER IN *MY MIND*...
...HOW SUSAN MUST HAVE TRIED TO *BREAK OFF* THEIR AFFAIR...
...HOW SHE LOVED *ME* TOO MUCH TO *DECEIVE* ME SO.
AND HOW THAT *BARBARIAN* HAD *KILLED* HER FOR IT!
KILLED MY SUSAN! MY DEAR, *SWEET* SUSAN!
BY DEITY, HE WAS GOING TO *PAY!*
EVERYONE WAS GOING TO *PAY!*

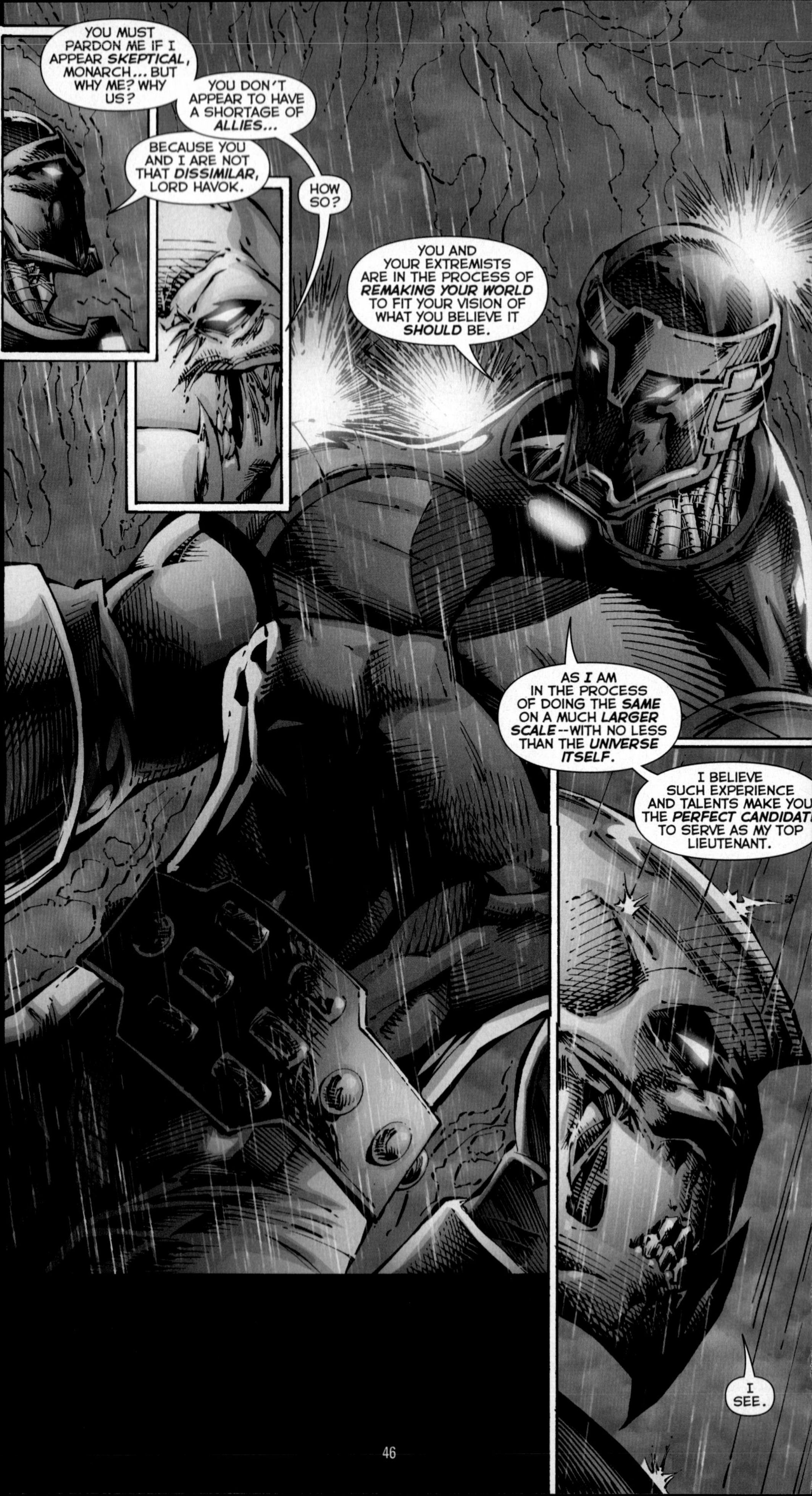

YOU MUST PARDON ME IF I APPEAR *SKEPTICAL*, MONARCH... BUT WHY ME? WHY US?
YOU DON'T APPEAR TO HAVE A SHORTAGE OF *ALLIES*...
BECAUSE YOU AND I ARE NOT THAT *DISSIMILAR*, LORD HAVOK.
HOW SO?
YOU AND YOUR EXTREMISTS ARE IN THE PROCESS OF *REMAKING YOUR WORLD* TO FIT YOUR VISION OF WHAT YOU BELIEVE IT *SHOULD* BE.
AS *I* AM IN THE PROCESS OF DOING THE *SAME* ON A MUCH *LARGER SCALE*--WITH NO LESS THAN THE *UNIVERSE ITSELF*.
I BELIEVE SUCH EXPERIENCE AND TALENTS MAKE YOU THE *PERFECT CANDIDATE* TO SERVE AS MY TOP LIEUTENANT.
I SEE.

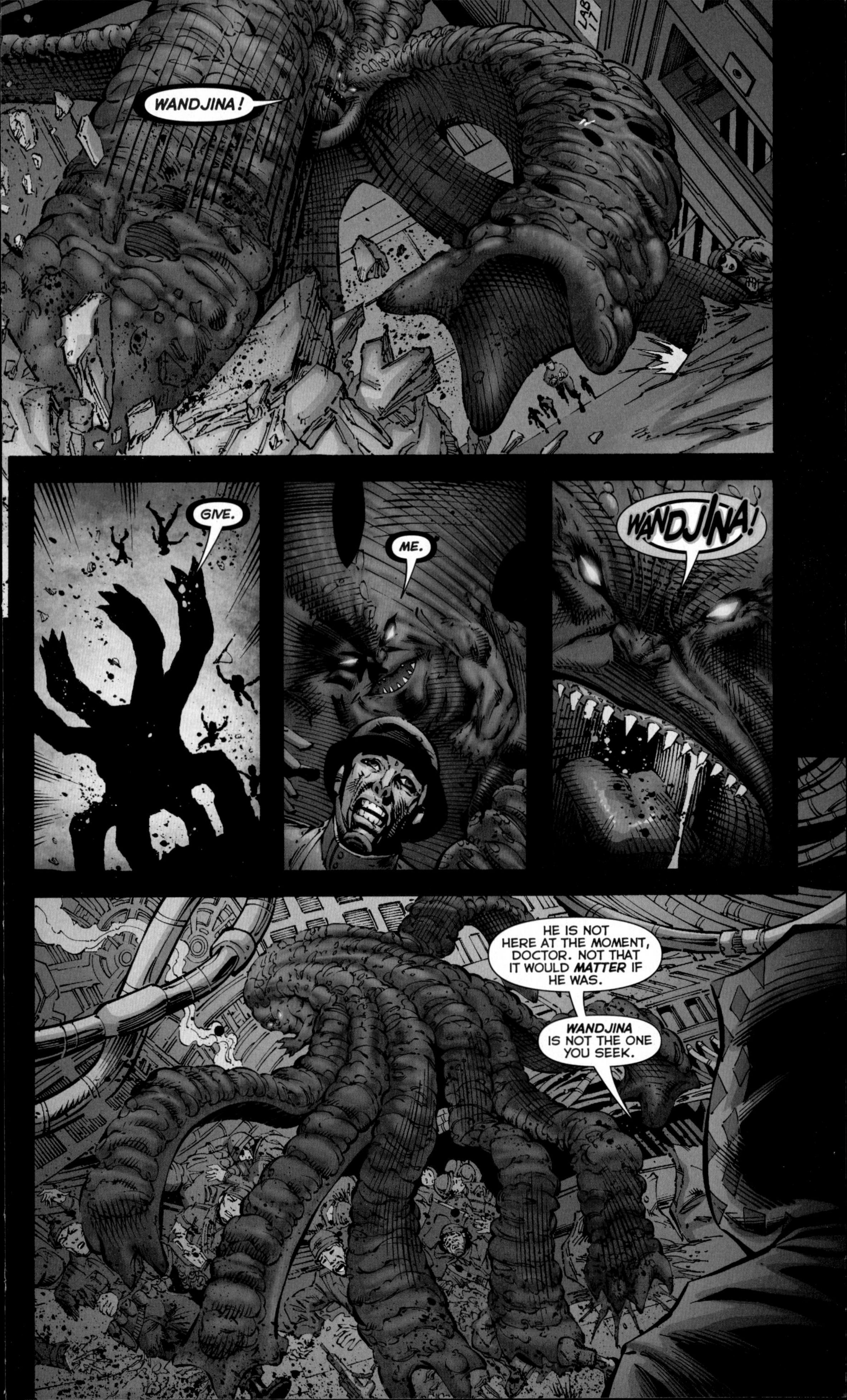
WANDJINA!
GIVE.
ME.
WANDJINA!
HE IS NOT HERE AT THE MOMENT, DOCTOR. NOT THAT IT WOULD MATTER IF HE WAS.
WANDJINA IS NOT THE ONE YOU SEEK.

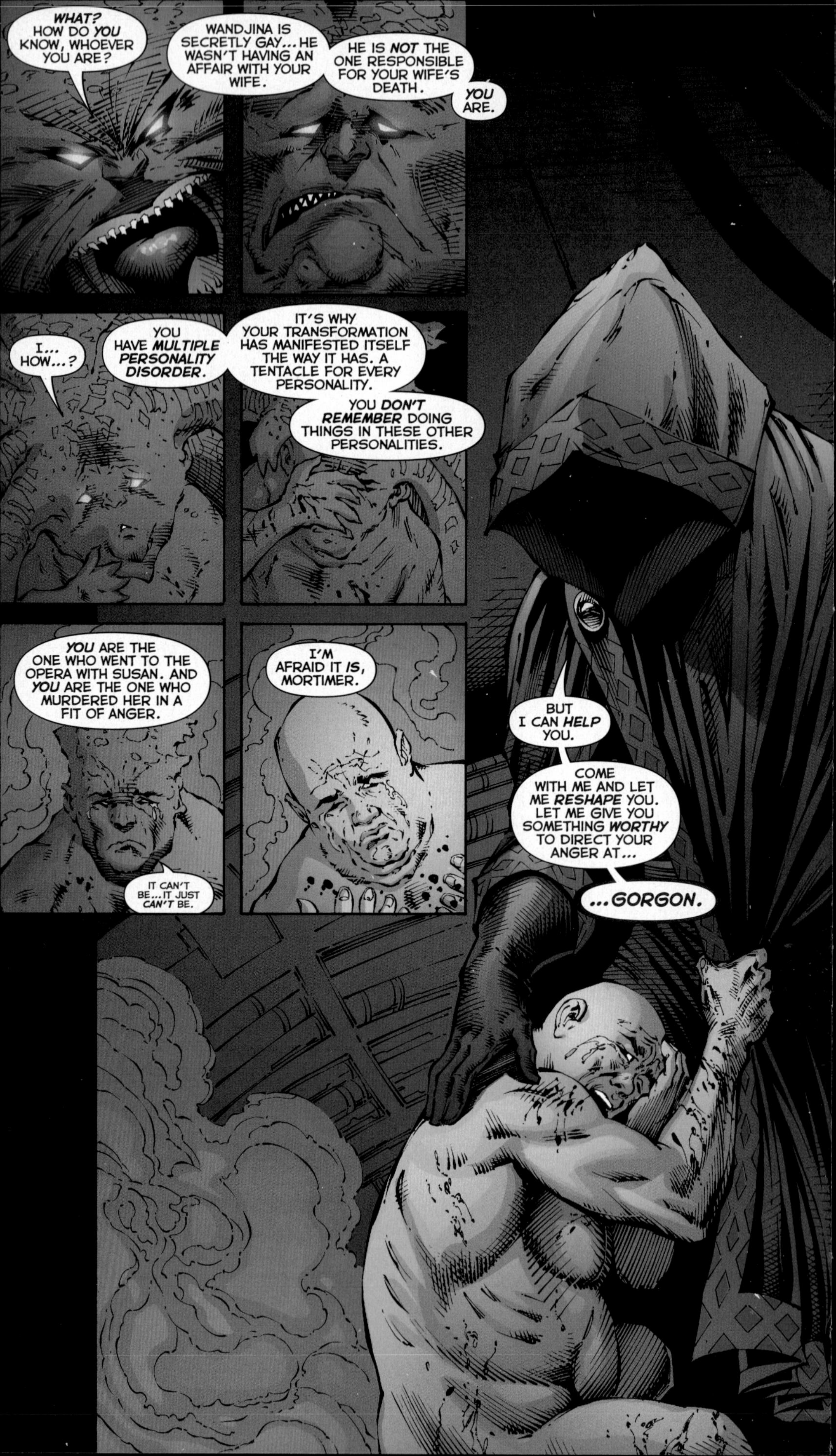
WHAT? HOW DO YOU KNOW, WHOEVER YOU ARE?
WANDJINA IS SECRETLY GAY... HE WASN'T HAVING AN AFFAIR WITH YOUR WIFE.
HE IS NOT THE ONE RESPONSIBLE FOR YOUR WIFE'S DEATH.
YOU ARE.
I... HOW...?
YOU HAVE MULTIPLE PERSONALITY DISORDER.
IT'S WHY YOUR TRANSFORMATION HAS MANIFESTED ITSELF THE WAY IT HAS. A TENTACLE FOR EVERY PERSONALITY.
YOU DON'T REMEMBER DOING THINGS IN THESE OTHER PERSONALITIES.
YOU ARE THE ONE WHO WENT TO THE OPERA WITH SUSAN. AND YOU ARE THE ONE WHO MURDERED HER IN A FIT OF ANGER.
IT CAN'T BE... IT JUST CAN'T BE.
I'M AFRAID IT IS, MORTIMER.
BUT I CAN HELP YOU.
COME WITH ME AND LET ME RESHAPE YOU. LET ME GIVE YOU SOMETHING WORTHY TO DIRECT YOUR ANGER AT...
...GORGON.

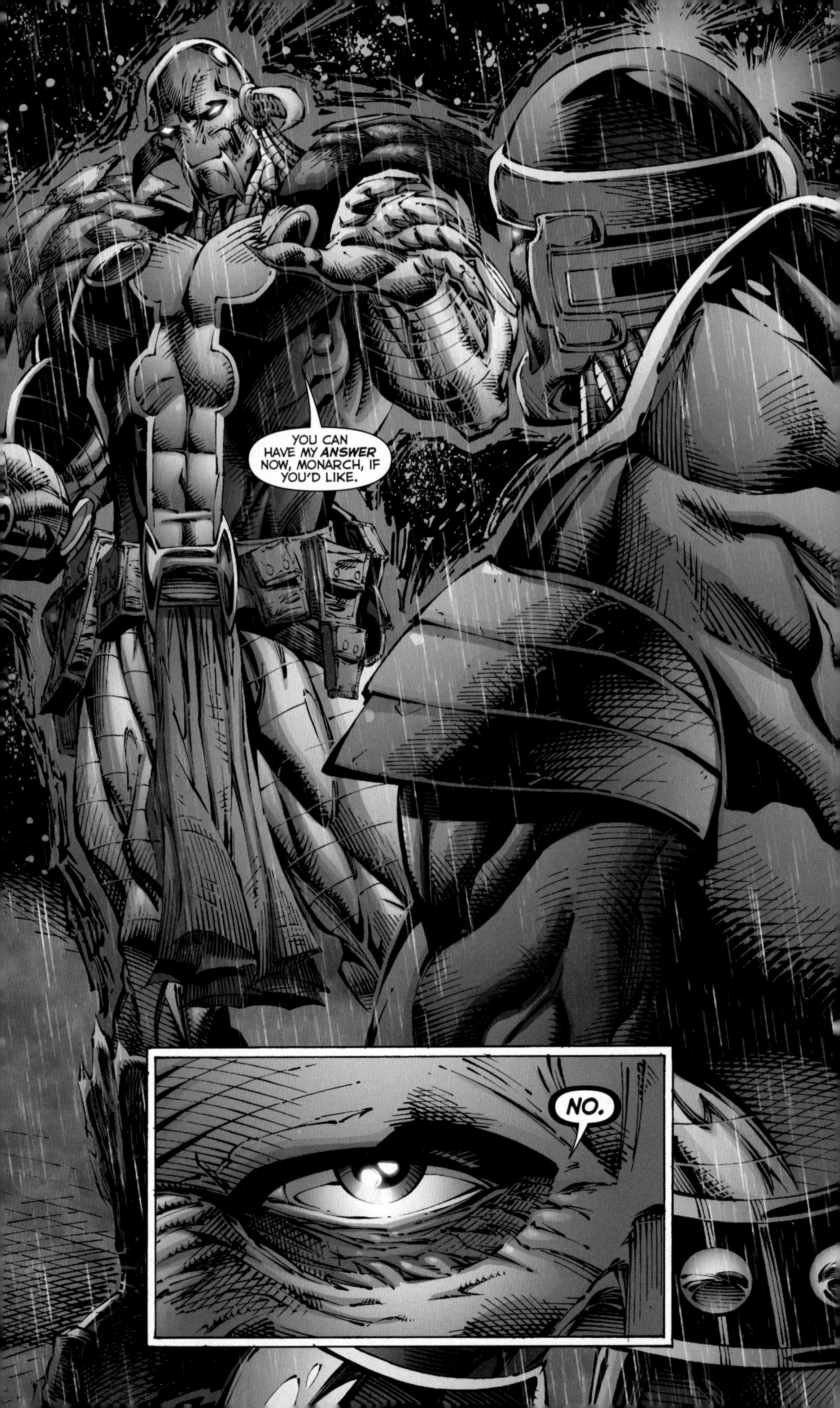
YOU CAN HAVE MY ANSWER NOW, MONARCH, IF YOU'D LIKE.
NO.

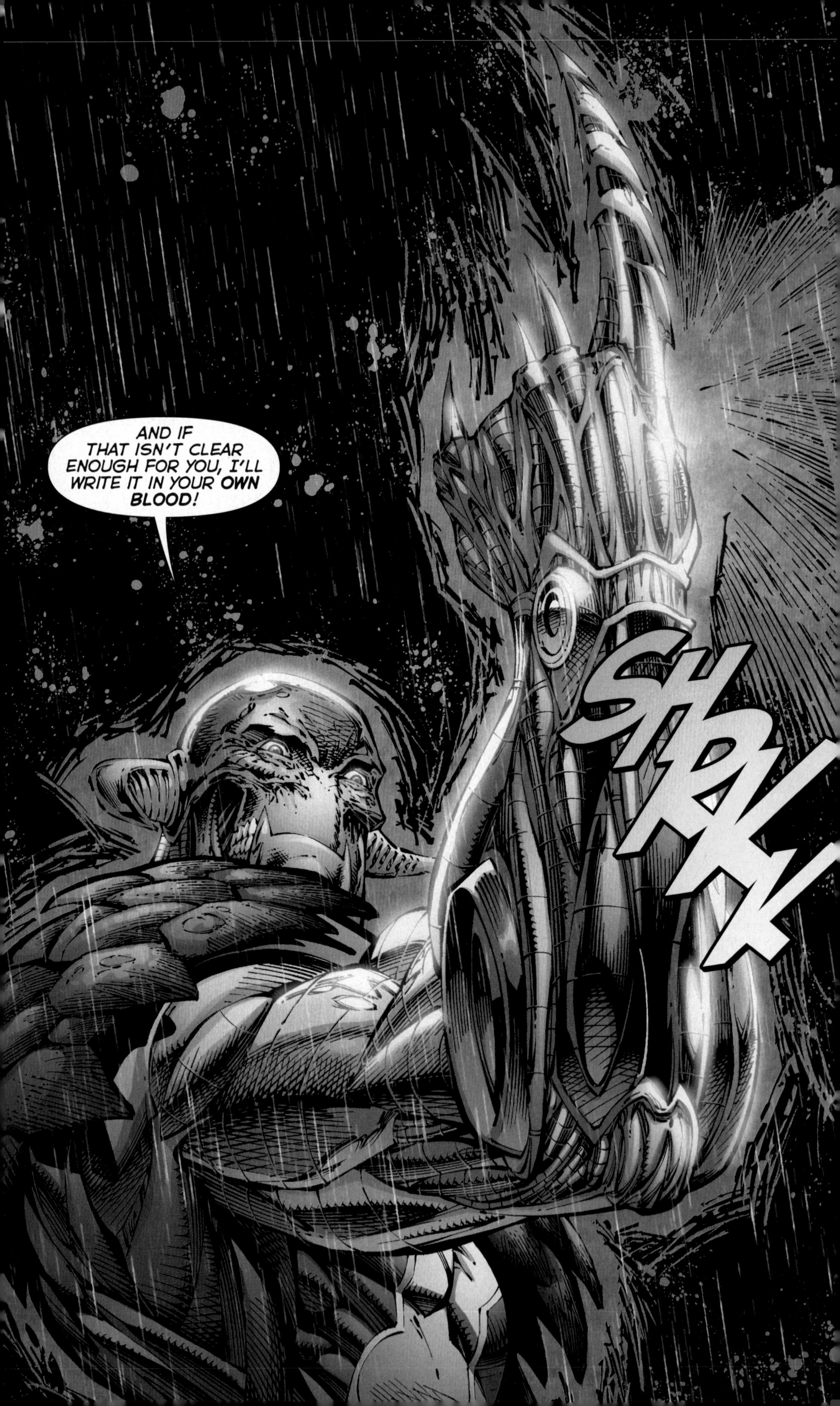

AND IF THAT ISN'T CLEAR ENOUGH FOR YOU, I'LL WRITE IT IN YOUR OWN BLOOD!
SHNK

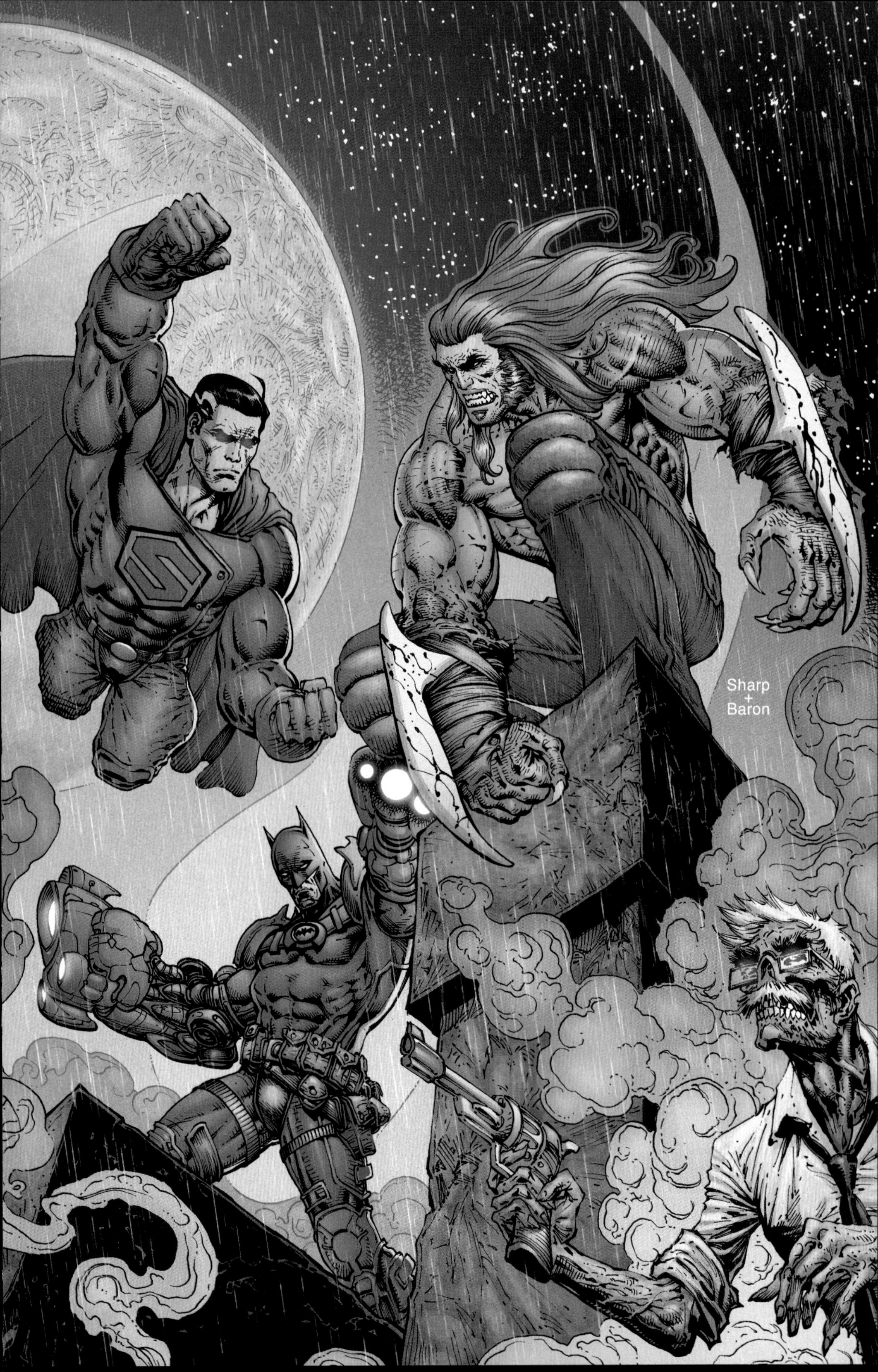
Sharp
+
Baron

Part 3: The Beast Within

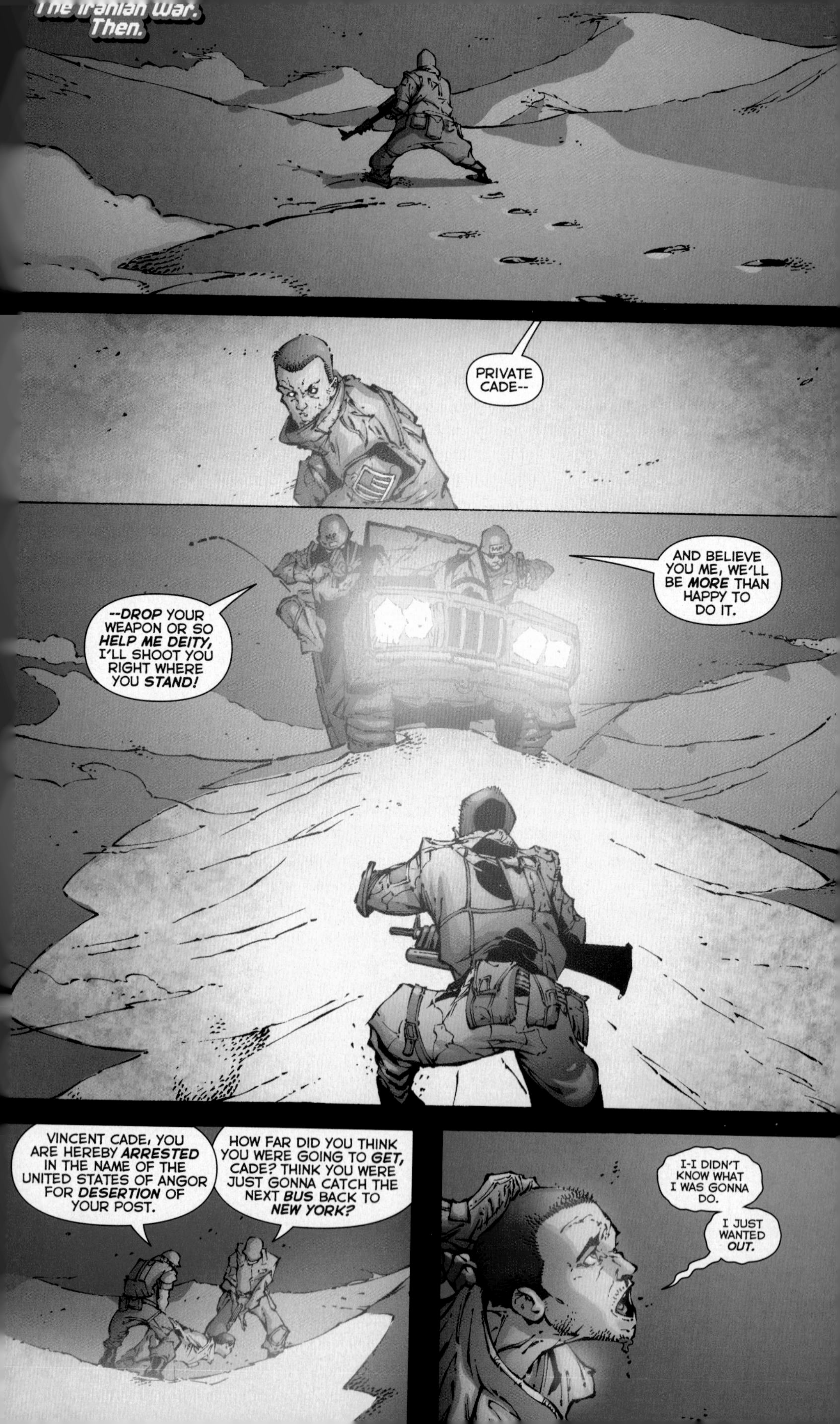
The Iranian War. Then.
PRIVATE CADE--
--DROP YOUR WEAPON OR SO HELP ME DEITY, I'LL SHOOT YOU RIGHT WHERE YOU STAND!
AND BELIEVE YOU ME, WE'LL BE MORE THAN HAPPY TO DO IT.
VINCENT CADE, YOU ARE HEREBY ARRESTED IN THE NAME OF THE UNITED STATES OF ANGOR FOR DESERTION OF YOUR POST.
HOW FAR DID YOU THINK YOU WERE GOING TO GET, CADE? THINK YOU WERE JUST GONNA CATCH THE NEXT BUS BACK TO NEW YORK?
I-I DIDN'T KNOW WHAT I WAS GONNA DO.
I JUST WANTED OUT.

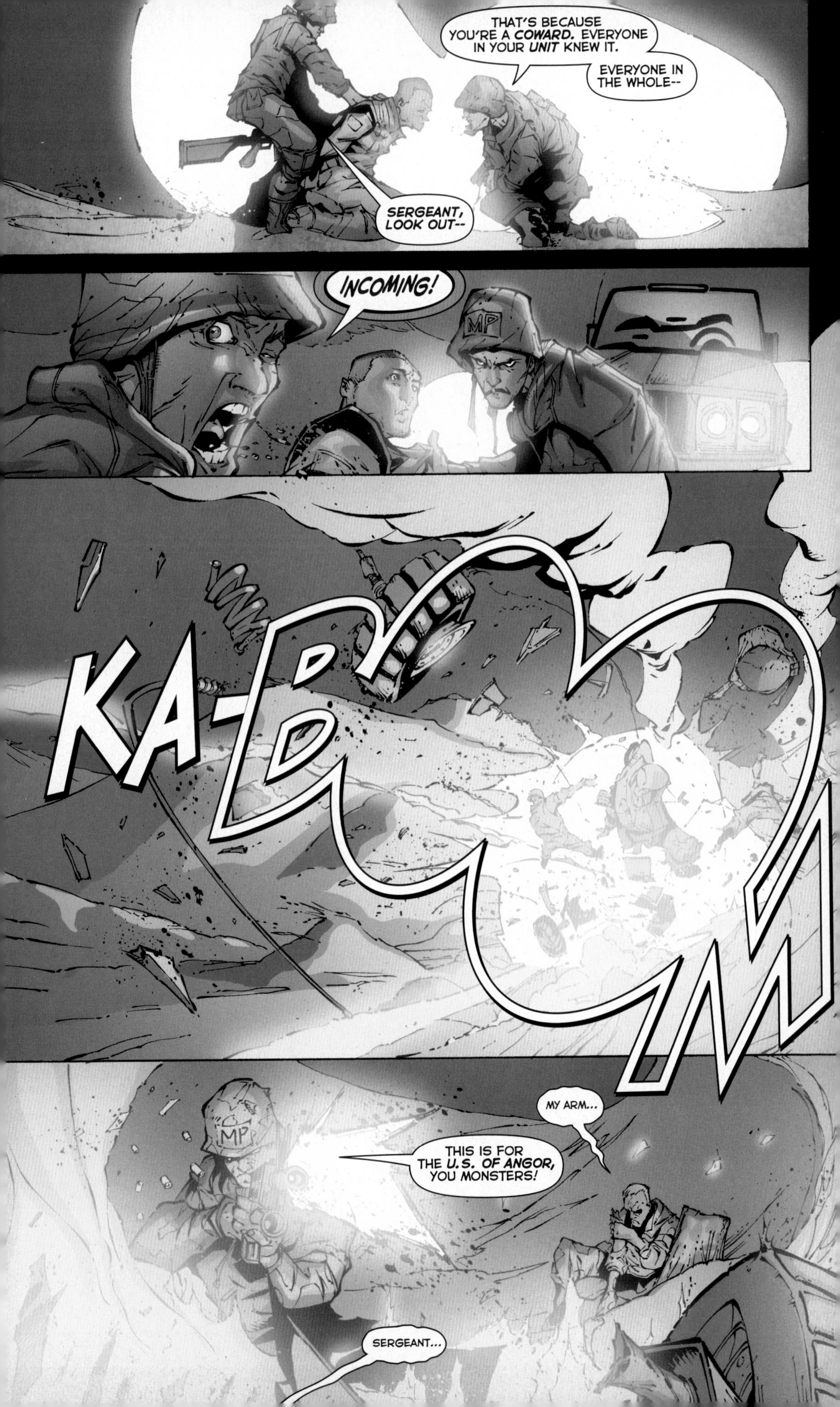
THAT'S BECAUSE YOU'RE A COWARD. EVERYONE IN YOUR UNIT KNEW IT.
EVERYONE IN THE WHOLE--
SERGEANT, LOOK OUT--
INCOMING!
KA-BOOM
MY ARM...
THIS IS FOR THE U.S. OF ANGOR, YOU MONSTERS!
SERGEANT...

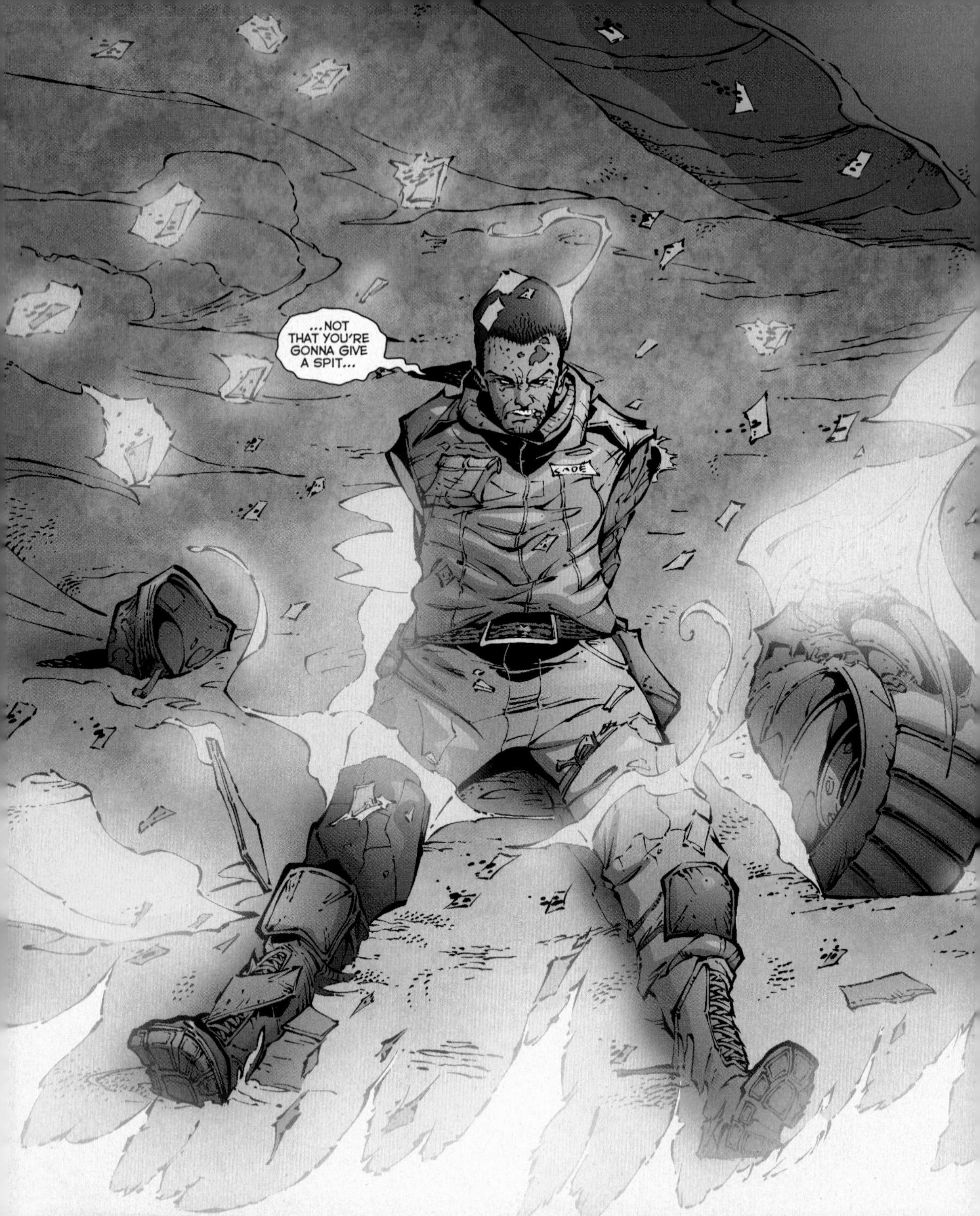
...NOT THAT YOU'RE GONNA GIVE A SPIT...
KADE

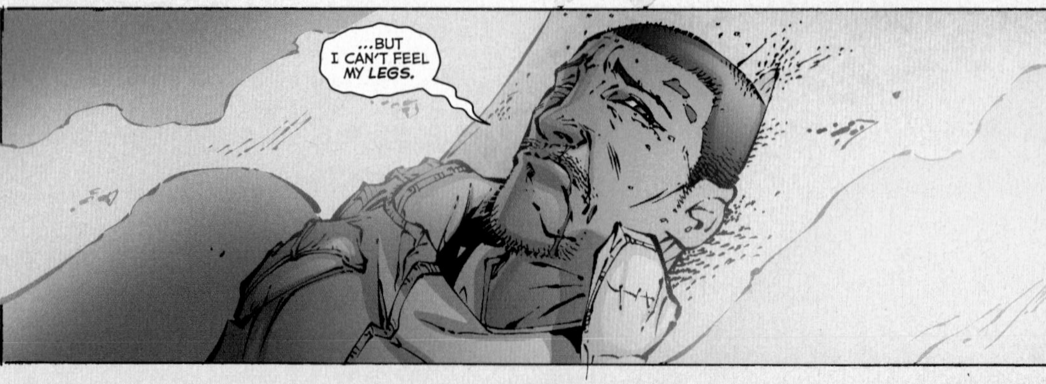
...BUT I CAN'T FEEL MY LEGS.

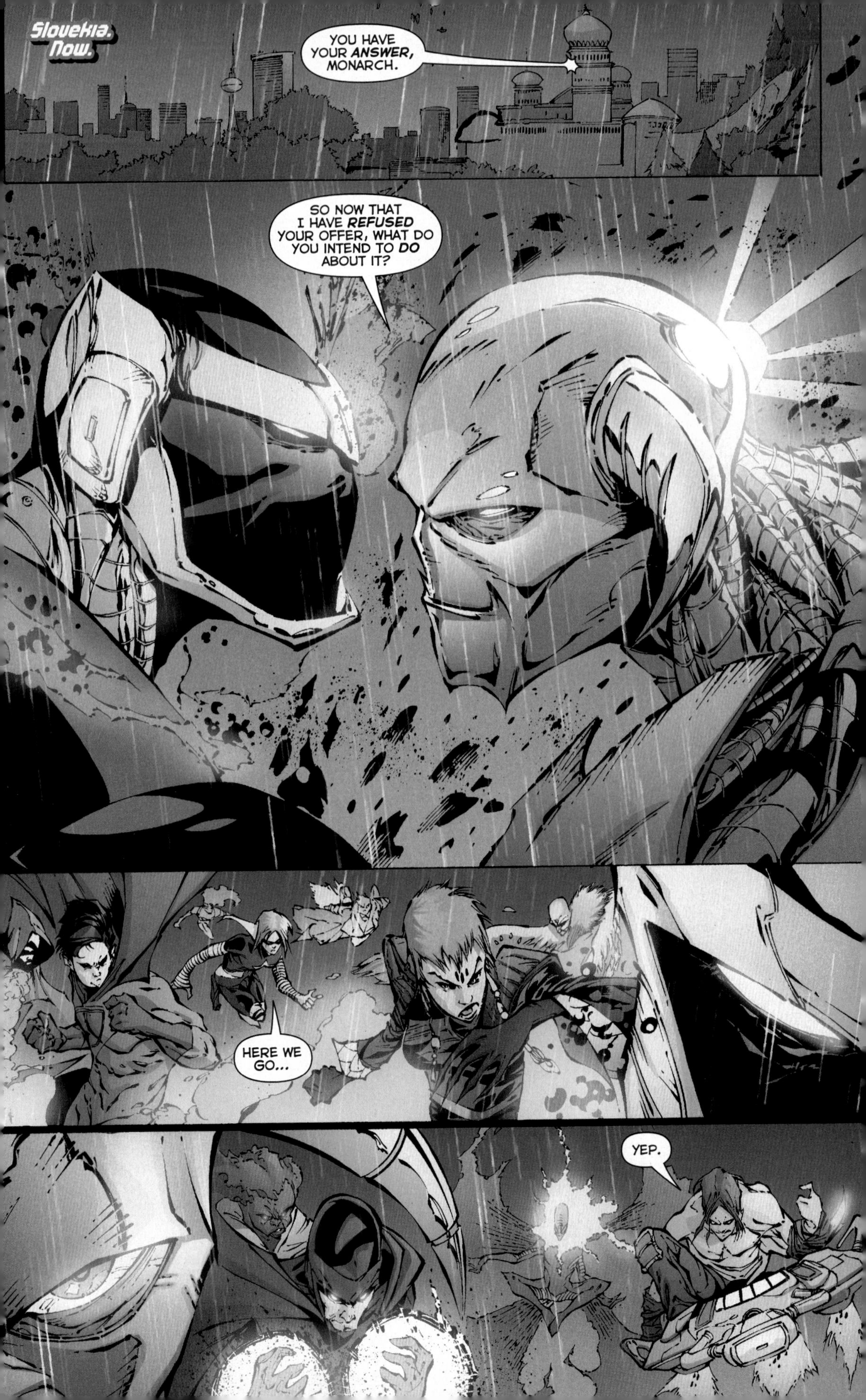
Slovekia. Now.
YOU HAVE YOUR ANSWER, MONARCH.
SO NOW THAT I HAVE REFUSED YOUR OFFER, WHAT DO YOU INTEND TO DO ABOUT IT?
HERE WE GO...
YEP.

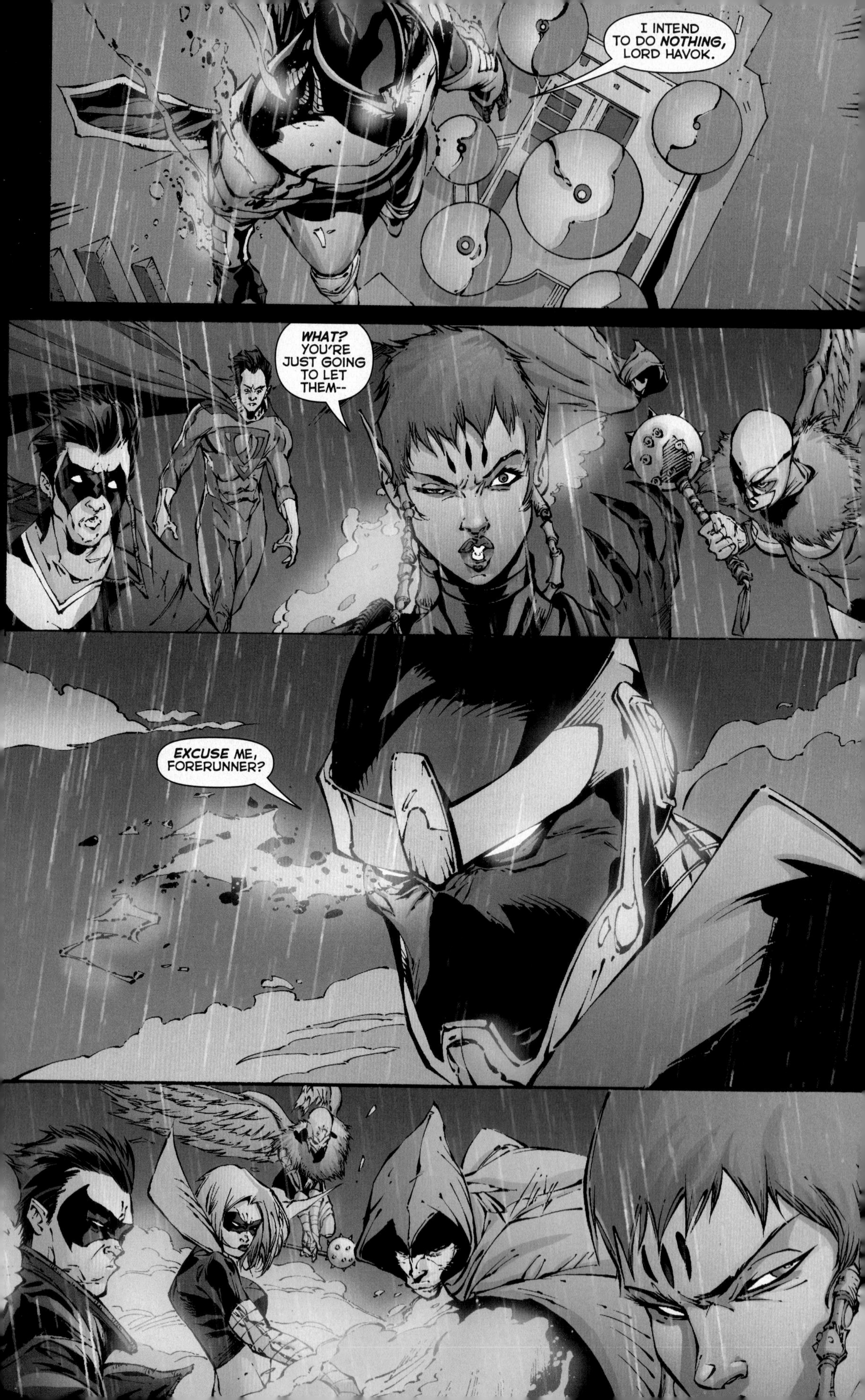
I INTEND TO DO NOTHING, LORD HAVOK.
WHAT? YOU'RE JUST GOING TO LET THEM--
EXCUSE ME, FORERUNNER?

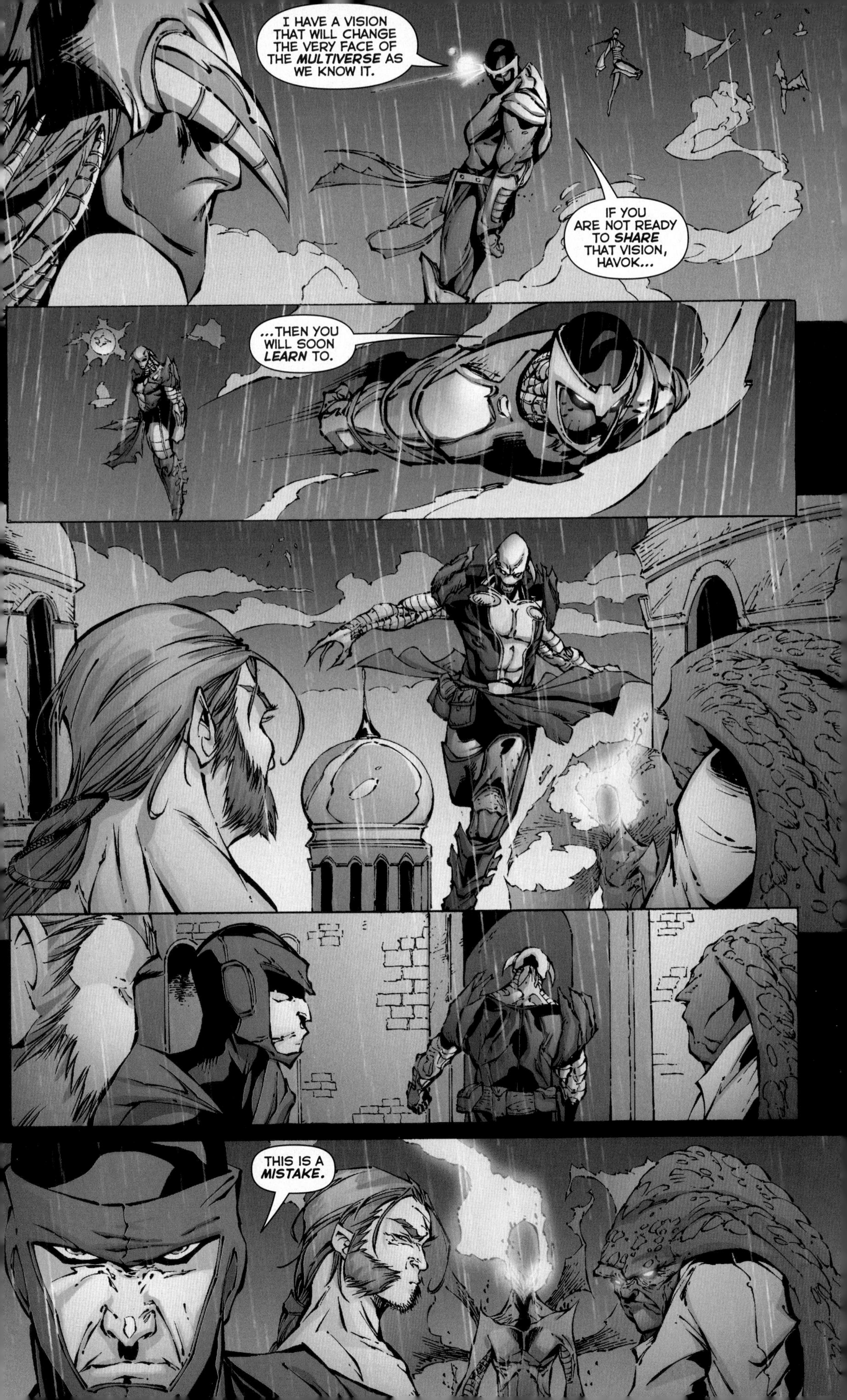
I HAVE A VISION THAT WILL CHANGE THE VERY FACE OF THE MULTIVERSE AS WE KNOW IT.
IF YOU ARE NOT READY TO SHARE THAT VISION, HAVOK...
...THEN YOU WILL SOON LEARN TO.
THIS IS A MISTAKE.

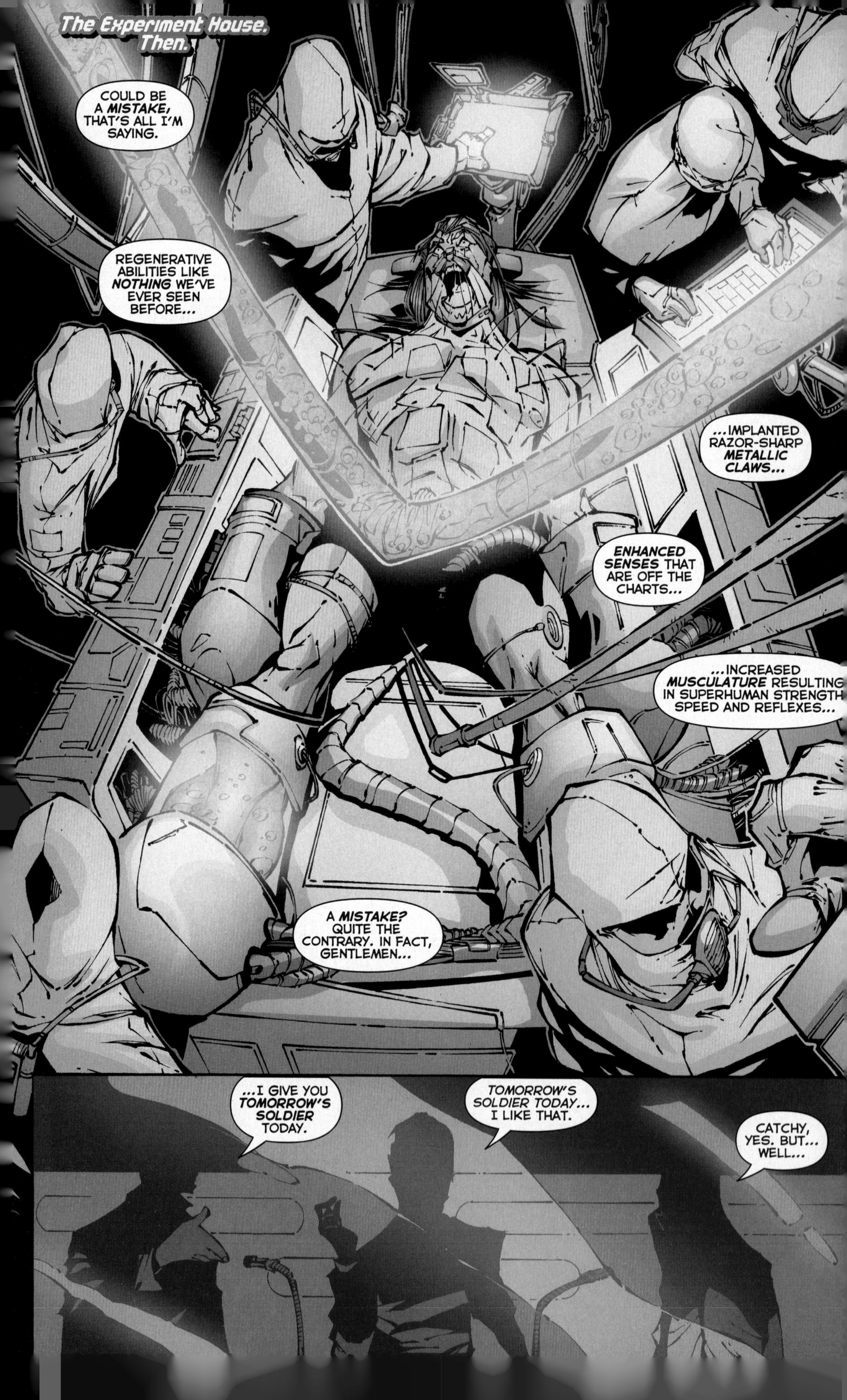
The Experiment House. Then.
COULD BE A MISTAKE, THAT'S ALL I'M SAYING.
REGENERATIVE ABILITIES LIKE NOTHING WE'VE EVER SEEN BEFORE...
...IMPLANTED RAZOR-SHARP METALLIC CLAWS...
ENHANCED SENSES THAT ARE OFF THE CHARTS...
...INCREASED MUSCULATURE RESULTING IN SUPERHUMAN STRENGTH SPEED AND REFLEXES...
A MISTAKE? QUITE THE CONTRARY. IN FACT, GENTLEMEN...
...I GIVE YOU TOMORROW'S SOLDIER TODAY.
TOMORROW'S SOLDIER TODAY... I LIKE THAT.
CATCHY, YES. BUT... WELL...

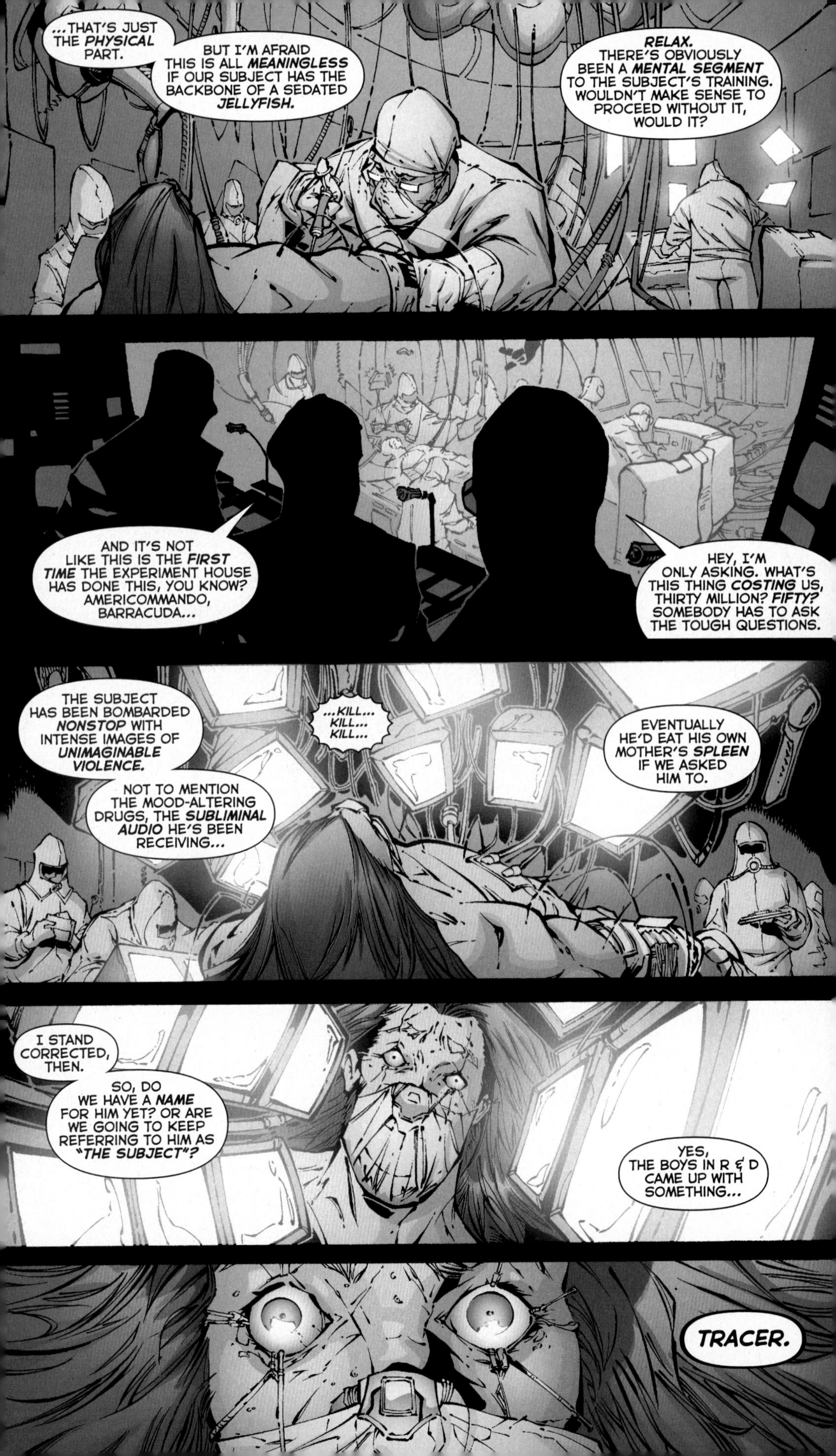
...THAT'S JUST THE PHYSICAL PART.
BUT I'M AFRAID THIS IS ALL MEANINGLESS IF OUR SUBJECT HAS THE BACKBONE OF A SEDATED JELLYFISH.
RELAX. THERE'S OBVIOUSLY BEEN A MENTAL SEGMENT TO THE SUBJECT'S TRAINING. WOULDN'T MAKE SENSE TO PROCEED WITHOUT IT, WOULD IT?
AND IT'S NOT LIKE THIS IS THE FIRST TIME THE EXPERIMENT HOUSE HAS DONE THIS, YOU KNOW? AMERICOMMANDO, BARRACUDA...
HEY, I'M ONLY ASKING. WHAT'S THIS THING COSTING US, THIRTY MILLION? FIFTY? SOMEBODY HAS TO ASK THE TOUGH QUESTIONS.
THE SUBJECT HAS BEEN BOMBARDED NONSTOP WITH INTENSE IMAGES OF UNIMAGINABLE VIOLENCE.
...KILL... KILL... KILL...
NOT TO MENTION THE MOOD-ALTERING DRUGS, THE SUBLIMINAL AUDIO HE'S BEEN RECEIVING...
EVENTUALLY HE'D EAT HIS OWN MOTHER'S SPLEEN IF WE ASKED HIM TO.
I STAND CORRECTED, THEN.
SO, DO WE HAVE A NAME FOR HIM YET? OR ARE WE GOING TO KEEP REFERRING TO HIM AS "THE SUBJECT"?
YES, THE BOYS IN R & D CAME UP WITH SOMETHING...
TRACER.

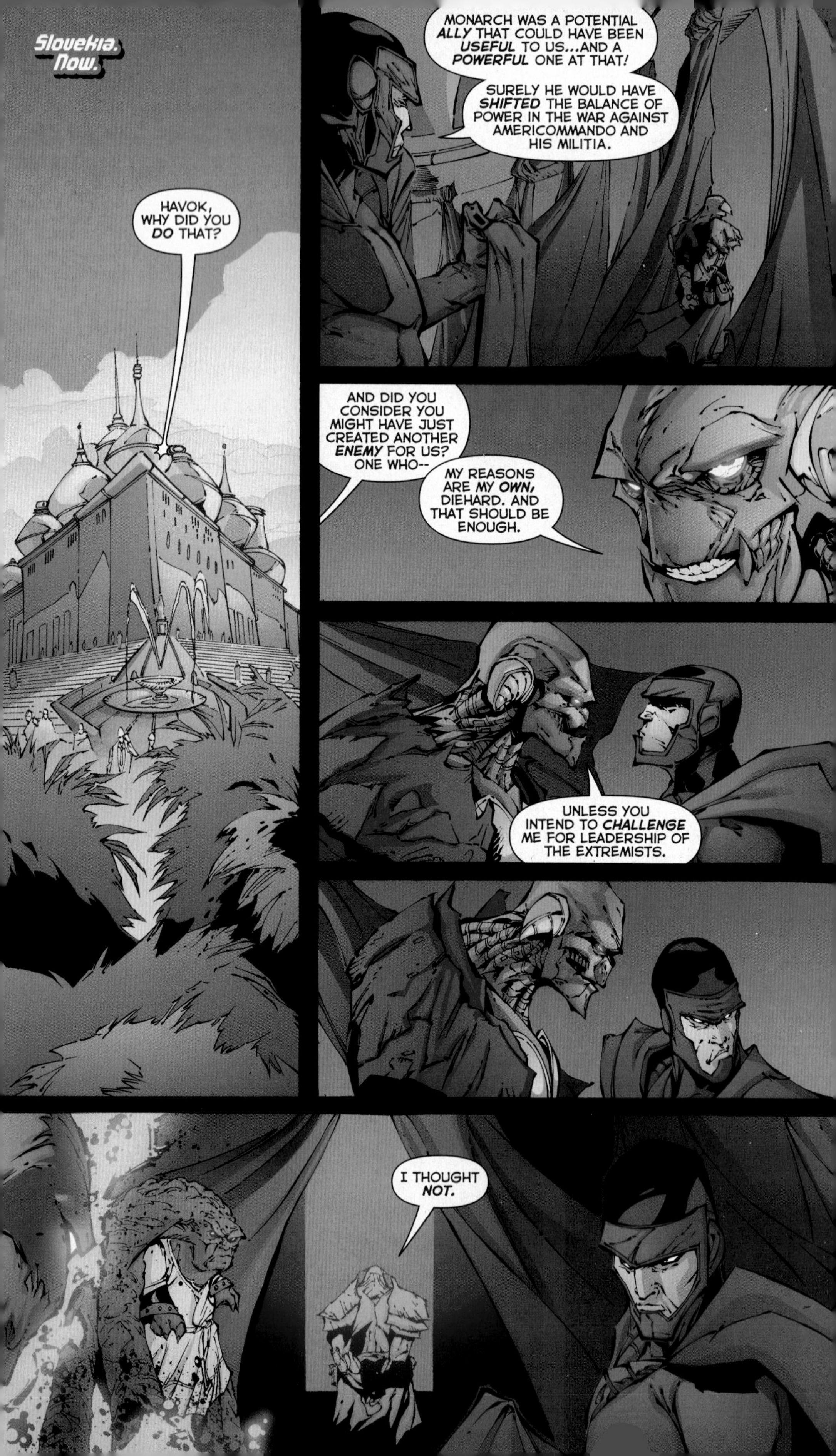
Slovekia. Now.
HAVOK, WHY DID YOU DO THAT?
MONARCH WAS A POTENTIAL ALLY THAT COULD HAVE BEEN USEFUL TO US...AND A POWERFUL ONE AT THAT!
SURELY HE WOULD HAVE SHIFTED THE BALANCE OF POWER IN THE WAR AGAINST AMERICOMMANDO AND HIS MILITIA.
AND DID YOU CONSIDER YOU MIGHT HAVE JUST CREATED ANOTHER ENEMY FOR US? ONE WHO--
MY REASONS ARE MY OWN, DIEHARD. AND THAT SHOULD BE ENOUGH.
UNLESS YOU INTEND TO CHALLENGE ME FOR LEADERSHIP OF THE EXTREMISTS.
I THOUGHT NOT.

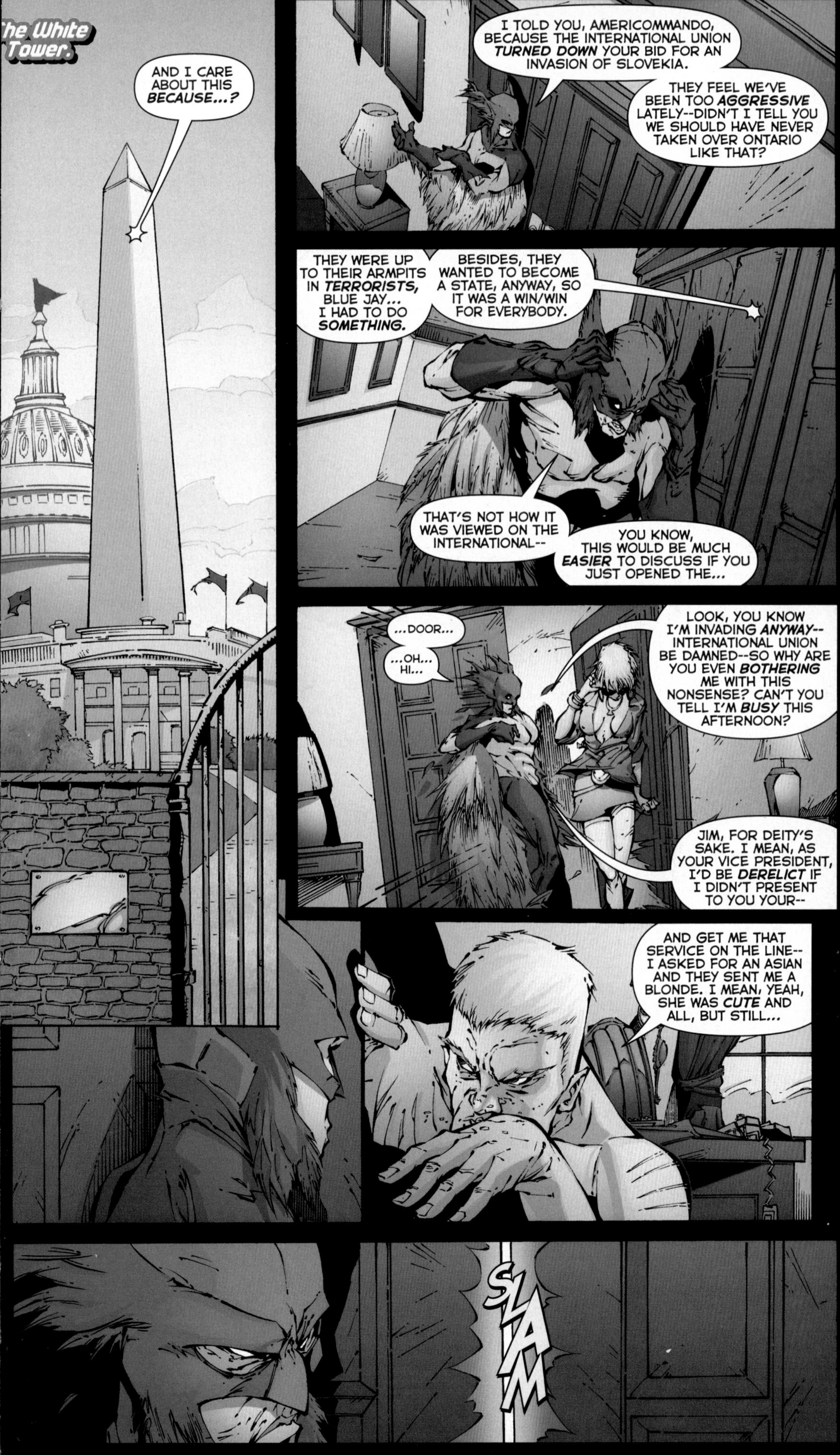
The White Tower.
AND I CARE ABOUT THIS BECAUSE...?
I TOLD YOU, AMERICOMMANDO, BECAUSE THE INTERNATIONAL UNION TURNED DOWN YOUR BID FOR AN INVASION OF SLOVEKIA.
THEY FEEL WE'VE BEEN TOO AGGRESSIVE LATELY--DIDN'T I TELL YOU WE SHOULD HAVE NEVER TAKEN OVER ONTARIO LIKE THAT?
THEY WERE UP TO THEIR ARMPITS IN TERRORISTS, BLUE JAY... I HAD TO DO SOMETHING.
BESIDES, THEY WANTED TO BECOME A STATE, ANYWAY, SO IT WAS A WIN/WIN FOR EVERYBODY.
THAT'S NOT HOW IT WAS VIEWED ON THE INTERNATIONAL--
YOU KNOW, THIS WOULD BE MUCH EASIER TO DISCUSS IF YOU JUST OPENED THE...
...DOOR...
...OH... HI...
LOOK, YOU KNOW I'M INVADING ANYWAY--INTERNATIONAL UNION BE DAMNED--SO WHY ARE YOU EVEN BOTHERING ME WITH THIS NONSENSE? CAN'T YOU TELL I'M BUSY THIS AFTERNOON?
JIM, FOR DEITY'S SAKE. I MEAN, AS YOUR VICE PRESIDENT, I'D BE DERELICT IF I DIDN'T PRESENT TO YOU YOUR--
AND GET ME THAT SERVICE ON THE LINE--I ASKED FOR AN ASIAN AND THEY SENT ME A BLONDE. I MEAN, YEAH, SHE WAS CUTE AND ALL, BUT STILL...
SLAM

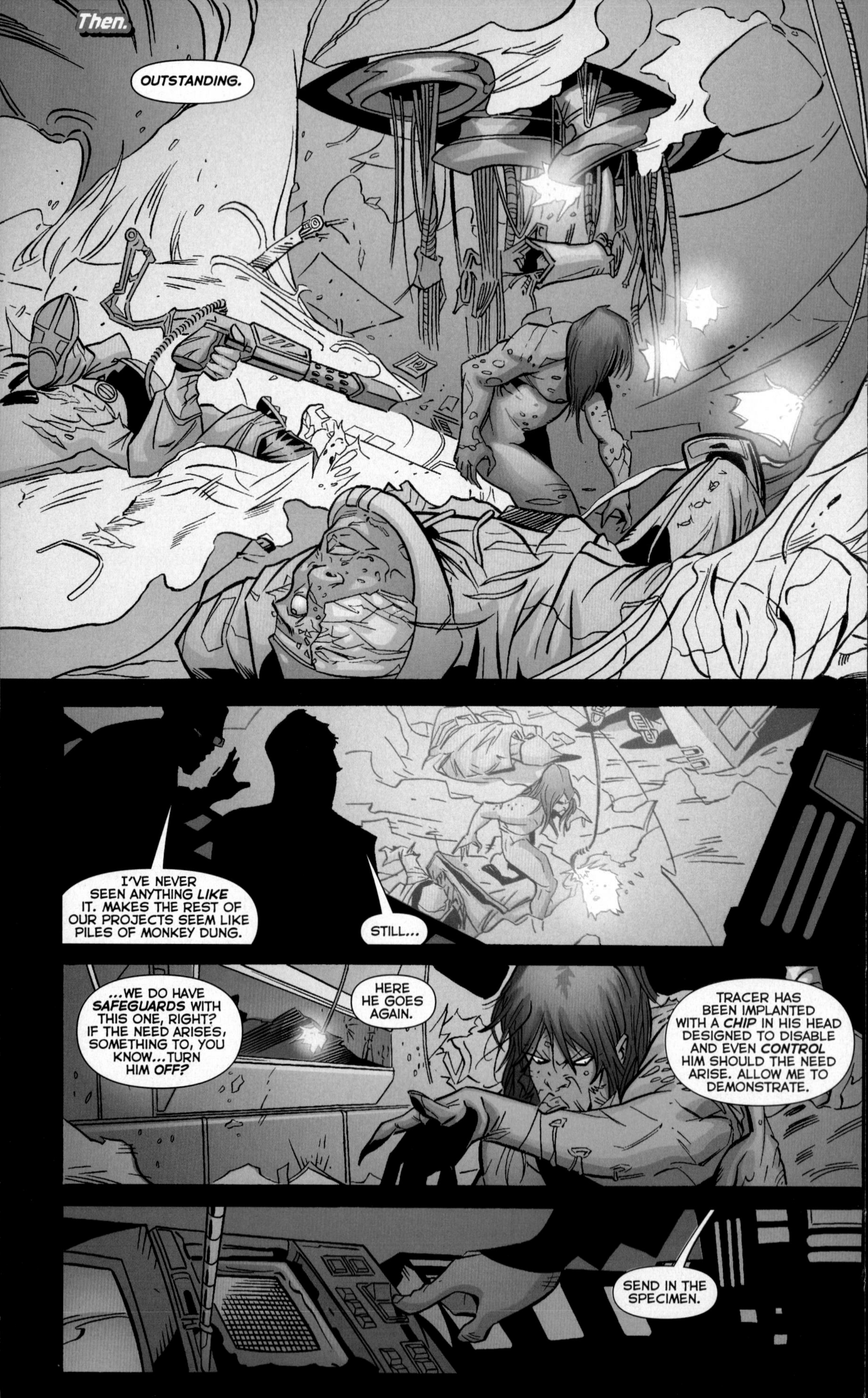
Then.
OUTSTANDING.
I'VE NEVER SEEN ANYTHING LIKE IT. MAKES THE REST OF OUR PROJECTS SEEM LIKE PILES OF MONKEY DUNG.
STILL...
...WE DO HAVE SAFEGUARDS WITH THIS ONE, RIGHT? IF THE NEED ARISES, SOMETHING TO, YOU KNOW...TURN HIM OFF?
HERE HE GOES AGAIN.
TRACER HAS BEEN IMPLANTED WITH A CHIP IN HIS HEAD DESIGNED TO DISABLE AND EVEN CONTROL HIM SHOULD THE NEED ARISE. ALLOW ME TO DEMONSTRATE.
SEND IN THE SPECIMEN.

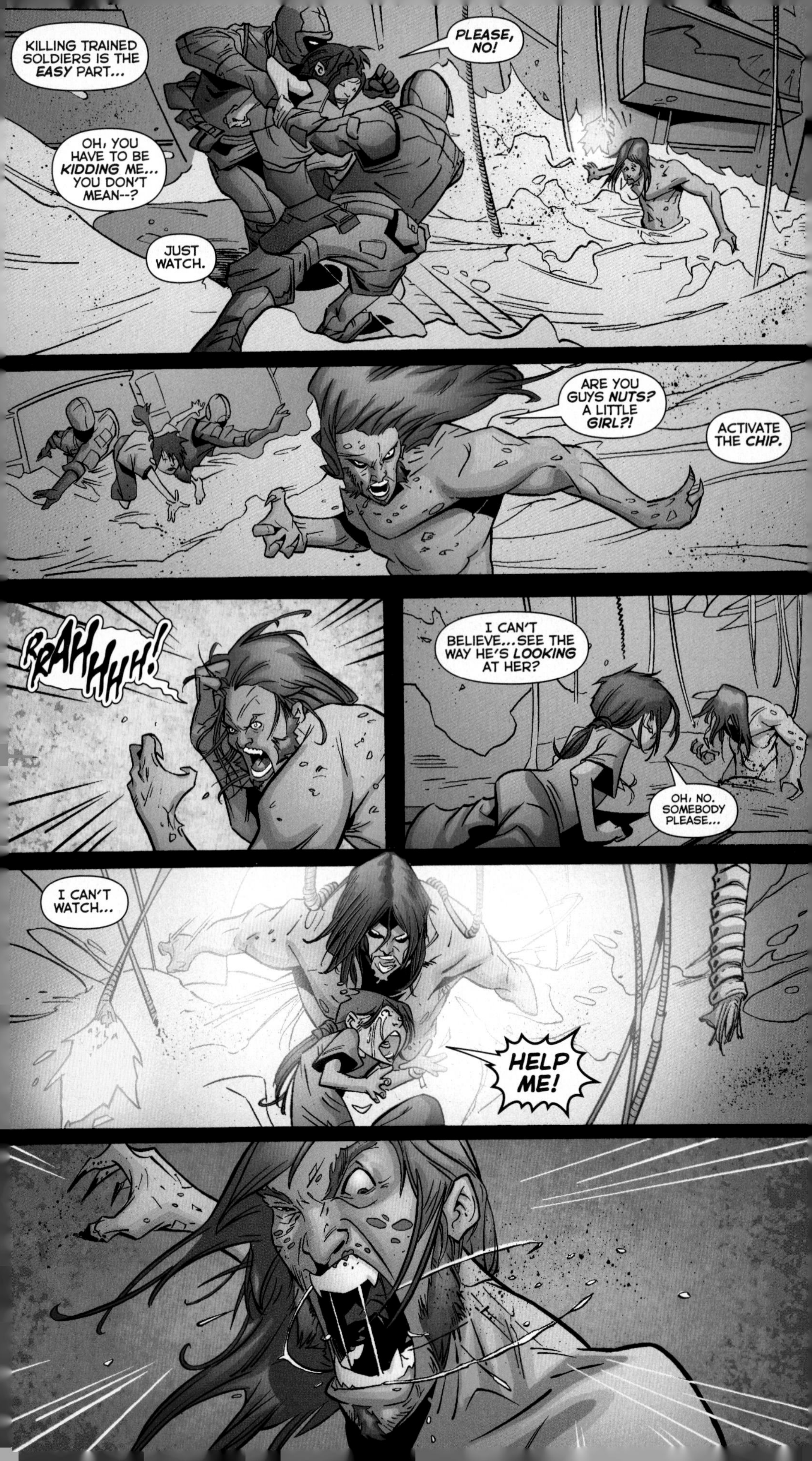
KILLING TRAINED SOLDIERS IS THE *EASY* PART...
PLEASE, NO!
OH, YOU HAVE TO BE *KIDDING* ME... YOU DON'T MEAN--?
JUST WATCH.
ARE YOU GUYS *NUTS?* A LITTLE *GIRL?!*
ACTIVATE THE *CHIP.*
RRAHHHH!
I CAN'T BELIEVE...SEE THE WAY HE'S *LOOKING* AT HER?
OH, NO. SOMEBODY PLEASE...
I CAN'T WATCH...
HELP ME!

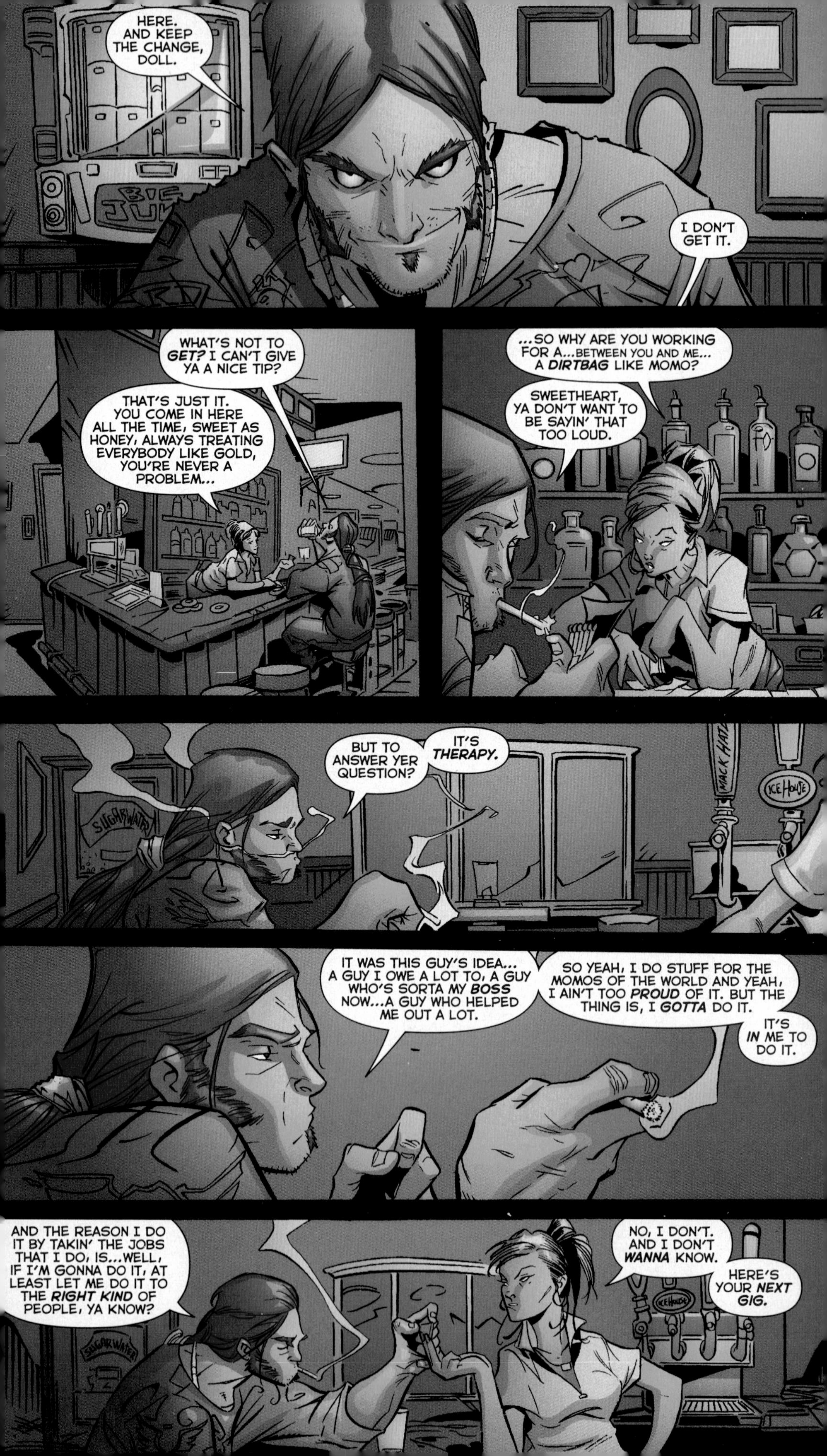
HERE. AND KEEP THE CHANGE, DOLL.
I DON'T GET IT.
WHAT'S NOT TO GET? I CAN'T GIVE YA A NICE TIP?
THAT'S JUST IT. YOU COME IN HERE ALL THE TIME, SWEET AS HONEY, ALWAYS TREATING EVERYBODY LIKE GOLD, YOU'RE NEVER A PROBLEM...
...SO WHY ARE YOU WORKING FOR A...BETWEEN YOU AND ME... A DIRTBAG LIKE MOMO?
SWEETHEART, YA DON'T WANT TO BE SAYIN' THAT TOO LOUD.
BUT TO ANSWER YER QUESTION?
IT'S THERAPY.
SUGARWATER
ICE HOUSE
IT WAS THIS GUY'S IDEA... A GUY I OWE A LOT TO, A GUY WHO'S SORTA MY BOSS NOW...A GUY WHO HELPED ME OUT A LOT.
SO YEAH, I DO STUFF FOR THE MOMOS OF THE WORLD AND YEAH, I AIN'T TOO PROUD OF IT. BUT THE THING IS, I GOTTA DO IT.
IT'S IN ME TO DO IT.
AND THE REASON I DO IT BY TAKIN' THE JOBS THAT I DO, IS...WELL, IF I'M GONNA DO IT, AT LEAST LET ME DO IT TO THE RIGHT KIND OF PEOPLE, YA KNOW?
NO, I DON'T. AND I DON'T WANNA KNOW.
HERE'S YOUR NEXT GIG.

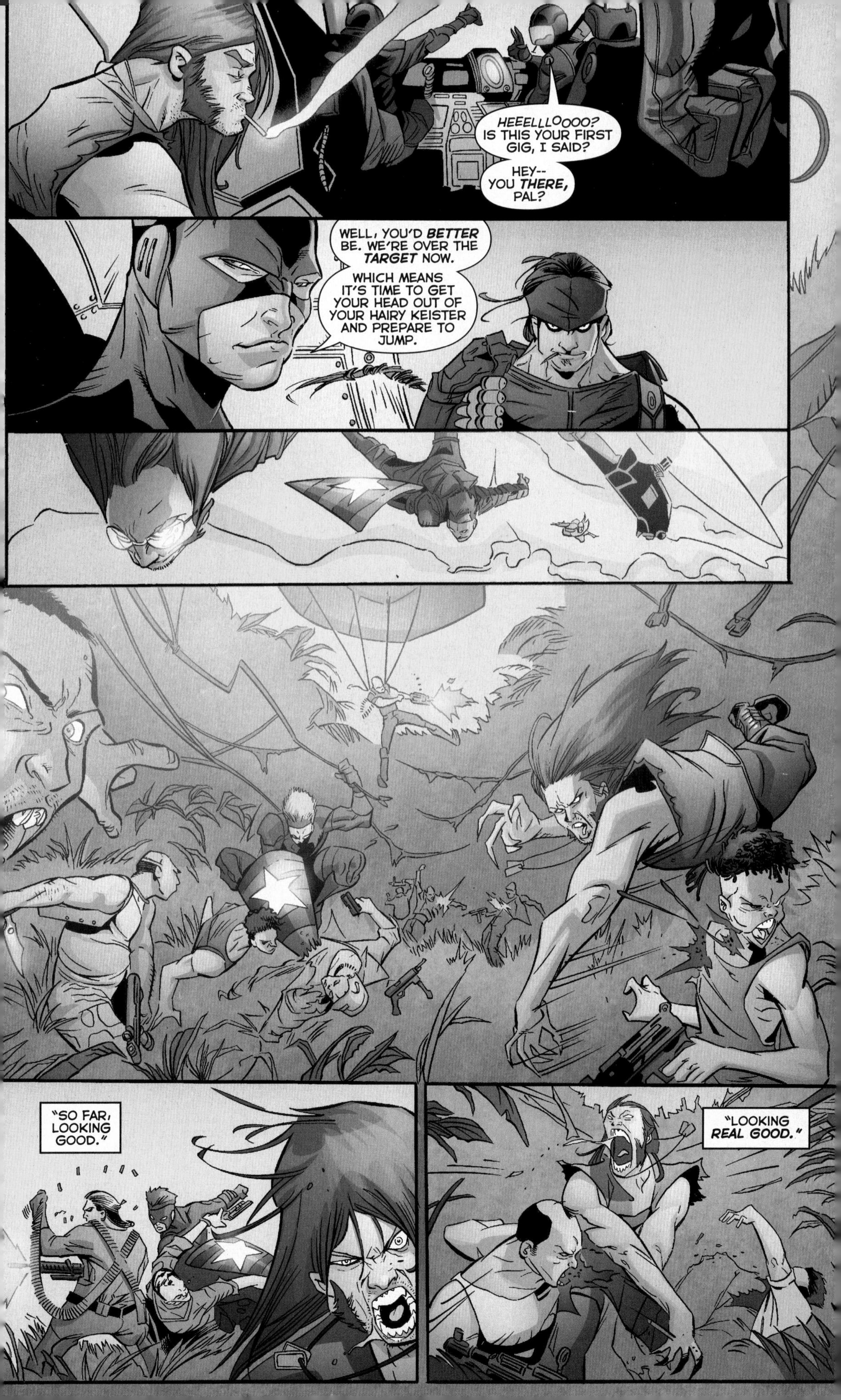
HEEELLLOOOO?
IS THIS YOUR FIRST GIG, I SAID?
HEY-- YOU THERE, PAL?
WELL, YOU'D BETTER BE. WE'RE OVER THE TARGET NOW.
WHICH MEANS IT'S TIME TO GET YOUR HEAD OUT OF YOUR HAIRY KEISTER AND PREPARE TO JUMP.
"SO FAR, LOOKING GOOD."
"LOOKING REAL GOOD."

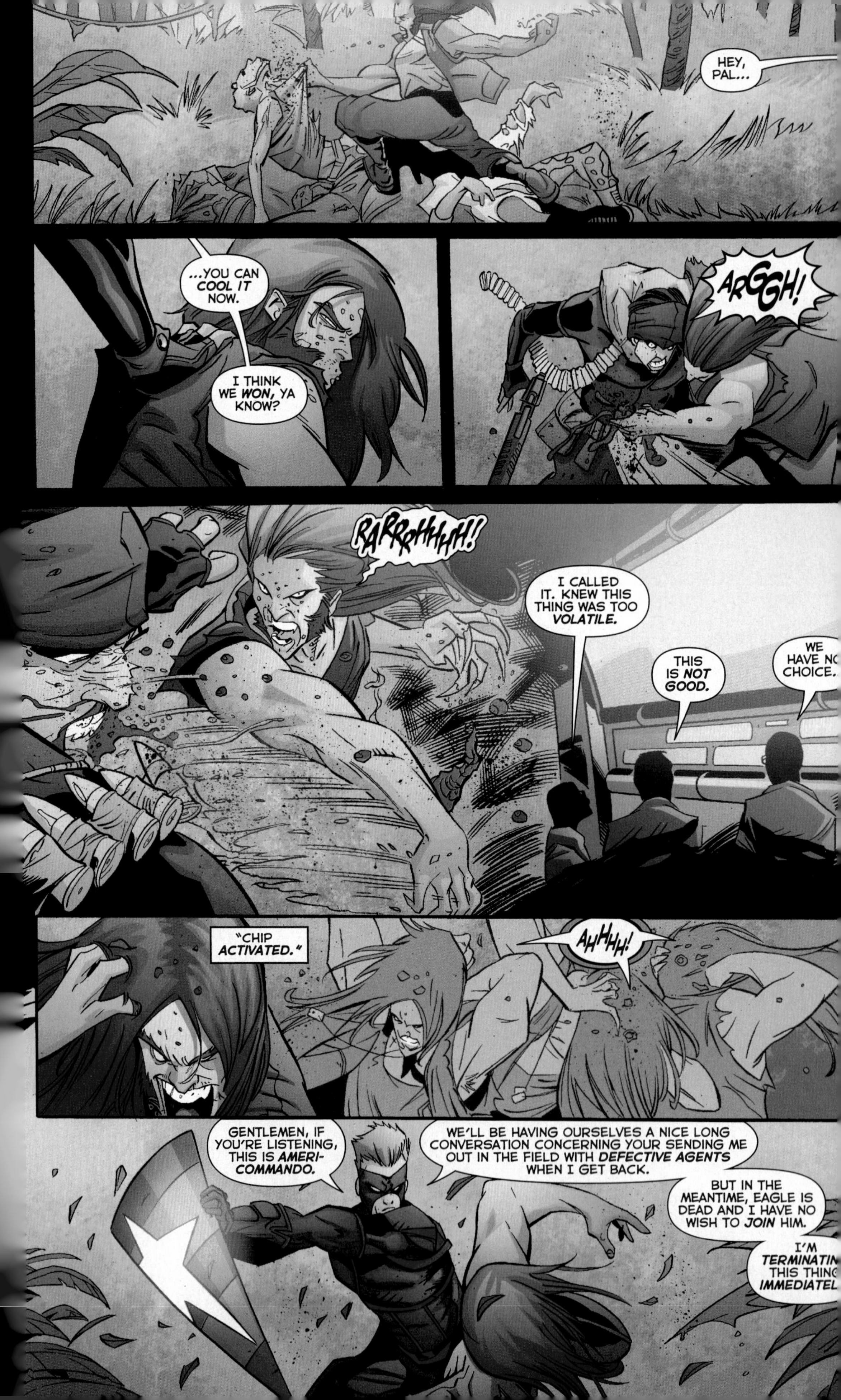
HEY, PAL...
...YOU CAN COOL IT NOW.
I THINK WE WON, YA KNOW?
ARGGH!
RARRRHHHH!
I CALLED IT. KNEW THIS THING WAS TOO VOLATILE.
THIS IS NOT GOOD.
WE HAVE NO CHOICE.
"CHIP ACTIVATED."
AHHHH!
GENTLEMEN, IF YOU'RE LISTENING, THIS IS AMERI-COMMANDO.
WE'LL BE HAVING OURSELVES A NICE LONG CONVERSATION CONCERNING YOUR SENDING ME OUT IN THE FIELD WITH DEFECTIVE AGENTS WHEN I GET BACK.
BUT IN THE MEANTIME, EAGLE IS DEAD AND I HAVE NO WISH TO JOIN HIM.
I'M TERMINATIN THIS THING IMMEDIATEL

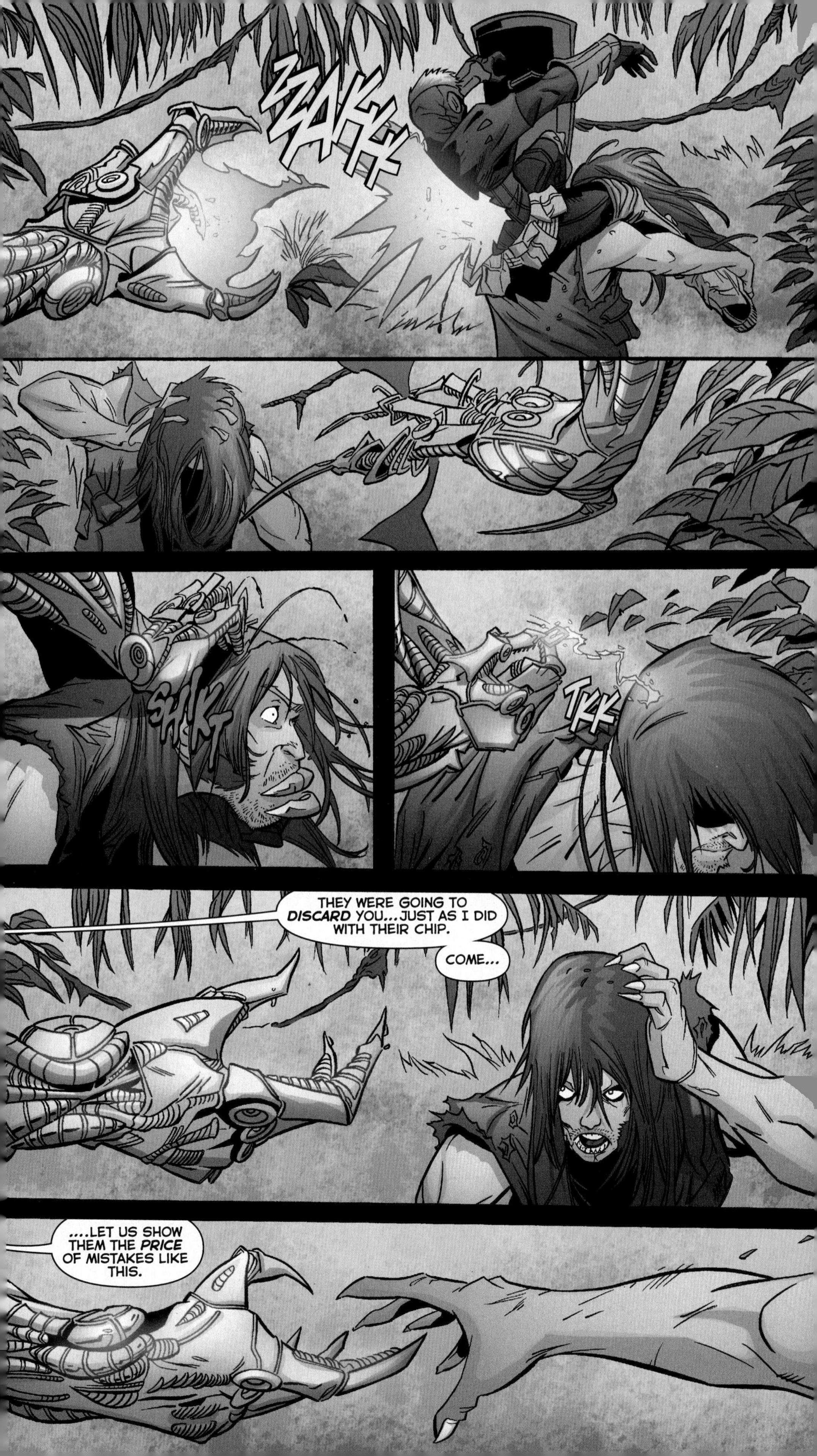
ZZAKKK
SHKT
TKK
THEY WERE GOING TO DISCARD YOU...JUST AS I DID WITH THEIR CHIP.
COME...
....LET US SHOW THEM THE PRICE OF MISTAKES LIKE THIS.

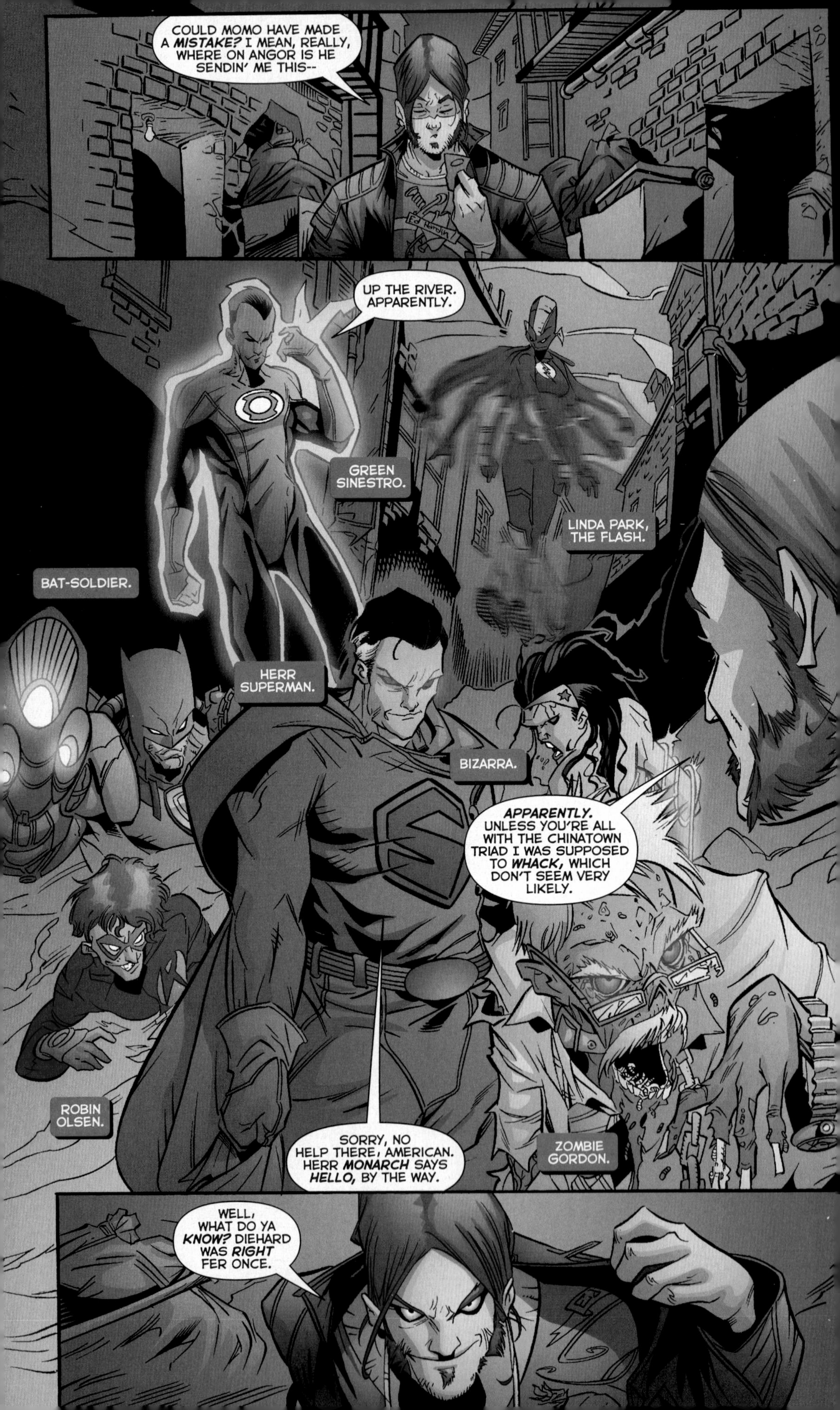
COULD MOMO HAVE MADE A *MISTAKE?* I MEAN, REALLY, WHERE ON ANGOR IS HE SENDIN' ME THIS--
UP THE RIVER. APPARENTLY.
GREEN SINESTRO.
LINDA PARK, THE FLASH.
BAT-SOLDIER.
HERR SUPERMAN.
BIZARRA.
APPARENTLY. UNLESS YOU'RE ALL WITH THE CHINATOWN TRIAD I WAS SUPPOSED TO *WHACK,* WHICH DON'T SEEM VERY LIKELY.
ROBIN OLSEN.
SORRY, NO HELP THERE, AMERICAN. HERR *MONARCH* SAYS *HELLO,* BY THE WAY.
ZOMBIE GORDON.
WELL, WHAT DO YA *KNOW?* DIEHARD WAS *RIGHT* FER ONCE.

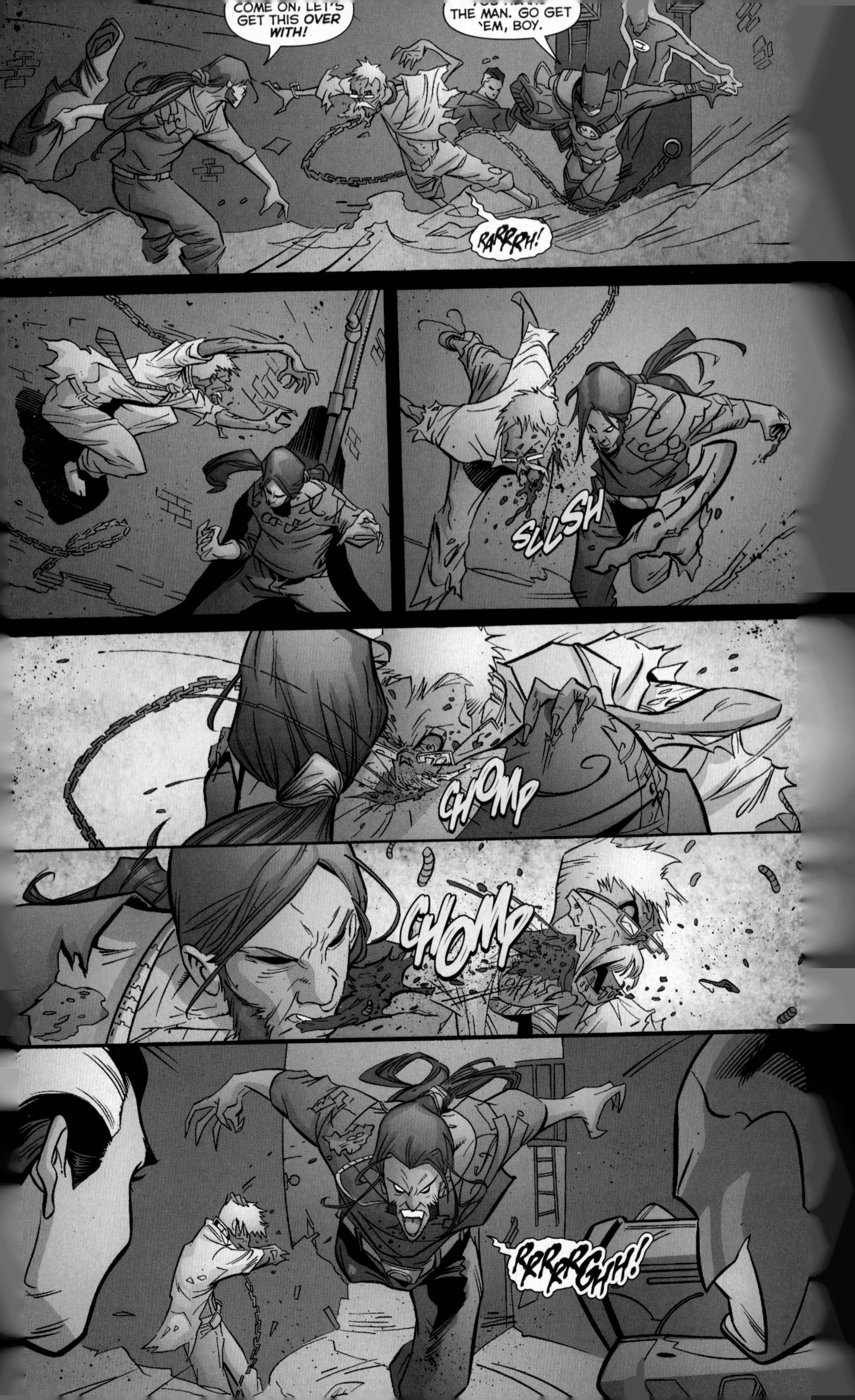
COME ON, LET'S GET THIS OVER WITH!
THE MAN. GO GET 'EM, BOY.
RARRRH!
SLLLSH
CHOMP
CHOMP
RRRRRRGHH!

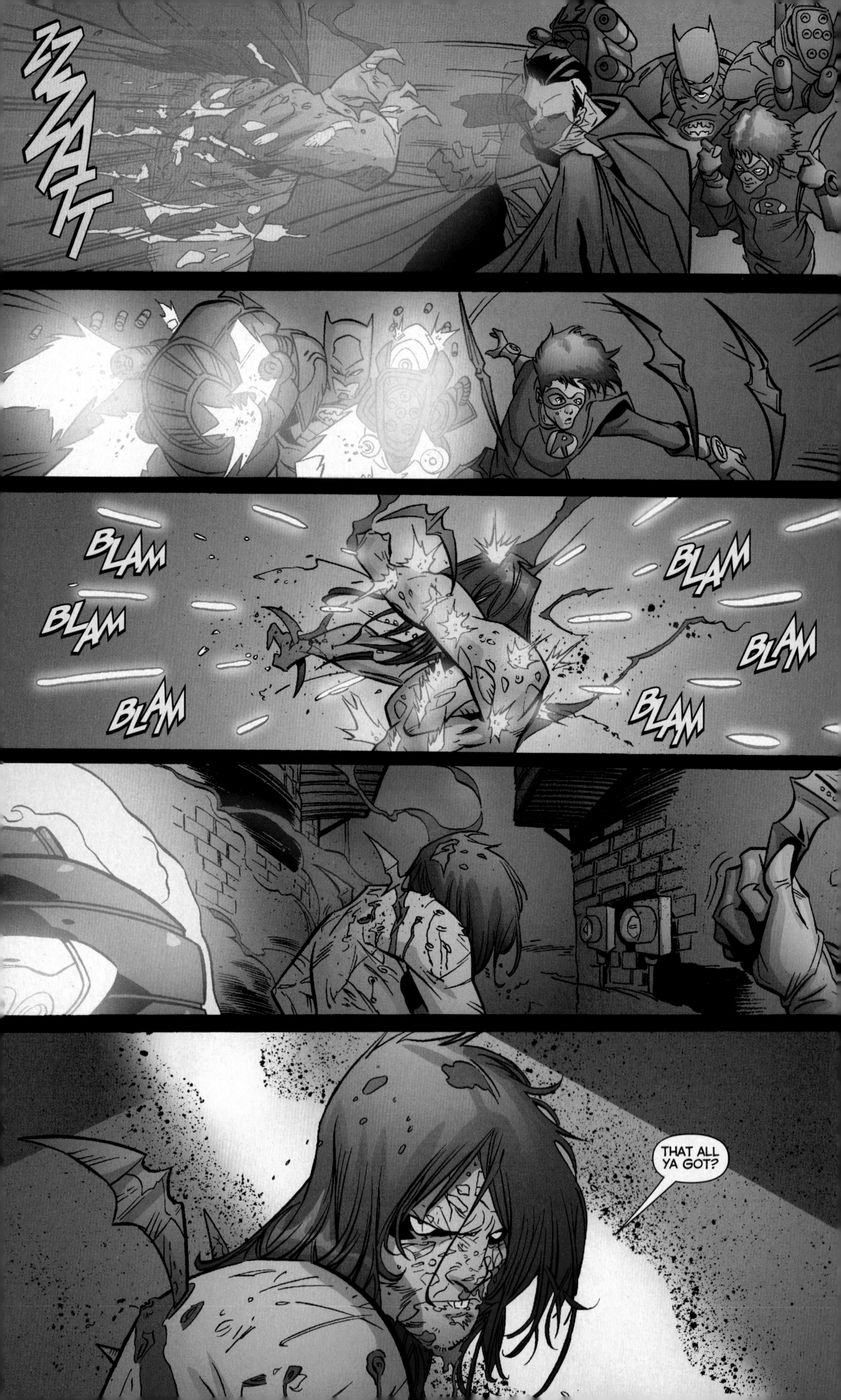
ZZZAKT
BLAM
BLAM
BLAM
BLAM
BLAM
BLAM
THAT ALL YA GOT?

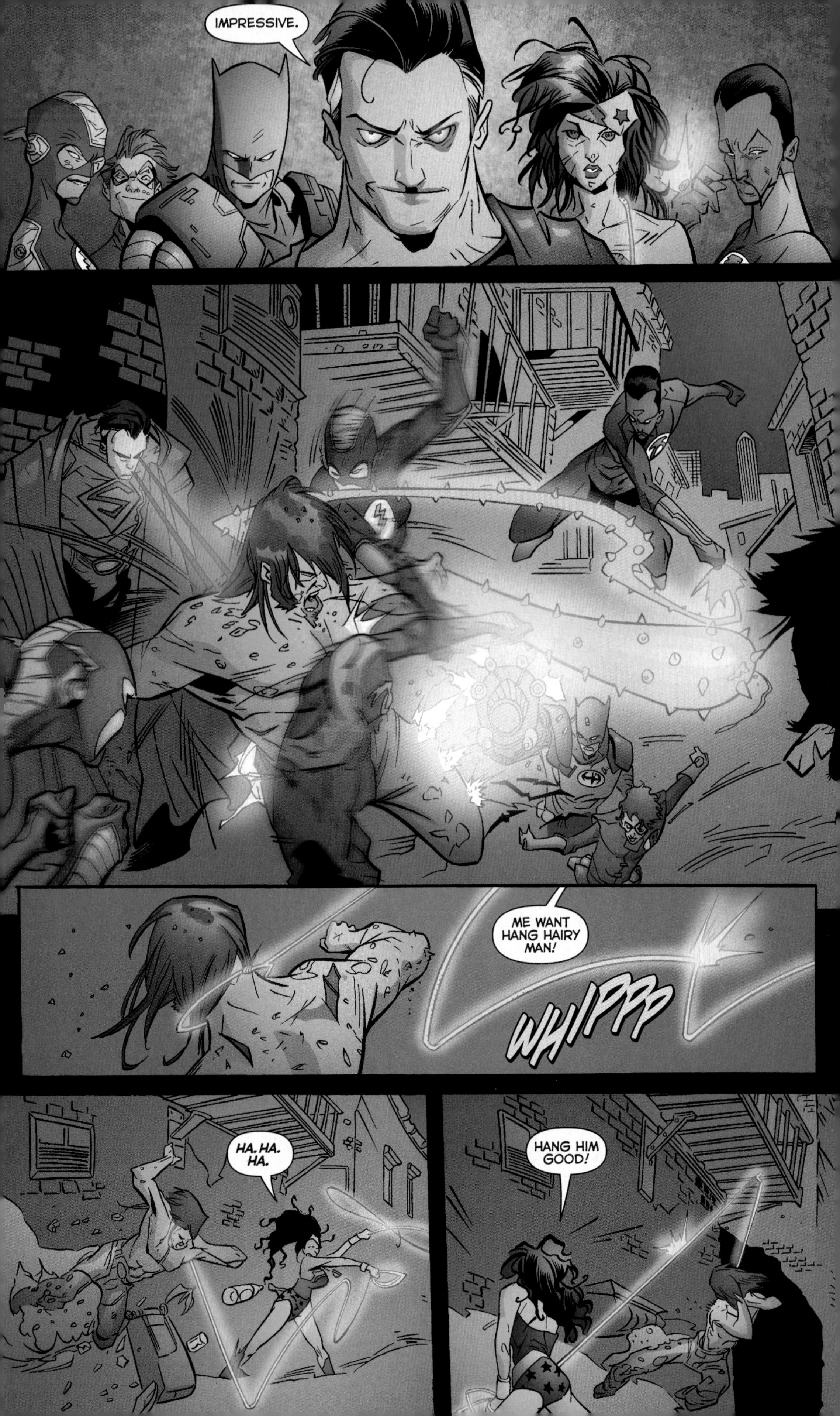
IMPRESSIVE.
ME WANT HANG HAIRY MAN!
WHIPPP
HA. HA. HA.
HANG HIM GOOD!

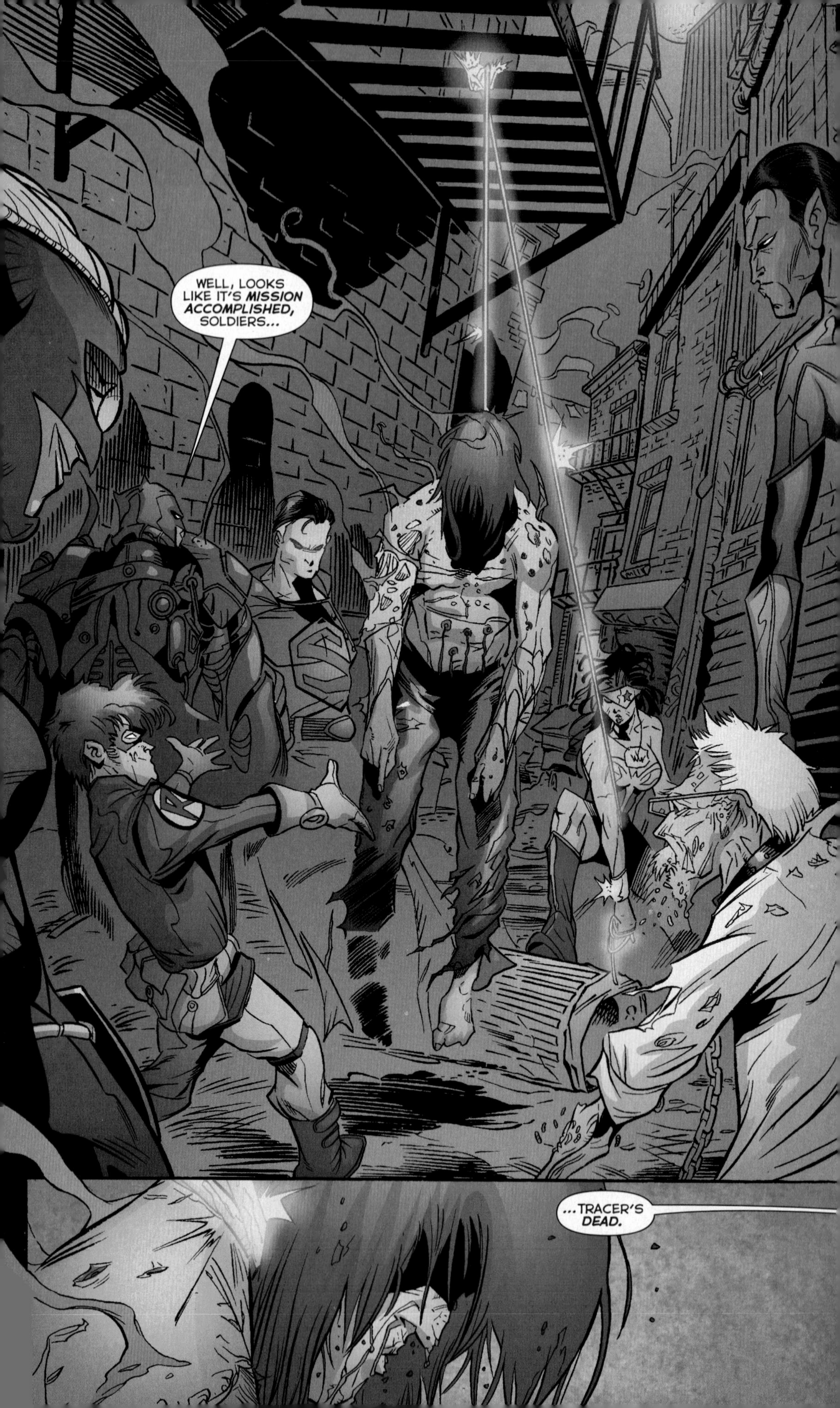

WELL, LOOKS LIKE IT'S MISSION ACCOMPLISHED, SOLDIERS...
...TRACER'S DEAD.

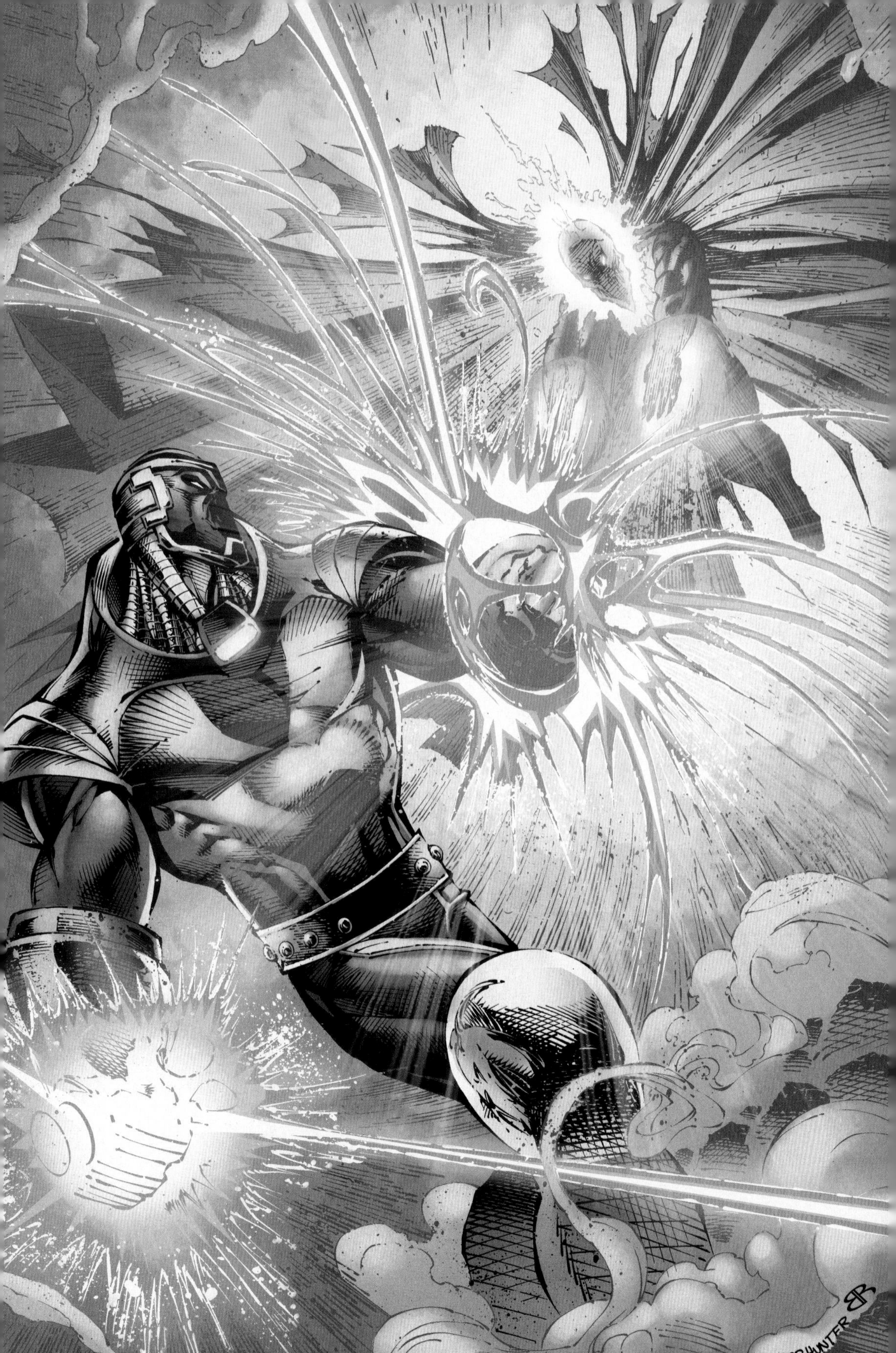
SHARP HUNTER

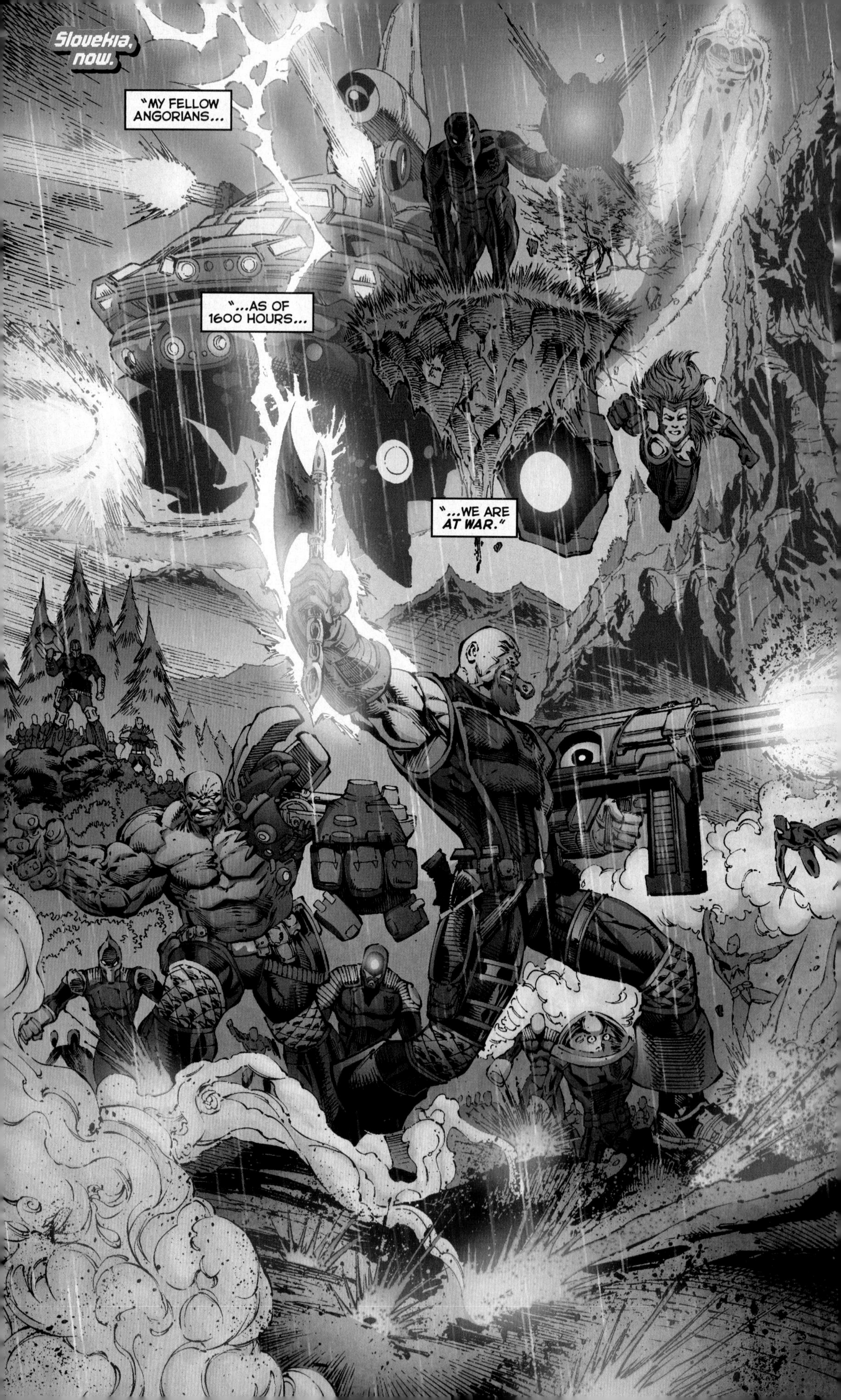
Slovekia, now.
"MY FELLOW ANGORIANS...
"...AS OF 1600 HOURS...
"...WE ARE AT WAR."

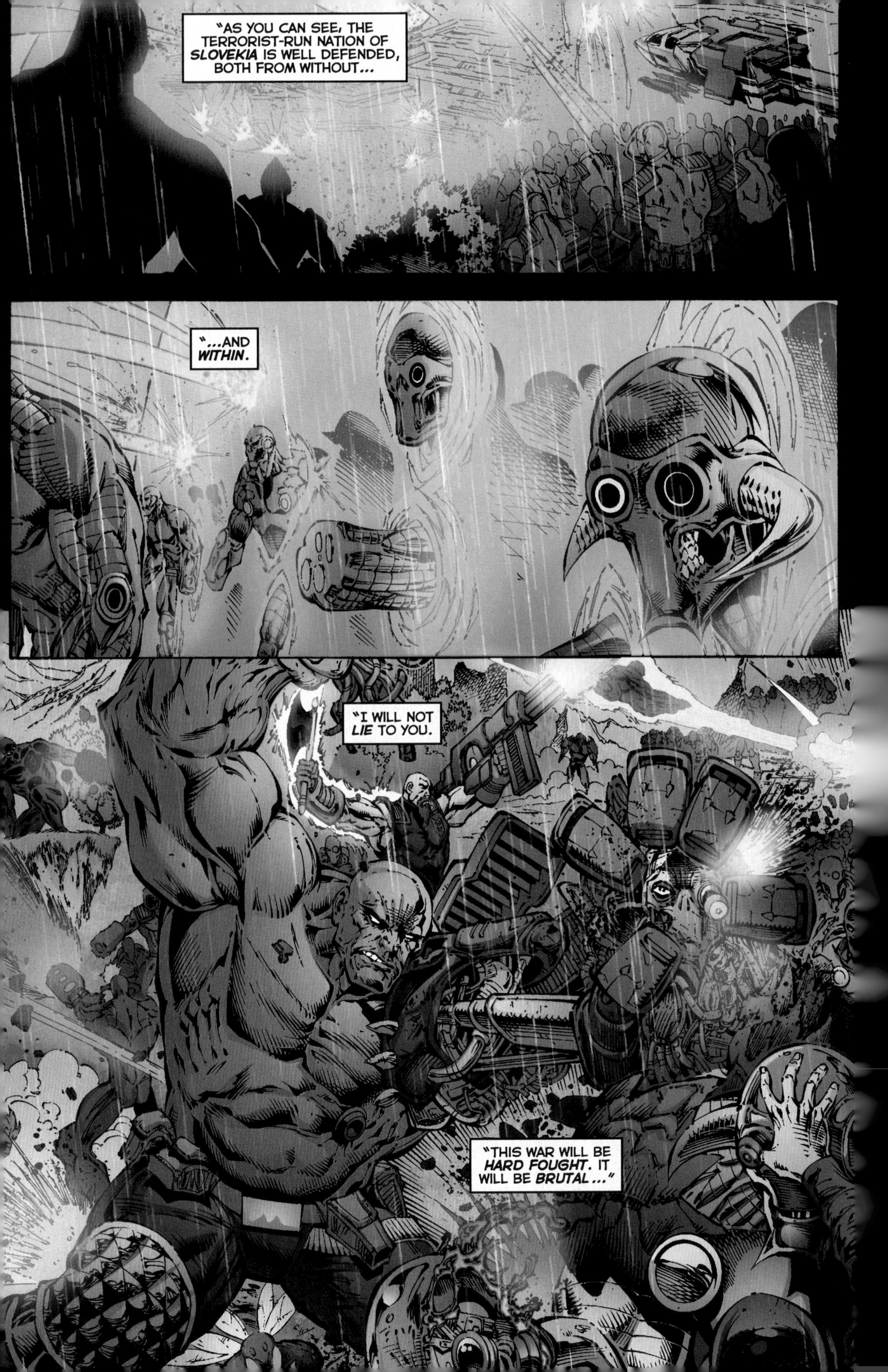
"AS YOU CAN SEE, THE TERRORIST-RUN NATION OF SLOVEKIA IS WELL DEFENDED, BOTH FROM WITHOUT...
"...AND WITHIN.
"I WILL NOT LIE TO YOU.
"THIS WAR WILL BE HARD FOUGHT. IT WILL BE BRUTAL..."

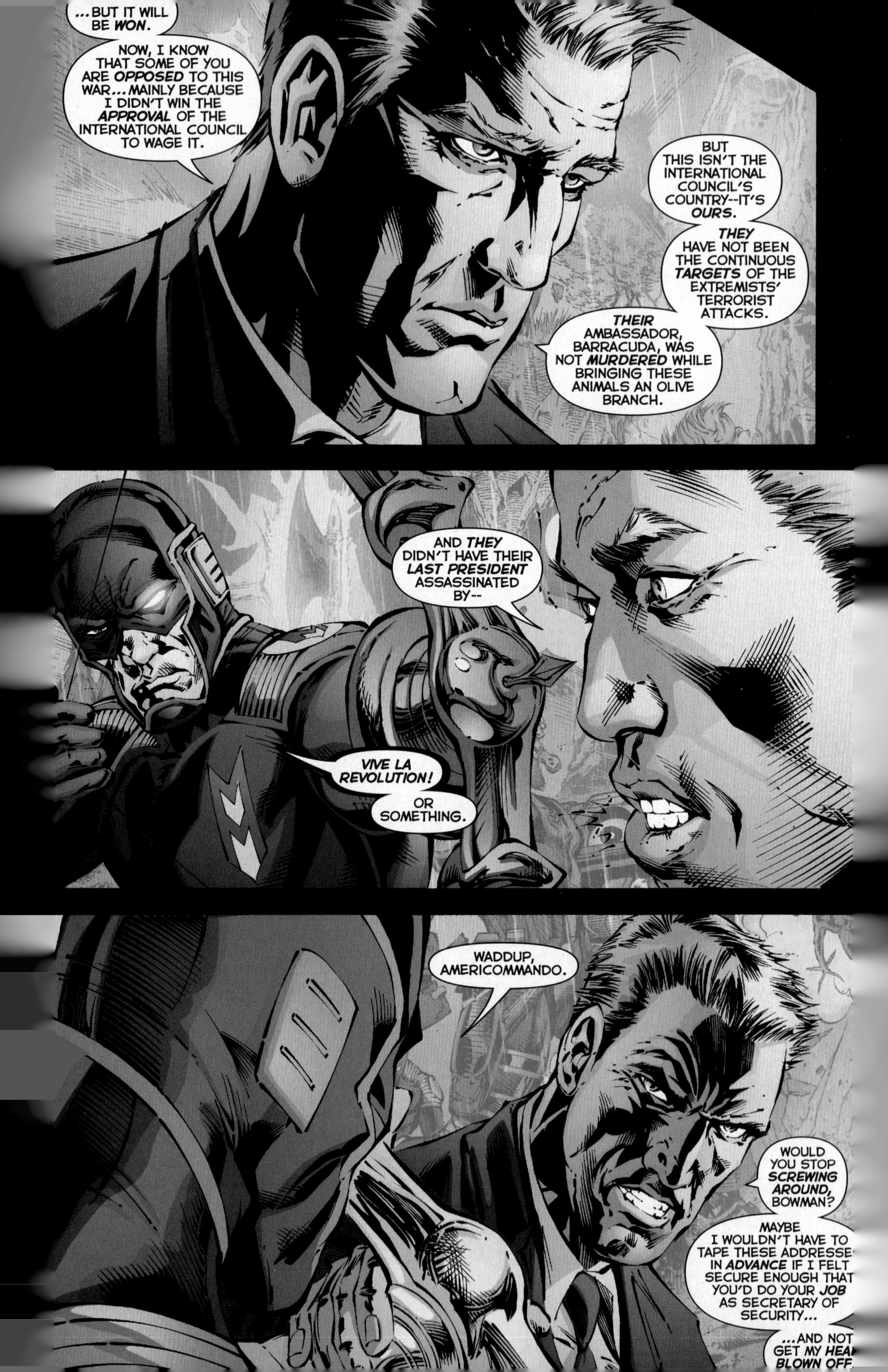
...BUT IT WILL BE *WON*.
NOW, I KNOW THAT SOME OF YOU ARE *OPPOSED* TO THIS WAR... MAINLY BECAUSE I DIDN'T WIN THE *APPROVAL* OF THE INTERNATIONAL COUNCIL TO WAGE IT.
BUT THIS ISN'T THE INTERNATIONAL COUNCIL'S COUNTRY--IT'S *OURS*.
THEY HAVE NOT BEEN THE CONTINUOUS *TARGETS* OF THE EXTREMISTS' TERRORIST ATTACKS.
THEIR AMBASSADOR, BARRACUDA, WAS NOT *MURDERED* WHILE BRINGING THESE ANIMALS AN OLIVE BRANCH.
AND *THEY* DIDN'T HAVE THEIR *LAST PRESIDENT* ASSASSINATED BY--
VIVE LA REVOLUTION!
OR SOMETHING.
WADDUP, AMERICOMMANDO.
WOULD YOU STOP *SCREWING AROUND*, BOWMAN?
MAYBE I WOULDN'T HAVE TO TAPE THESE ADDRESSE IN *ADVANCE* IF I FELT SECURE ENOUGH THAT YOU'D DO YOUR *JOB* AS SECRETARY OF SECURITY...
...AND NOT GET MY *HEA BLOWN OFF.*

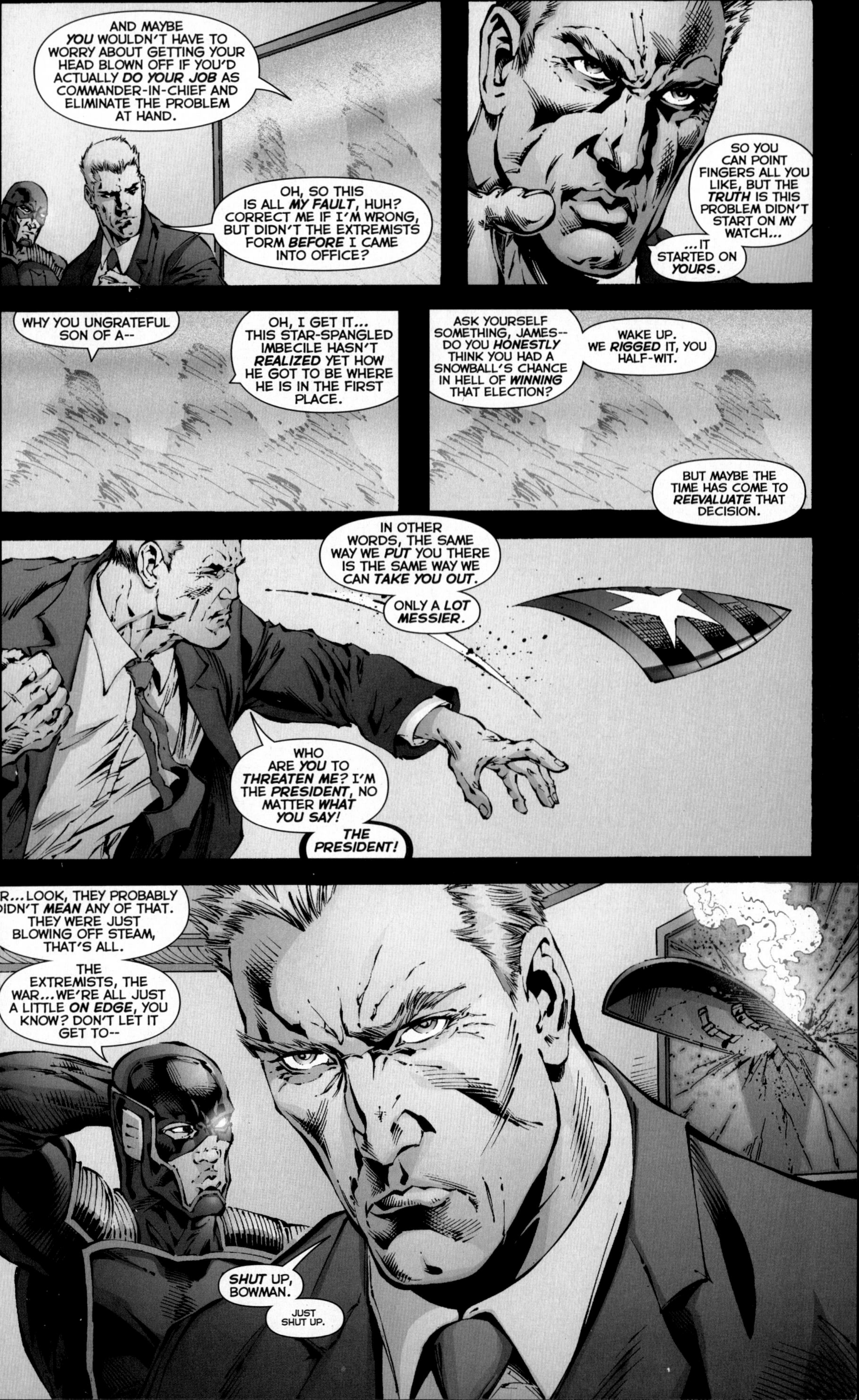
AND MAYBE YOU WOULDN'T HAVE TO WORRY ABOUT GETTING YOUR HEAD BLOWN OFF IF YOU'D ACTUALLY DO YOUR JOB AS COMMANDER-IN-CHIEF AND ELIMINATE THE PROBLEM AT HAND.
OH, SO THIS IS ALL MY FAULT, HUH? CORRECT ME IF I'M WRONG, BUT DIDN'T THE EXTREMISTS FORM BEFORE I CAME INTO OFFICE?
SO YOU CAN POINT FINGERS ALL YOU LIKE, BUT THE TRUTH IS THIS PROBLEM DIDN'T START ON MY WATCH...
...IT STARTED ON YOURS.
WHY YOU UNGRATEFUL SON OF A--
OH, I GET IT... THIS STAR-SPANGLED IMBECILE HASN'T REALIZED YET HOW HE GOT TO BE WHERE HE IS IN THE FIRST PLACE.
ASK YOURSELF SOMETHING, JAMES-- DO YOU HONESTLY THINK YOU HAD A SNOWBALL'S CHANCE IN HELL OF WINNING THAT ELECTION?
WAKE UP. WE RIGGED IT, YOU HALF-WIT.
BUT MAYBE THE TIME HAS COME TO REEVALUATE THAT DECISION.
IN OTHER WORDS, THE SAME WAY WE PUT YOU THERE IS THE SAME WAY WE CAN TAKE YOU OUT.
ONLY A LOT MESSIER.
WHO ARE YOU TO THREATEN ME? I'M THE PRESIDENT, NO MATTER WHAT YOU SAY!
THE PRESIDENT!
R...LOOK, THEY PROBABLY IDN'T MEAN ANY OF THAT. THEY WERE JUST BLOWING OFF STEAM, THAT'S ALL.
THE EXTREMISTS, THE WAR...WE'RE ALL JUST A LITTLE ON EDGE, YOU KNOW? DON'T LET IT GET TO--
SHUT UP, BOWMAN.
JUST SHUT UP.

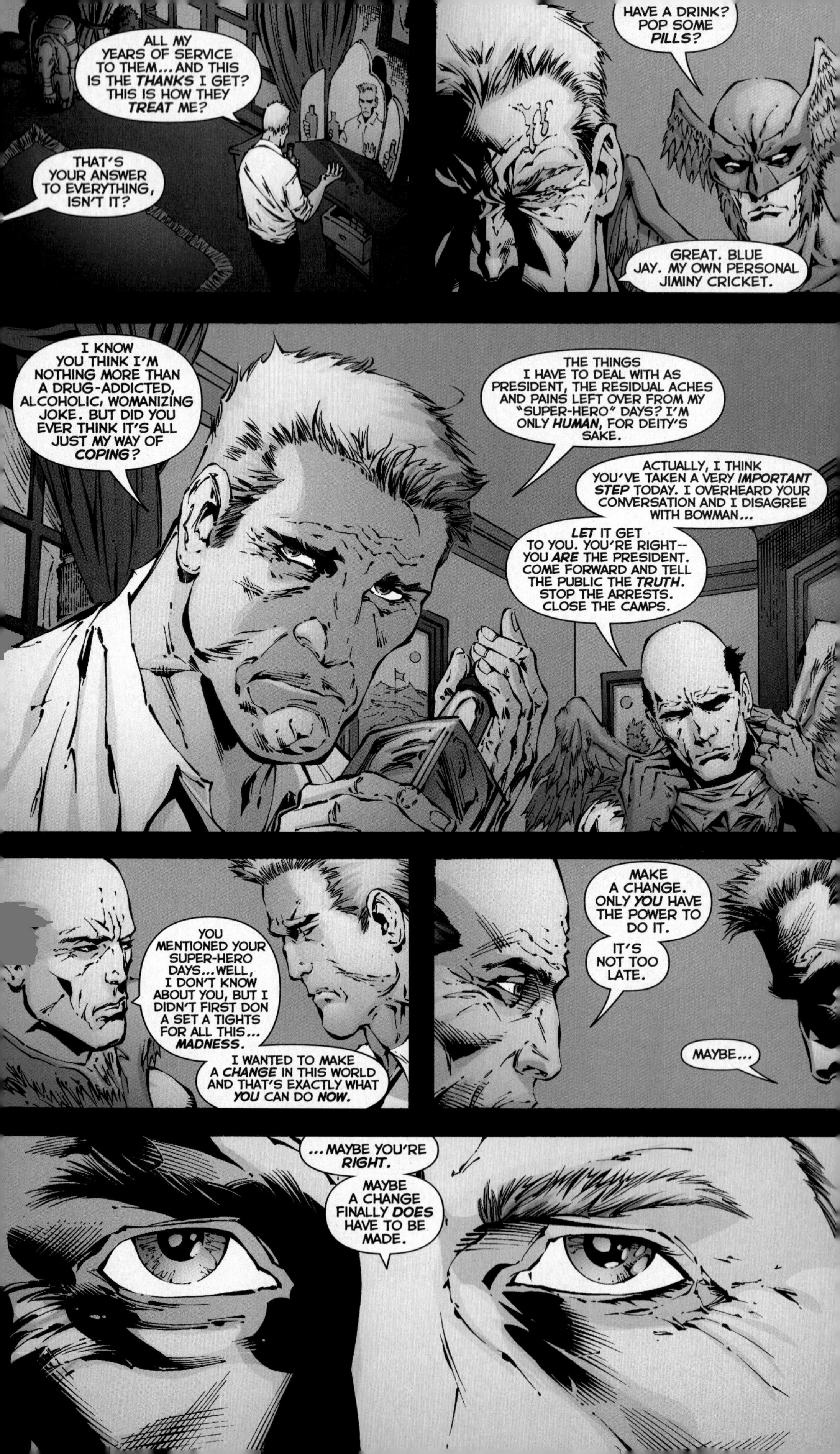
ALL MY YEARS OF SERVICE TO THEM... AND THIS IS THE *THANKS* I GET? THIS IS HOW THEY *TREAT* ME?
THAT'S YOUR ANSWER TO EVERYTHING, ISN'T IT?
HAVE A DRINK? POP SOME *PILLS*?
GREAT. BLUE JAY. MY OWN PERSONAL JIMINY CRICKET.
I KNOW YOU THINK I'M NOTHING MORE THAN A DRUG-ADDICTED, ALCOHOLIC, WOMANIZING JOKE. BUT DID YOU EVER THINK IT'S ALL JUST MY WAY OF *COPING*?
THE THINGS I HAVE TO DEAL WITH AS PRESIDENT, THE RESIDUAL ACHES AND PAINS LEFT OVER FROM MY "SUPER-HERO" DAYS? I'M ONLY *HUMAN*, FOR DEITY'S SAKE.
ACTUALLY, I THINK YOU'VE TAKEN A VERY *IMPORTANT STEP* TODAY. I OVERHEARD YOUR CONVERSATION AND I DISAGREE WITH BOWMAN...
LET IT GET TO YOU. YOU'RE RIGHT-- YOU *ARE* THE PRESIDENT. COME FORWARD AND TELL THE PUBLIC THE *TRUTH*. STOP THE ARRESTS. CLOSE THE CAMPS.
YOU MENTIONED YOUR SUPER-HERO DAYS... WELL, I DON'T KNOW ABOUT YOU, BUT I DIDN'T FIRST DON A SET A TIGHTS FOR ALL THIS... *MADNESS*.
I WANTED TO MAKE A *CHANGE* IN THIS WORLD AND THAT'S EXACTLY WHAT *YOU* CAN DO *NOW*.
MAKE A CHANGE. ONLY *YOU* HAVE THE POWER TO DO IT.
IT'S NOT TOO LATE.
MAYBE...
...MAYBE YOU'RE *RIGHT*.
MAYBE A CHANGE FINALLY *DOES* HAVE TO BE MADE.

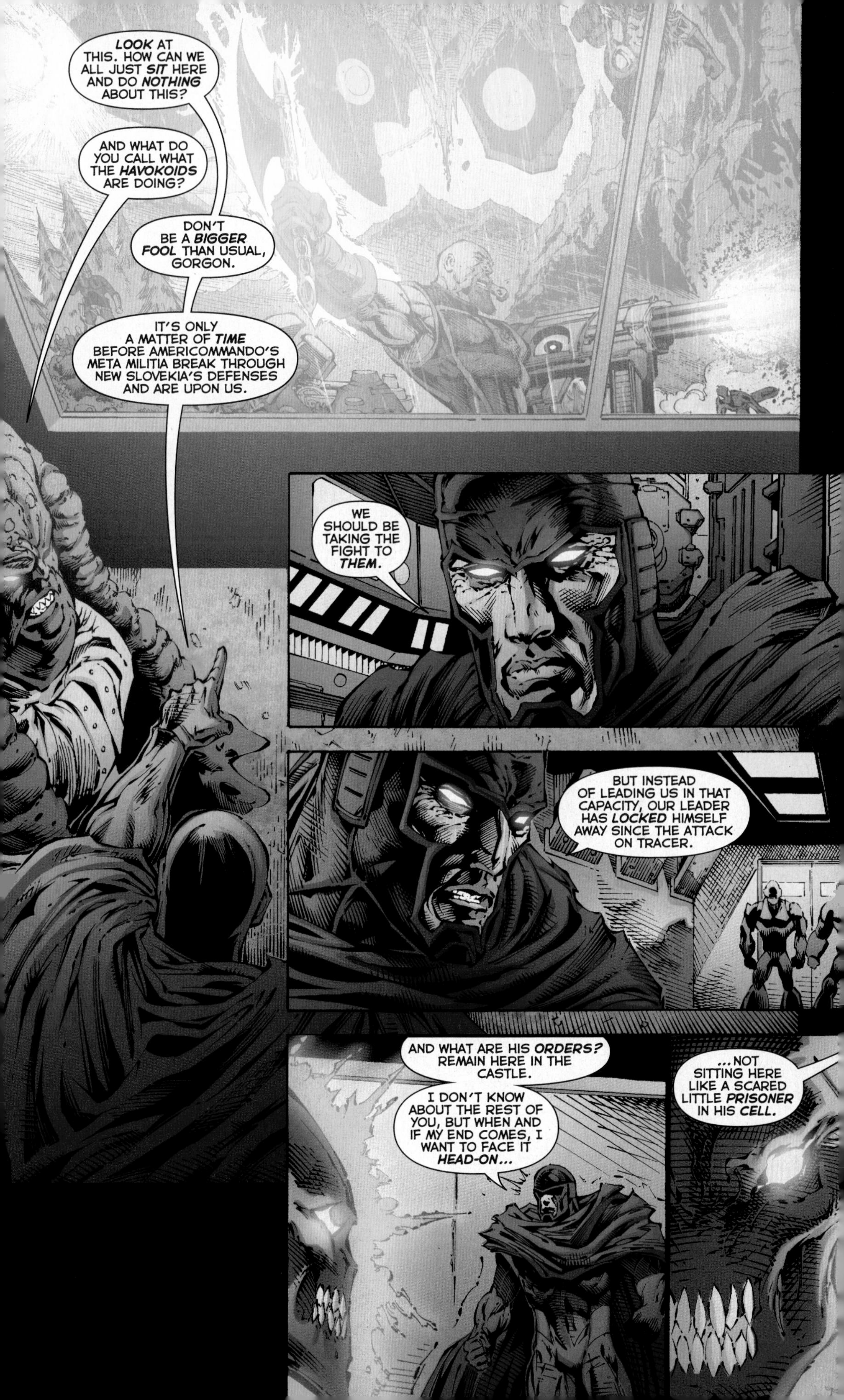
LOOK AT THIS. HOW CAN WE ALL JUST SIT HERE AND DO NOTHING ABOUT THIS?
AND WHAT DO YOU CALL WHAT THE HAVOKOIDS ARE DOING?
DON'T BE A BIGGER FOOL THAN USUAL, GORGON.
IT'S ONLY A MATTER OF TIME BEFORE AMERICOMMANDO'S META MILITIA BREAK THROUGH NEW SLOVEKIA'S DEFENSES AND ARE UPON US.
WE SHOULD BE TAKING THE FIGHT TO THEM.
BUT INSTEAD OF LEADING US IN THAT CAPACITY, OUR LEADER HAS LOCKED HIMSELF AWAY SINCE THE ATTACK ON TRACER.
AND WHAT ARE HIS ORDERS? REMAIN HERE IN THE CASTLE.
I DON'T KNOW ABOUT THE REST OF YOU, BUT WHEN AND IF MY END COMES, I WANT TO FACE IT HEAD-ON...
...NOT SITTING HERE LIKE A SCARED LITTLE PRISONER IN HIS CELL.

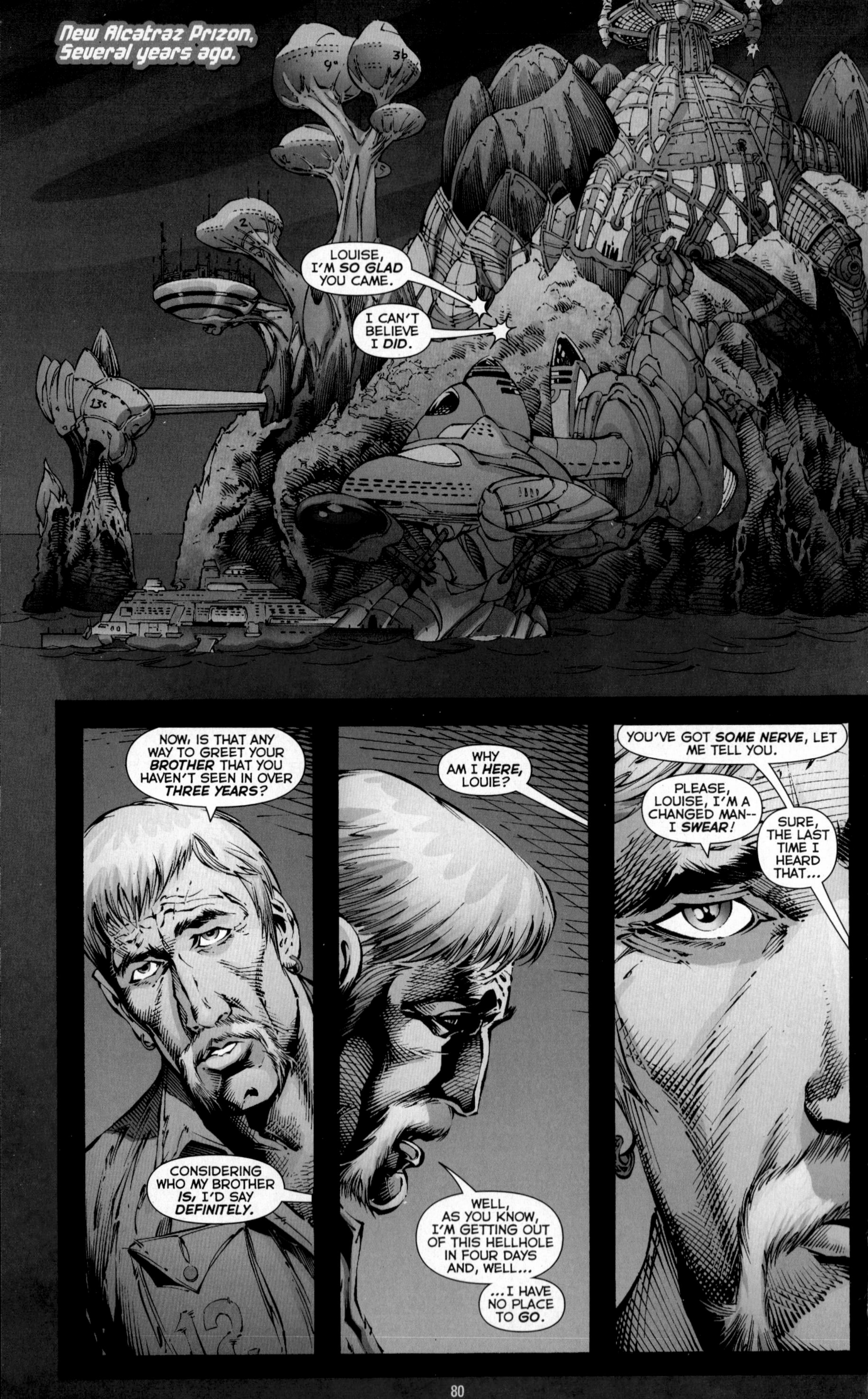
New Alcatraz Prizon,
Several years ago.
LOUISE, I'M SO GLAD YOU CAME.
I CAN'T BELIEVE I DID.
NOW, IS THAT ANY WAY TO GREET YOUR BROTHER THAT YOU HAVEN'T SEEN IN OVER THREE YEARS?
CONSIDERING WHO MY BROTHER IS, I'D SAY DEFINITELY.
WHY AM I HERE, LOUIE?
WELL, AS YOU KNOW, I'M GETTING OUT OF THIS HELLHOLE IN FOUR DAYS AND, WELL...
...I HAVE NO PLACE TO GO.
YOU'VE GOT SOME NERVE, LET ME TELL YOU.
PLEASE, LOUISE, I'M A CHANGED MAN-- I SWEAR!
SURE, THE LAST TIME I HEARD THAT...

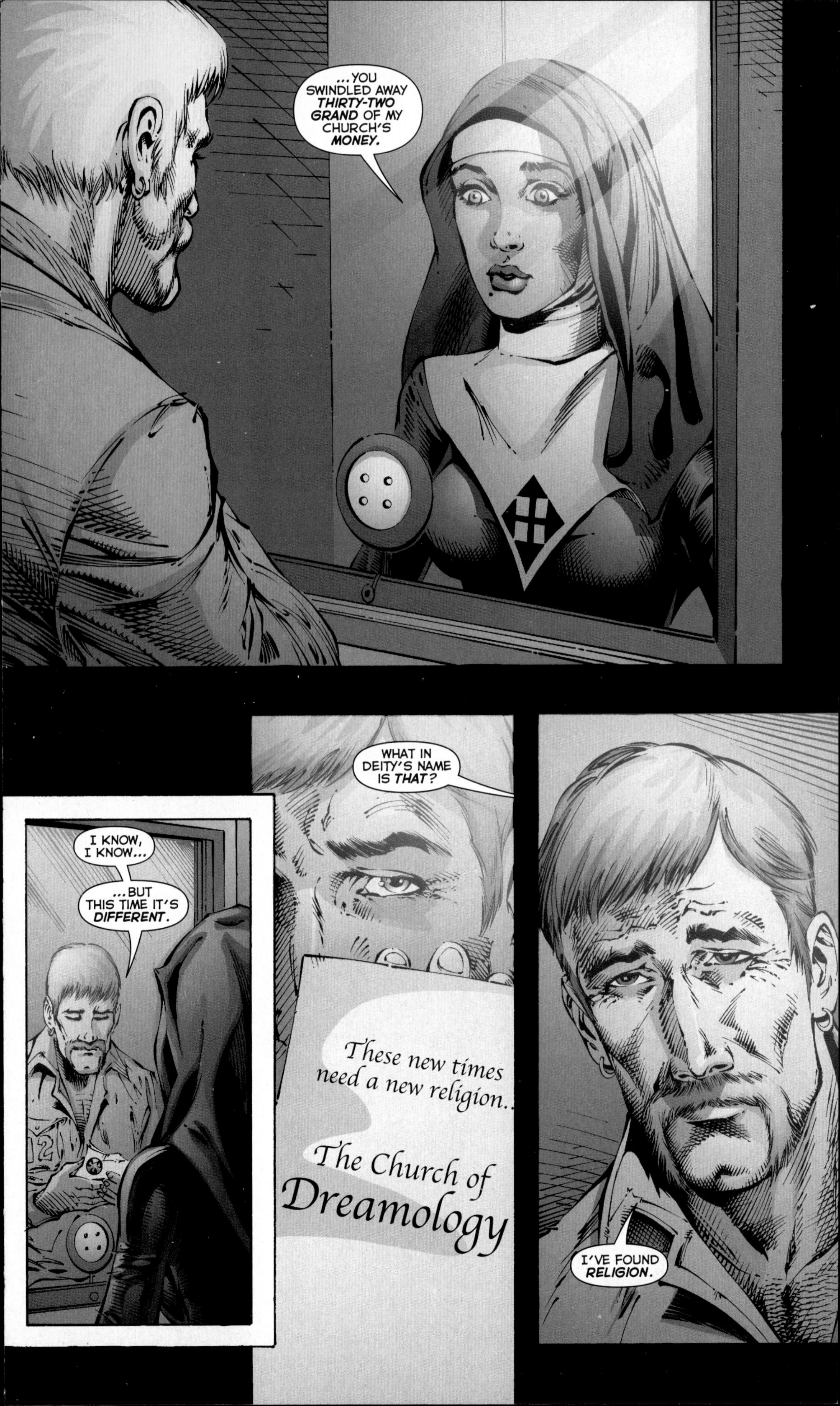
...YOU SWINDLED AWAY THIRTY-TWO GRAND OF MY CHURCH'S MONEY.
I KNOW, I KNOW...
...BUT THIS TIME IT'S DIFFERENT.
WHAT IN DEITY'S NAME IS THAT?
These new times need a new religion...
The Church of Dreamology
I'VE FOUND RELIGION.

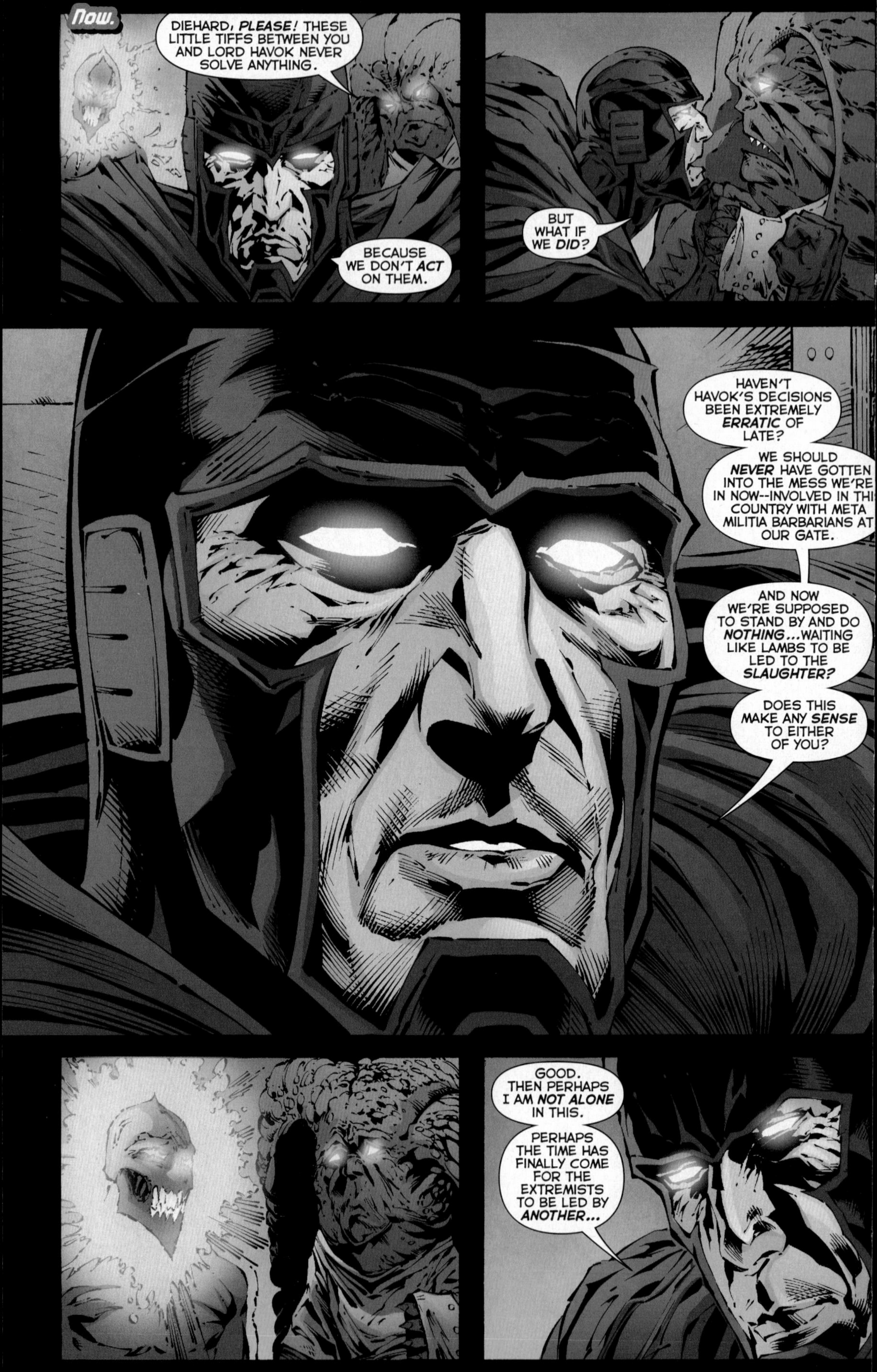
Now.
DIEHARD, PLEASE! THESE LITTLE TIFFS BETWEEN YOU AND LORD HAVOK NEVER SOLVE ANYTHING.
BECAUSE WE DON'T ACT ON THEM.
BUT WHAT IF WE DID?
HAVEN'T HAVOK'S DECISIONS BEEN EXTREMELY ERRATIC OF LATE?
WE SHOULD NEVER HAVE GOTTEN INTO THE MESS WE'RE IN NOW--INVOLVED IN THIS COUNTRY WITH META MILITIA BARBARIANS AT OUR GATE.
AND NOW WE'RE SUPPOSED TO STAND BY AND DO NOTHING...WAITING LIKE LAMBS TO BE LED TO THE SLAUGHTER?
DOES THIS MAKE ANY SENSE TO EITHER OF YOU?
GOOD. THEN PERHAPS I AM NOT ALONE IN THIS.
PERHAPS THE TIME HAS FINALLY COME FOR THE EXTREMISTS TO BE LED BY ANOTHER...

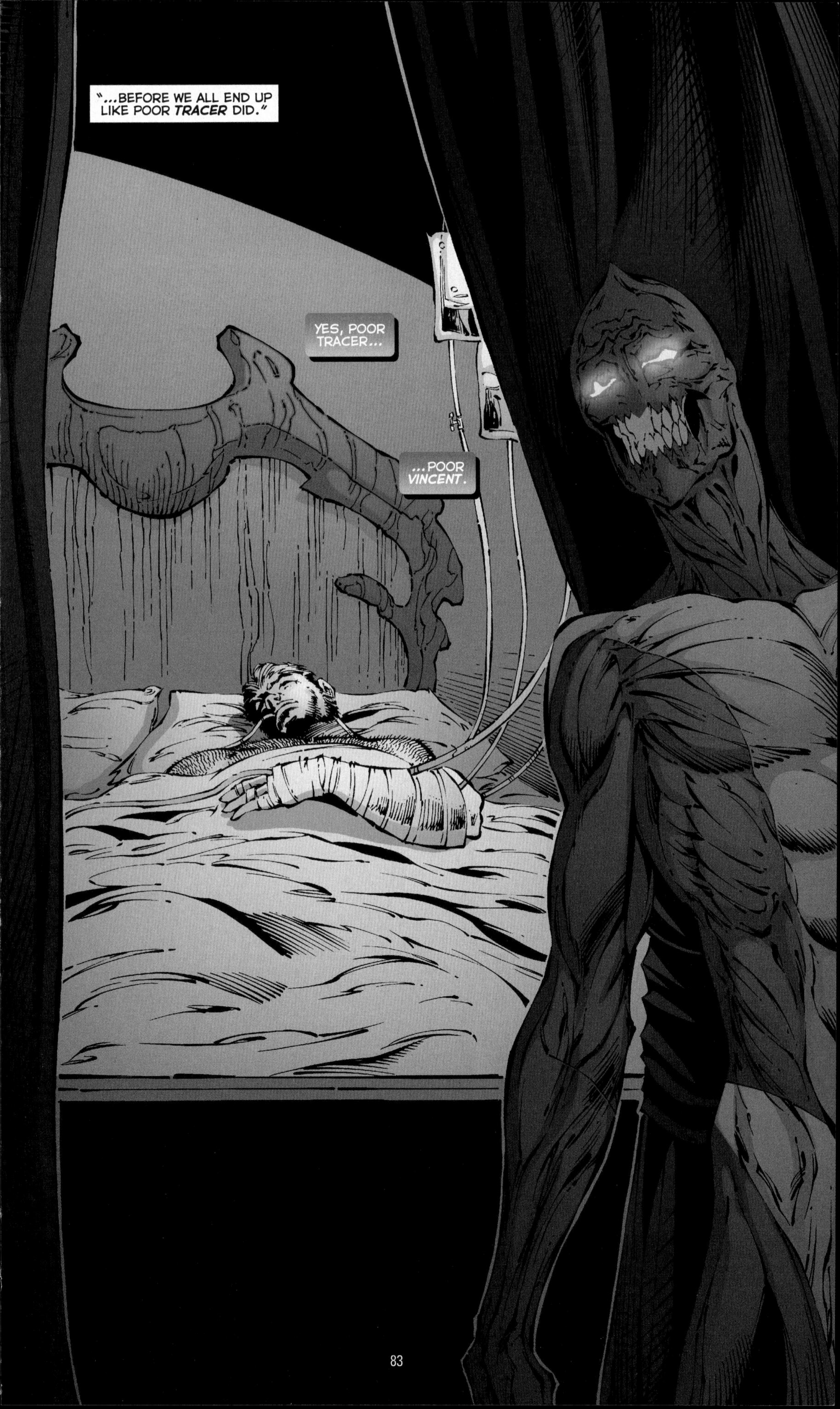
"...BEFORE WE ALL END UP LIKE POOR TRACER DID."
YES, POOR TRACER...
...POOR VINCENT.

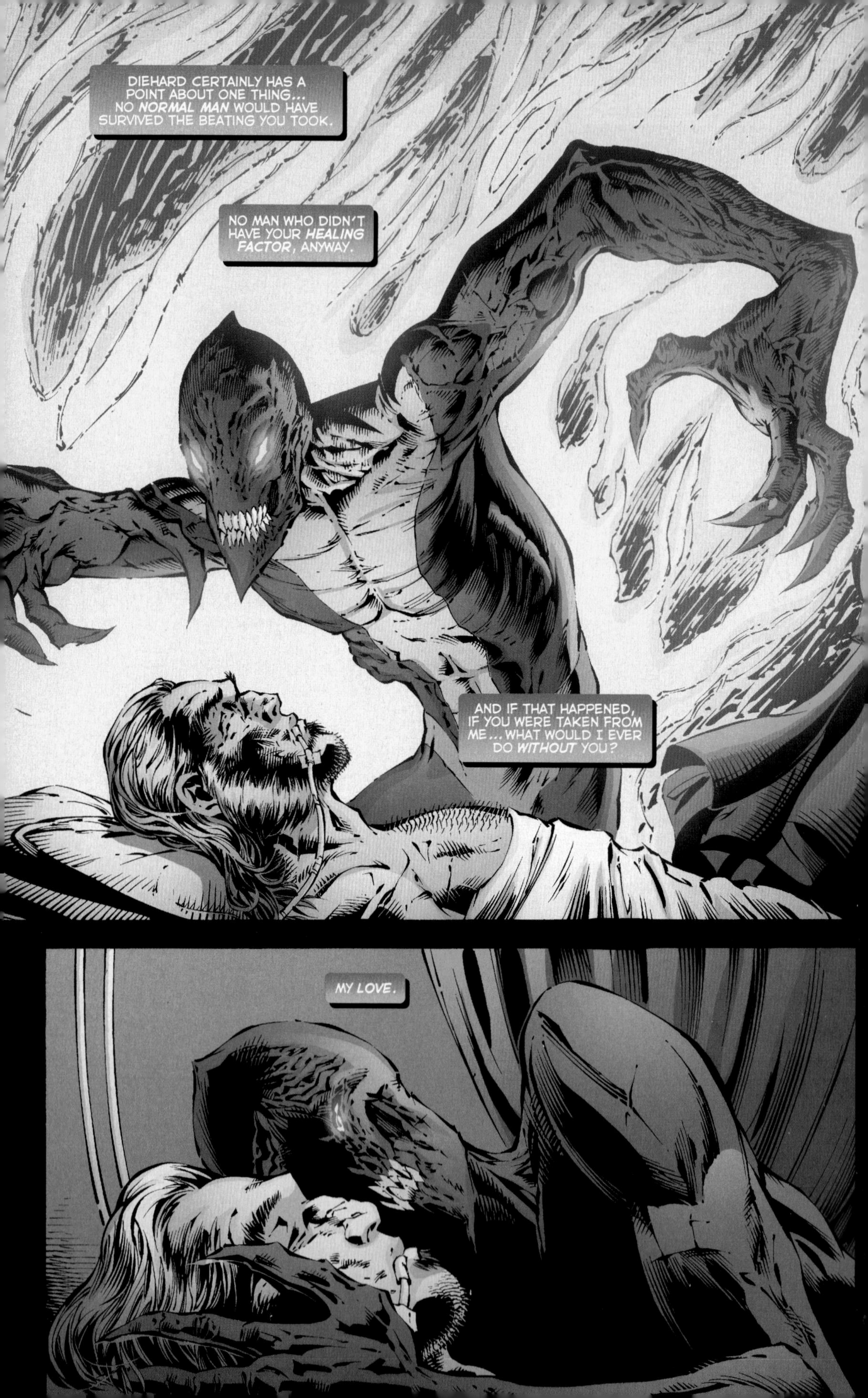
DIEHARD CERTAINLY HAS A POINT ABOUT ONE THING... NO *NORMAL MAN* WOULD HAVE SURVIVED THE BEATING YOU TOOK.
NO MAN WHO DIDN'T HAVE YOUR *HEALING FACTOR*, ANYWAY.
AND IF THAT HAPPENED, IF YOU WERE TAKEN FROM ME... WHAT WOULD I EVER DO *WITHOUT* YOU?
MY LOVE.

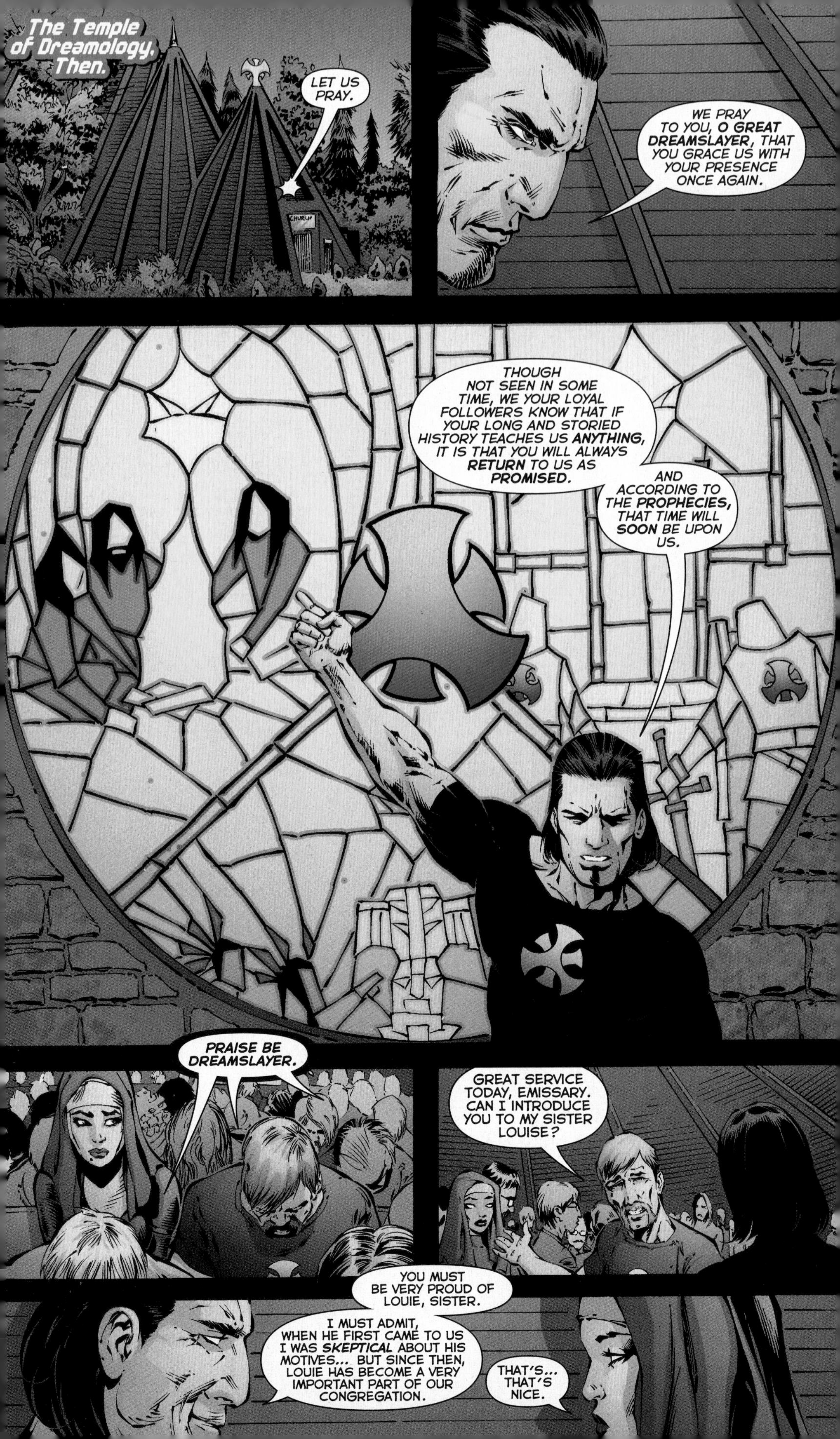
The Temple of Dreamology, Then.
LET US PRAY.
CHURCH
WE PRAY TO YOU, O GREAT DREAMSLAYER, THAT YOU GRACE US WITH YOUR PRESENCE ONCE AGAIN.
THOUGH NOT SEEN IN SOME TIME, WE YOUR LOYAL FOLLOWERS KNOW THAT IF YOUR LONG AND STORIED HISTORY TEACHES US ANYTHING, IT IS THAT YOU WILL ALWAYS RETURN TO US AS PROMISED.
AND ACCORDING TO THE PROPHECIES, THAT TIME WILL SOON BE UPON US.
PRAISE BE DREAMSLAYER.
GREAT SERVICE TODAY, EMISSARY. CAN I INTRODUCE YOU TO MY SISTER LOUISE?
YOU MUST BE VERY PROUD OF LOUIE, SISTER.
I MUST ADMIT, WHEN HE FIRST CAME TO US I WAS SKEPTICAL ABOUT HIS MOTIVES... BUT SINCE THEN, LOUIE HAS BECOME A VERY IMPORTANT PART OF OUR CONGREGATION.
THAT'S... THAT'S NICE.

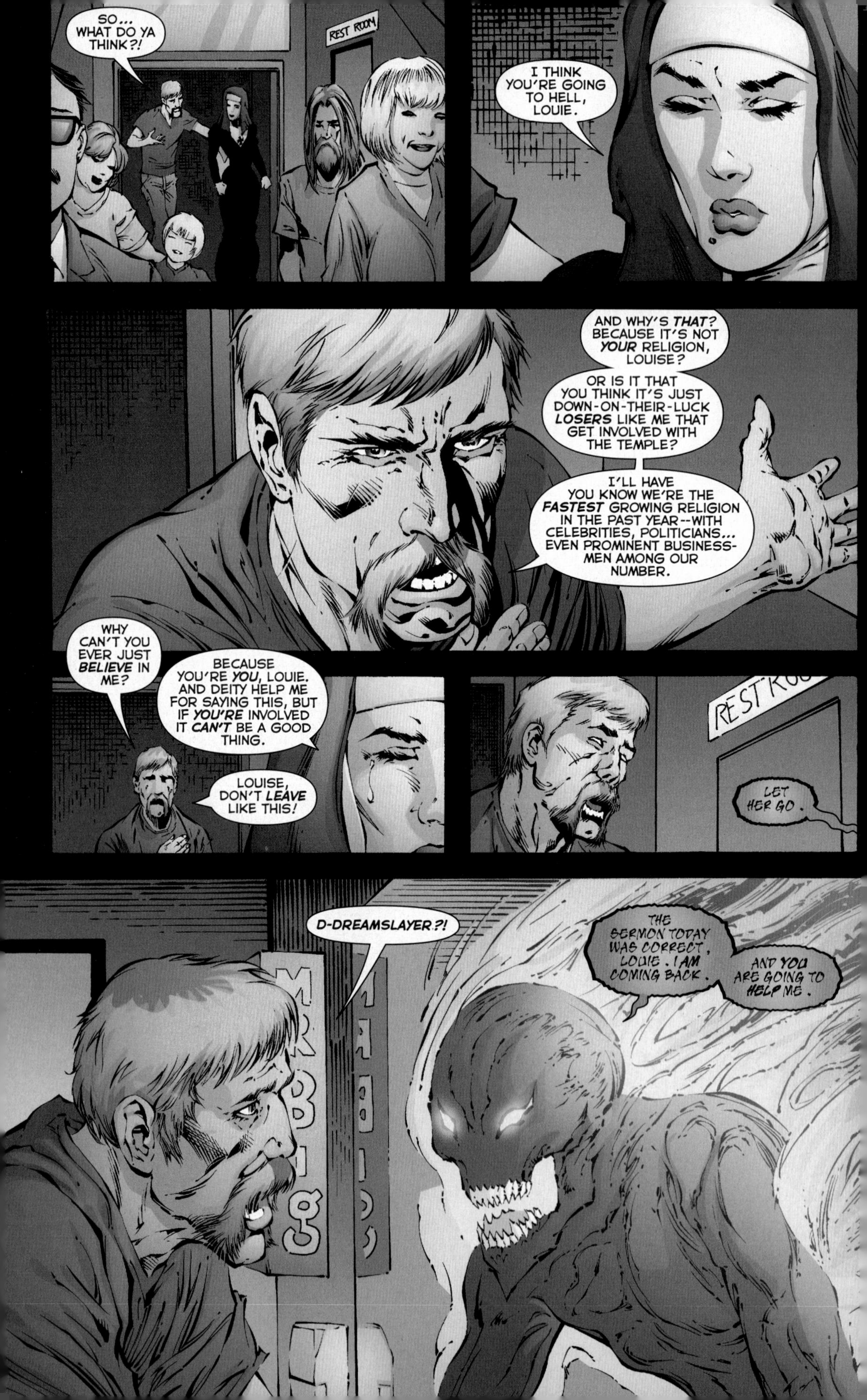
REST ROOM
SO... WHAT DO YA THINK?!
I THINK YOU'RE GOING TO HELL, LOUIE.
AND WHY'S *THAT*? BECAUSE IT'S NOT *YOUR* RELIGION, LOUISE?
OR IS IT THAT YOU THINK IT'S JUST DOWN-ON-THEIR-LUCK *LOSERS* LIKE ME THAT GET INVOLVED WITH THE TEMPLE?
I'LL HAVE YOU KNOW WE'RE THE *FASTEST* GROWING RELIGION IN THE PAST YEAR--WITH CELEBRITIES, POLITICIANS... EVEN PROMINENT BUSINESS-MEN AMONG OUR NUMBER.
WHY CAN'T YOU EVER JUST *BELIEVE* IN ME?
BECAUSE YOU'RE *YOU*, LOUIE. AND DEITY HELP ME FOR SAYING THIS, BUT IF *YOU'RE* INVOLVED IT *CAN'T* BE A GOOD THING.
LOUISE, DON'T *LEAVE* LIKE THIS!
LET HER GO.
D-DREAMSLAYER?!
THE SERMON TODAY WAS CORRECT, LOUIE. I *AM* COMING BACK.
AND *YOU* ARE GOING TO *HELP* ME.

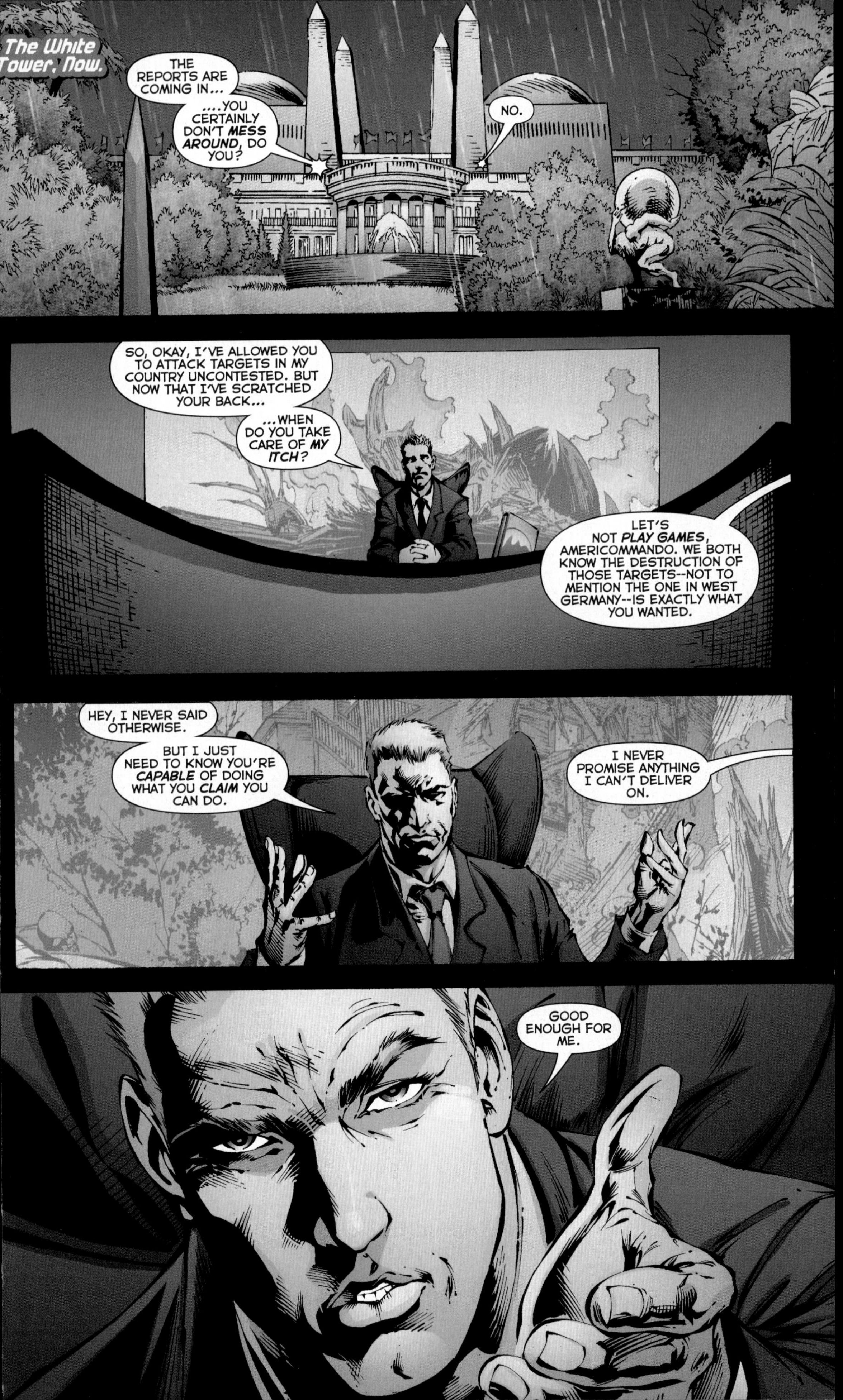
The White Tower, Now.
THE REPORTS ARE COMING IN...
....YOU CERTAINLY DON'T MESS AROUND, DO YOU?
NO.
SO, OKAY, I'VE ALLOWED YOU TO ATTACK TARGETS IN MY COUNTRY UNCONTESTED. BUT NOW THAT I'VE SCRATCHED YOUR BACK...
...WHEN DO YOU TAKE CARE OF MY ITCH?
LET'S NOT PLAY GAMES, AMERICOMMANDO. WE BOTH KNOW THE DESTRUCTION OF THOSE TARGETS--NOT TO MENTION THE ONE IN WEST GERMANY--IS EXACTLY WHAT YOU WANTED.
HEY, I NEVER SAID OTHERWISE.
BUT I JUST NEED TO KNOW YOU'RE CAPABLE OF DOING WHAT YOU CLAIM YOU CAN DO.
I NEVER PROMISE ANYTHING I CAN'T DELIVER ON.
GOOD ENOUGH FOR ME.

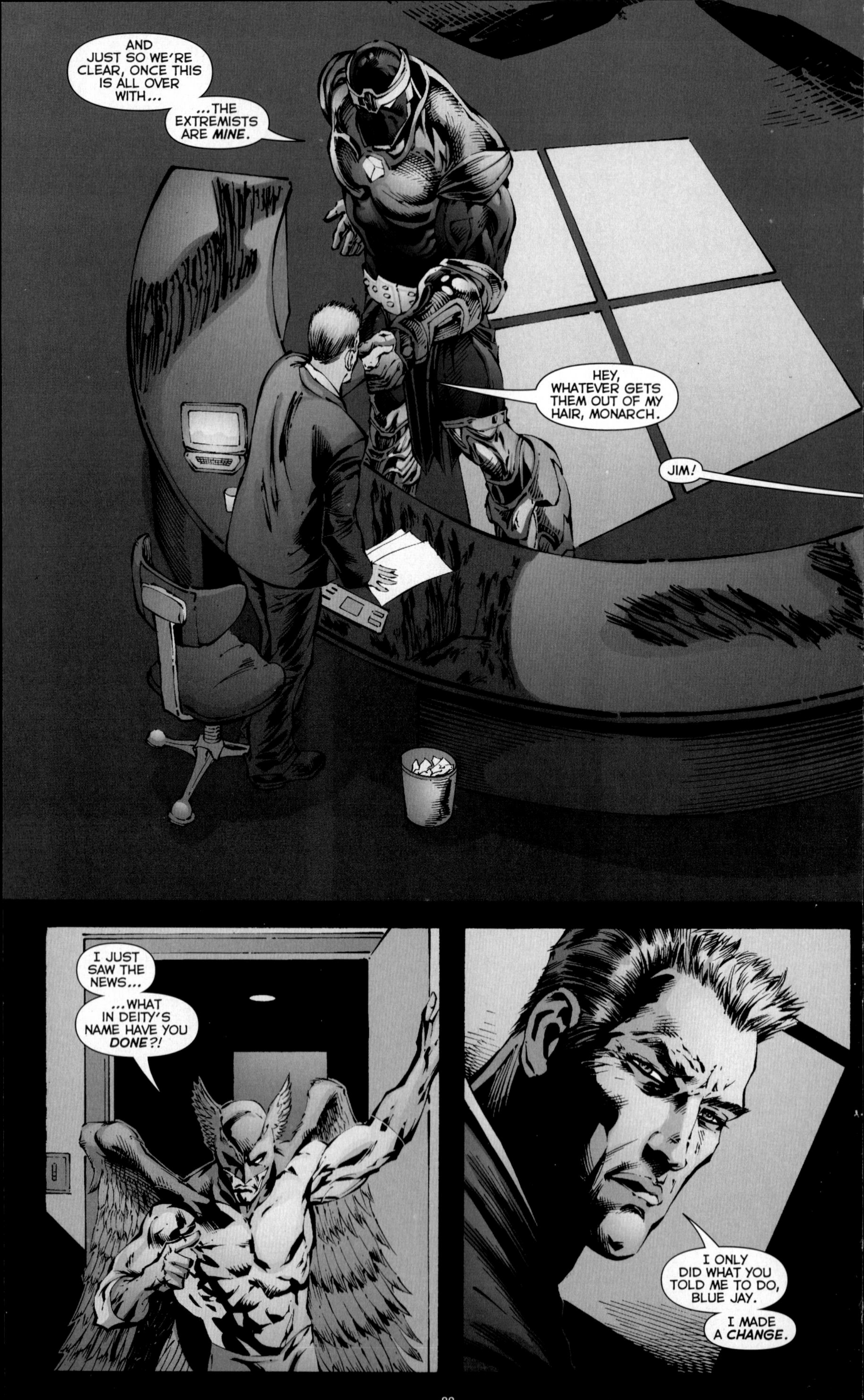
AND JUST SO WE'RE CLEAR, ONCE THIS IS ALL OVER WITH...
...THE EXTREMISTS ARE *MINE*.
HEY, WHATEVER GETS THEM OUT OF MY HAIR, MONARCH.
JIM!
I JUST SAW THE NEWS...
...WHAT IN DEITY'S NAME HAVE YOU *DONE*?!
I ONLY DID WHAT YOU TOLD ME TO DO, BLUE JAY.
I MADE A *CHANGE*.

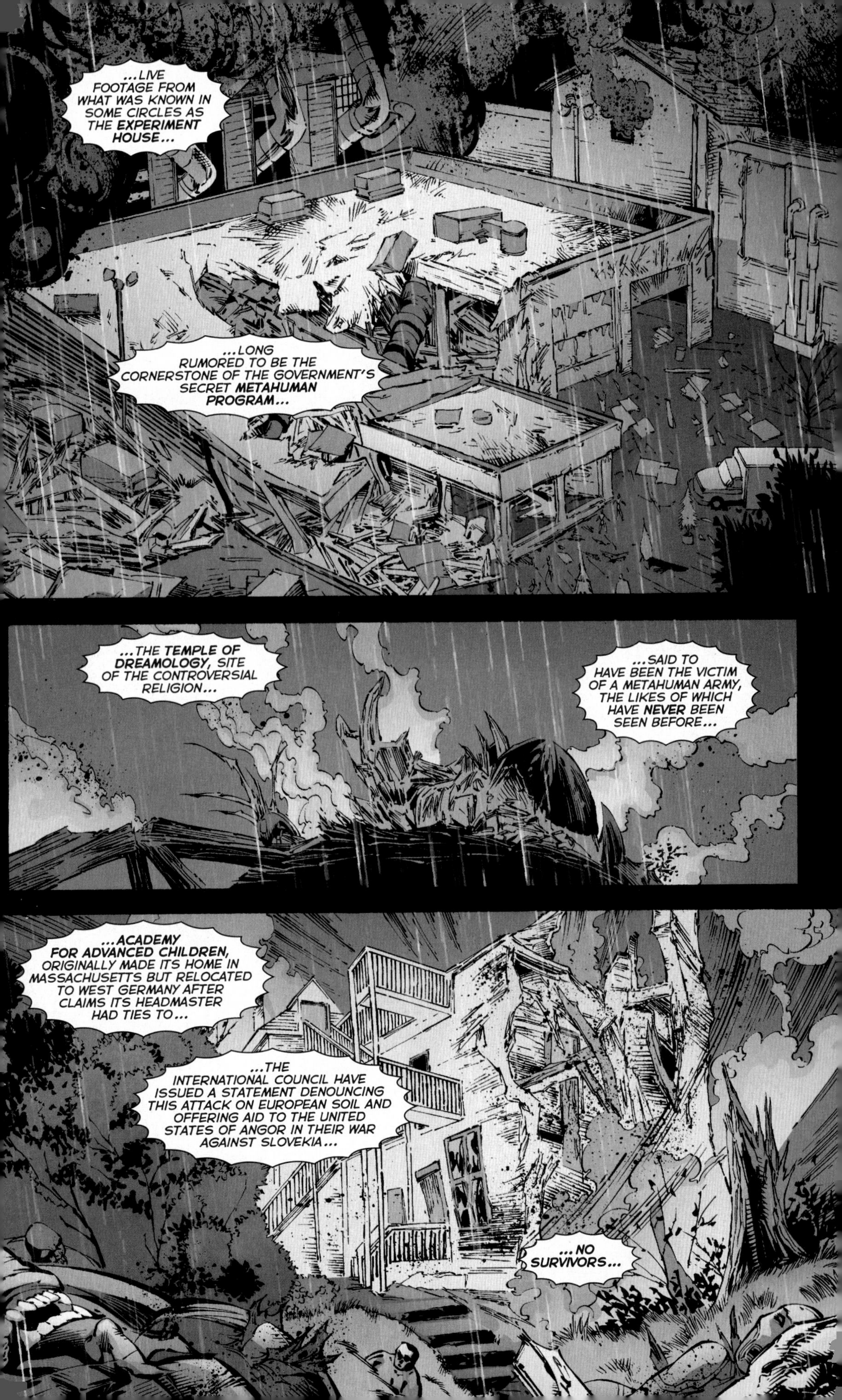
...LIVE FOOTAGE FROM WHAT WAS KNOWN IN SOME CIRCLES AS THE **EXPERIMENT HOUSE**...
...LONG RUMORED TO BE THE CORNERSTONE OF THE GOVERNMENT'S SECRET **METAHUMAN PROGRAM**...
...THE **TEMPLE OF DREAMOLOGY**, SITE OF THE CONTROVERSIAL RELIGION...
...SAID TO HAVE BEEN THE VICTIM OF A METAHUMAN ARMY, THE LIKES OF WHICH HAVE **NEVER** BEEN SEEN BEFORE...
...**ACADEMY FOR ADVANCED CHILDREN**, ORIGINALLY MADE ITS HOME IN MASSACHUSETTS BUT RELOCATED TO WEST GERMANY AFTER CLAIMS ITS HEADMASTER HAD TIES TO...
...THE INTERNATIONAL COUNCIL HAVE ISSUED A STATEMENT DENOUNCING THIS ATTACK ON EUROPEAN SOIL AND OFFERING AID TO THE UNITED STATES OF ANGOR IN THEIR WAR AGAINST SLOVEKIA...
...**NO SURVIVORS**...

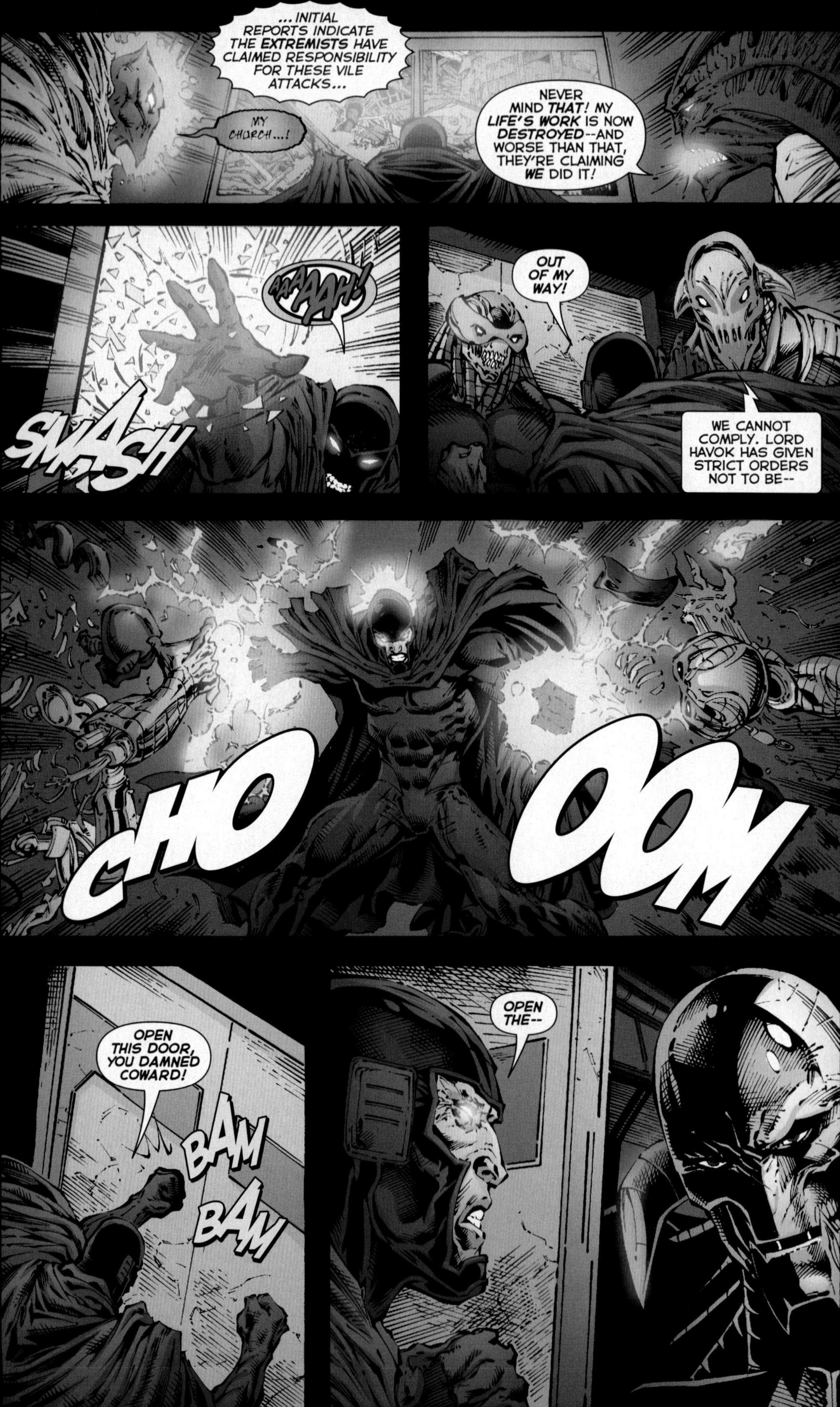
...INITIAL REPORTS INDICATE THE EXTREMISTS HAVE CLAIMED RESPONSIBILITY FOR THESE VILE ATTACKS...
MY CHURCH...!
NEVER MIND THAT! MY LIFE'S WORK IS NOW DESTROYED--AND WORSE THAN THAT, THEY'RE CLAIMING WE DID IT!
AAAAAH!
SMASH
OUT OF MY WAY!
WE CANNOT COMPLY. LORD HAVOK HAS GIVEN STRICT ORDERS NOT TO BE--
CHOOOM
OPEN THIS DOOR, YOU DAMNED COWARD!
BAM
BAM
OPEN THE--

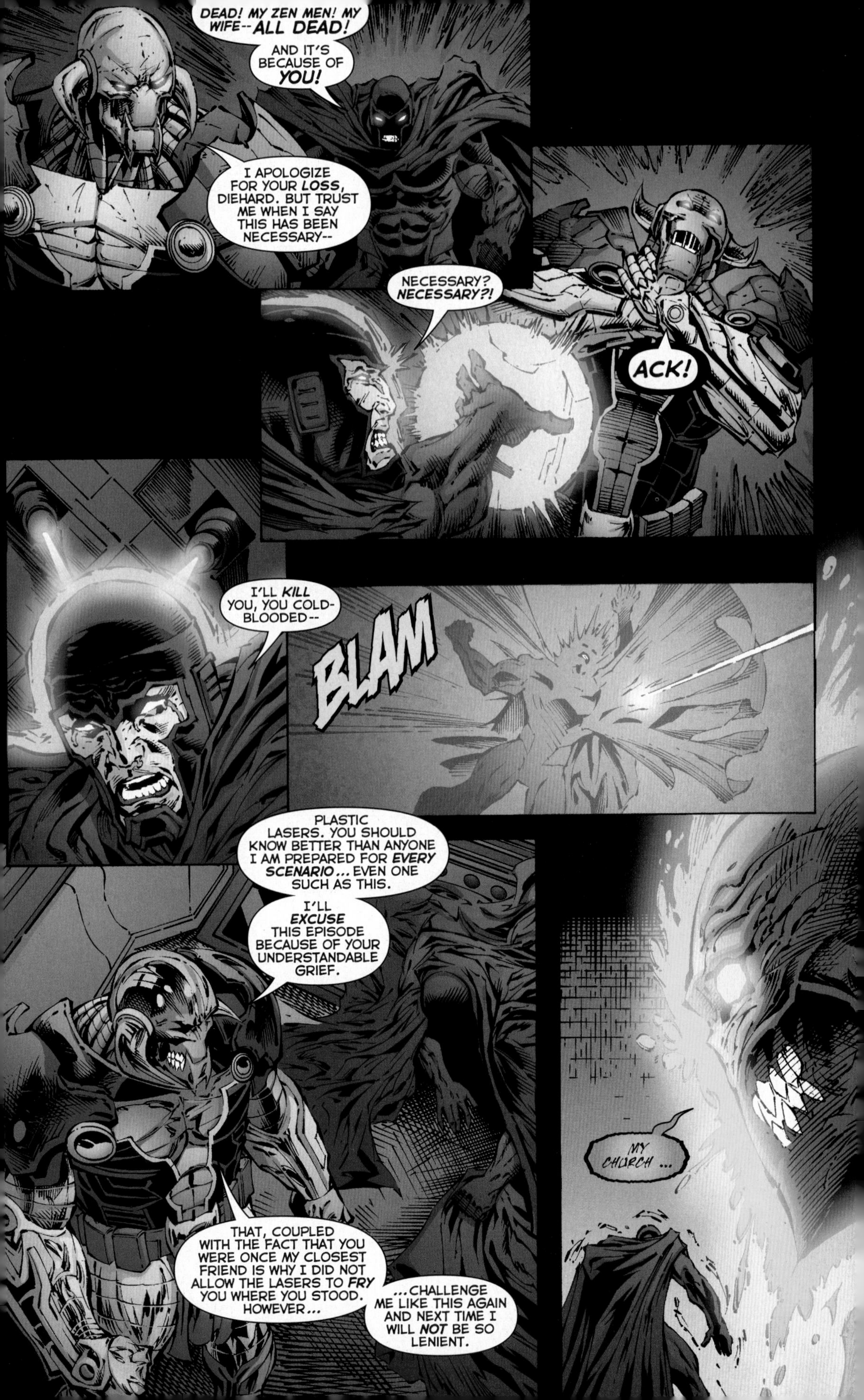
DEAD! MY ZEN MEN! MY WIFE--ALL DEAD!
AND IT'S BECAUSE OF YOU!
I APOLOGIZE FOR YOUR LOSS, DIEHARD. BUT TRUST ME WHEN I SAY THIS HAS BEEN NECESSARY--
NECESSARY? NECESSARY?!
ACK!
I'LL KILL YOU, YOU COLD-BLOODED--
BLAM
PLASTIC LASERS. YOU SHOULD KNOW BETTER THAN ANYONE I AM PREPARED FOR EVERY SCENARIO... EVEN ONE SUCH AS THIS.
I'LL EXCUSE THIS EPISODE BECAUSE OF YOUR UNDERSTANDABLE GRIEF.
THAT, COUPLED WITH THE FACT THAT YOU WERE ONCE MY CLOSEST FRIEND IS WHY I DID NOT ALLOW THE LASERS TO FRY YOU WHERE YOU STOOD. HOWEVER...
...CHALLENGE ME LIKE THIS AGAIN AND NEXT TIME I WILL NOT BE SO LENIENT.
MY CHURCH...

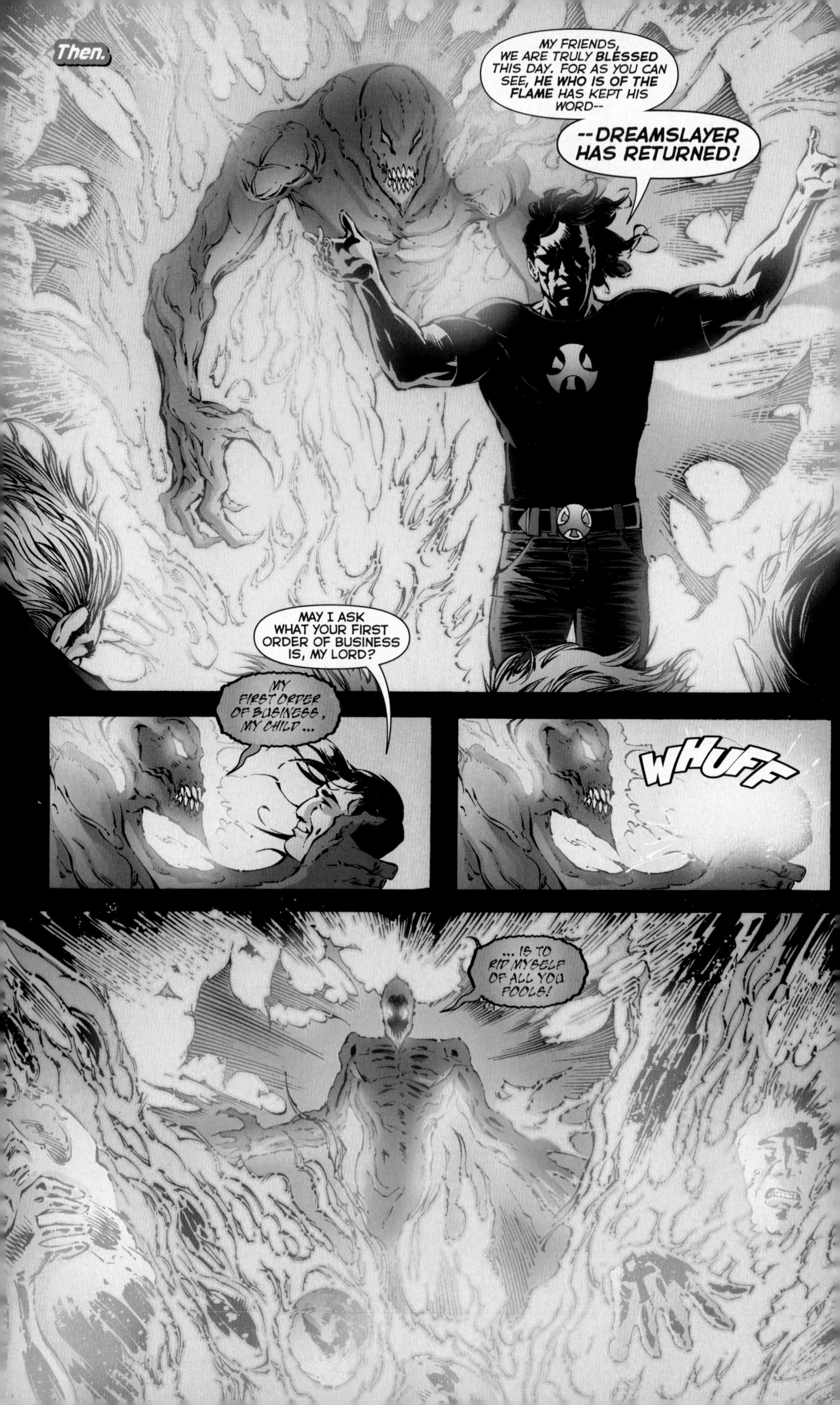
Then.
MY FRIENDS, WE ARE TRULY BLESSED THIS DAY. FOR AS YOU CAN SEE, HE WHO IS OF THE FLAME HAS KEPT HIS WORD--
--DREAMSLAYER HAS RETURNED!
MAY I ASK WHAT YOUR FIRST ORDER OF BUSINESS IS, MY LORD?
MY FIRST ORDER OF BUSINESS, MY CHILD...
WHUFF
...IS TO RID MYSELF OF ALL YOU FOOLS!

HA! HA!

WON YDOB SIHT EVAEL!

WHAT'S...

...HAPPENING?!

THE DREAMSLAYER ENTITY HAS BEEN *DRIVEN* FROM YOUR BODY, LOUIS MARINO.

BUT WE MUST *HURRY*. I AM BUT A *NOVICE* IN THE MYSTIC ARTS, AND THE INCANTATION I SPOKE WILL NOT KEEP HIM AT BAY FOR LONG.

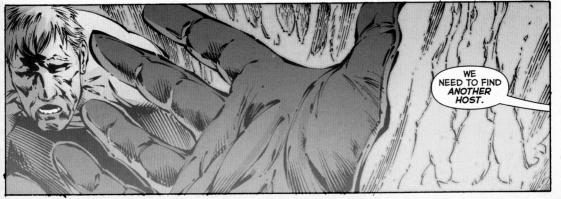

WE NEED TO FIND *ANOTHER* HOST.

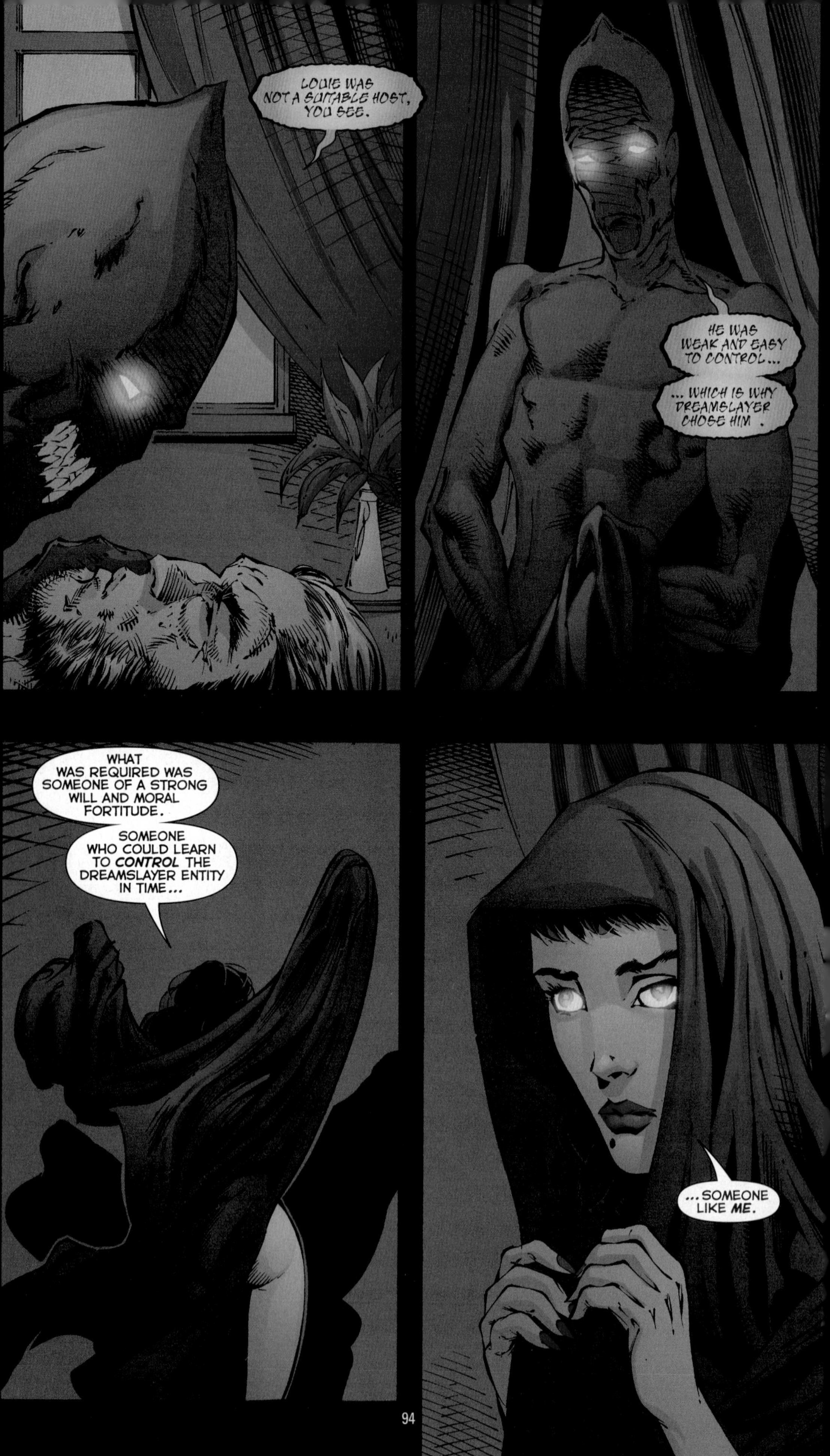
LOUIE WAS NOT A SUITABLE HOST, YOU SEE.
HE WAS WEAK AND EASY TO CONTROL...
...WHICH IS WHY DREAMSLAYER CHOSE HIM.
WHAT WAS REQUIRED WAS SOMEONE OF A STRONG WILL AND MORAL FORTITUDE.
SOMEONE WHO COULD LEARN TO CONTROL THE DREAMSLAYER ENTITY IN TIME...
...SOMEONE LIKE ME.

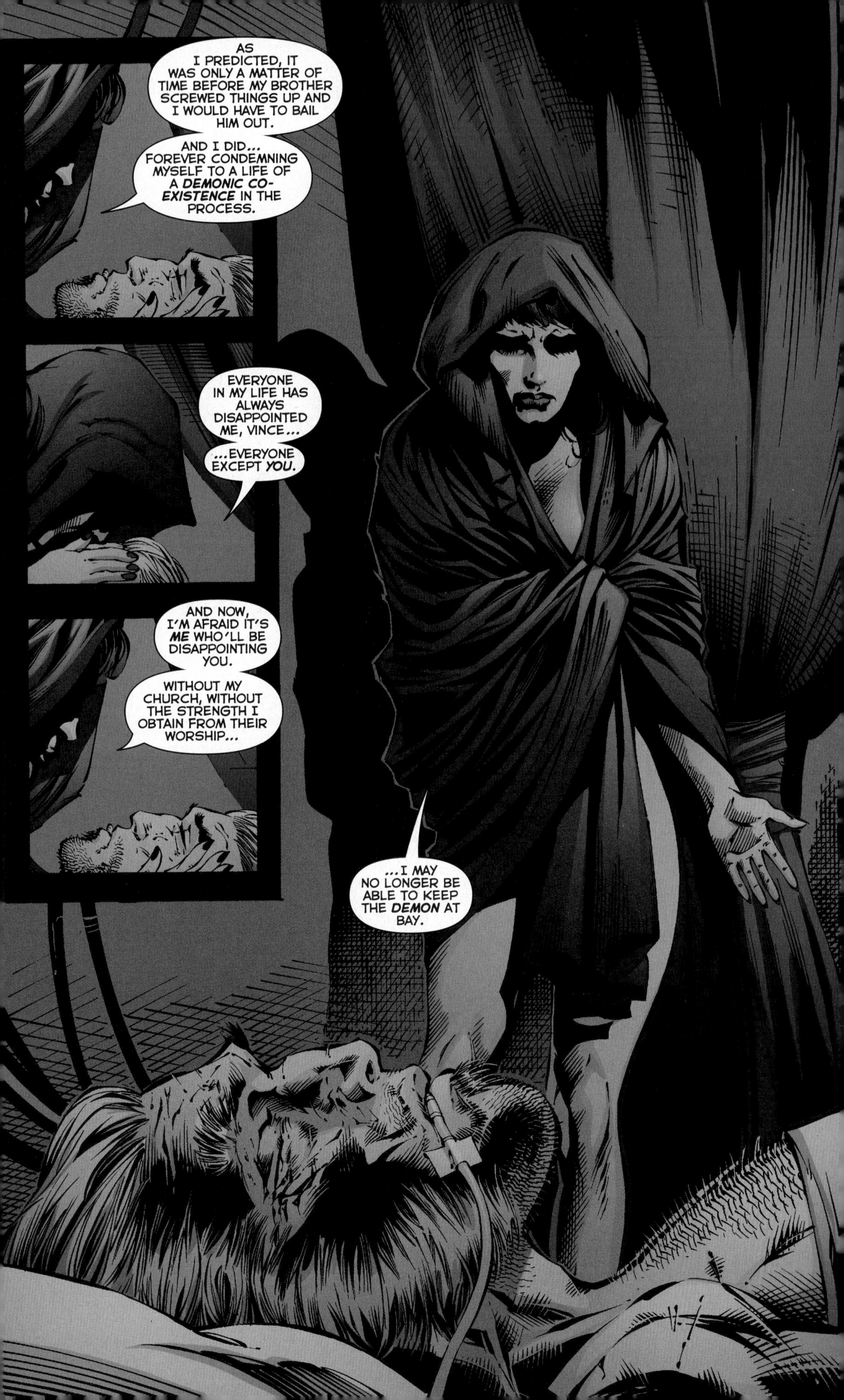
AS I PREDICTED, IT WAS ONLY A MATTER OF TIME BEFORE MY BROTHER SCREWED THINGS UP AND I WOULD HAVE TO BAIL HIM OUT.
AND I DID... FOREVER CONDEMNING MYSELF TO A LIFE OF A DEMONIC CO-EXISTENCE IN THE PROCESS.
EVERYONE IN MY LIFE HAS ALWAYS DISAPPOINTED ME, VINCE...
...EVERYONE EXCEPT YOU.
AND NOW, I'M AFRAID IT'S ME WHO'LL BE DISAPPOINTING YOU.
WITHOUT MY CHURCH, WITHOUT THE STRENGTH I OBTAIN FROM THEIR WORSHIP...
...I MAY NO LONGER BE ABLE TO KEEP THE DEMON AT BAY.

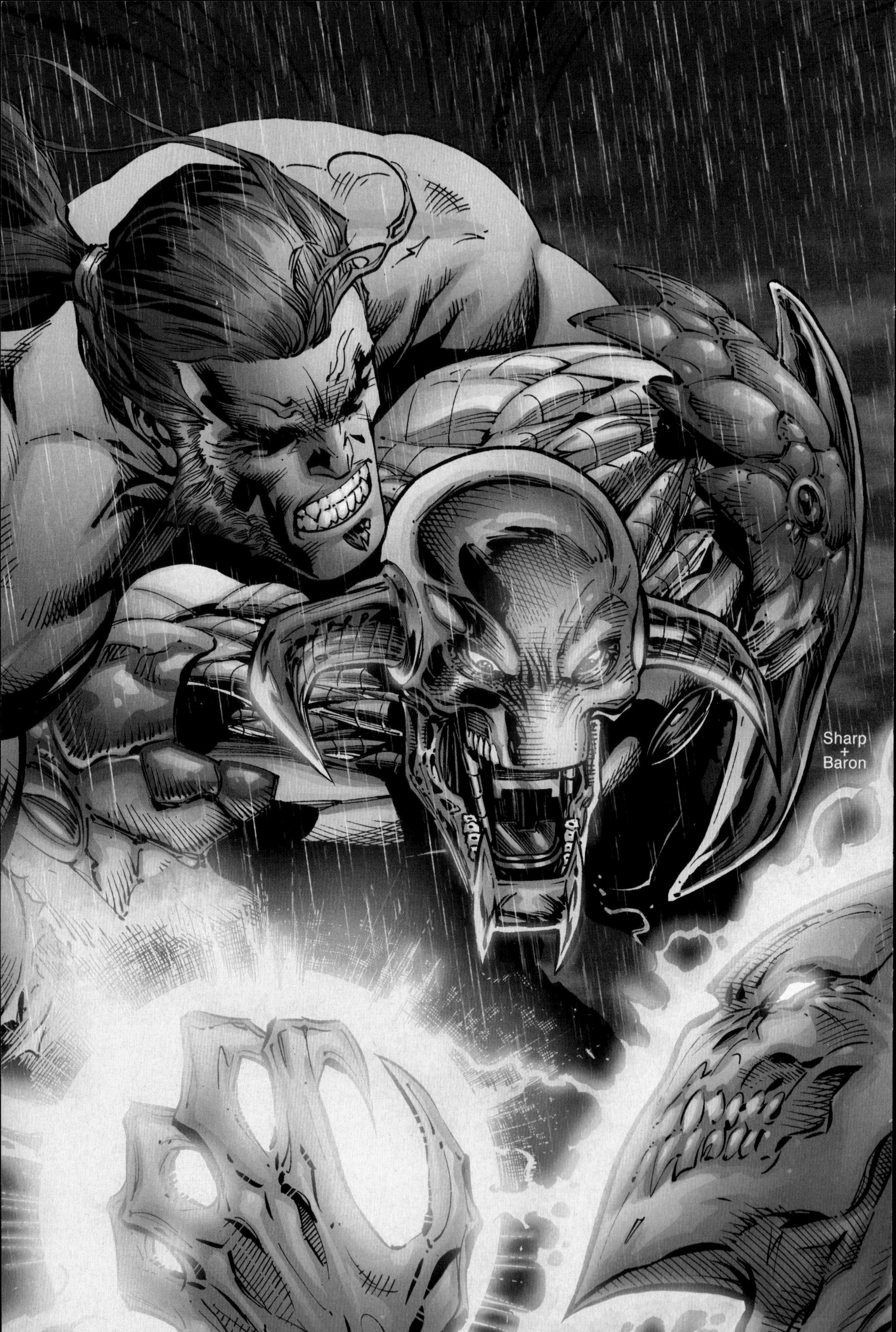
Sharp
+
Baron

Part 5: Man of Peace. Man of War.

Chapter pencilled by Liam Sharp with Mark Robinson

Chapter inked by Rob Hunter, Mark Irwin, Mark Pennington and Sandu Florea   Cover art by Liam Sharp & Dave Baron

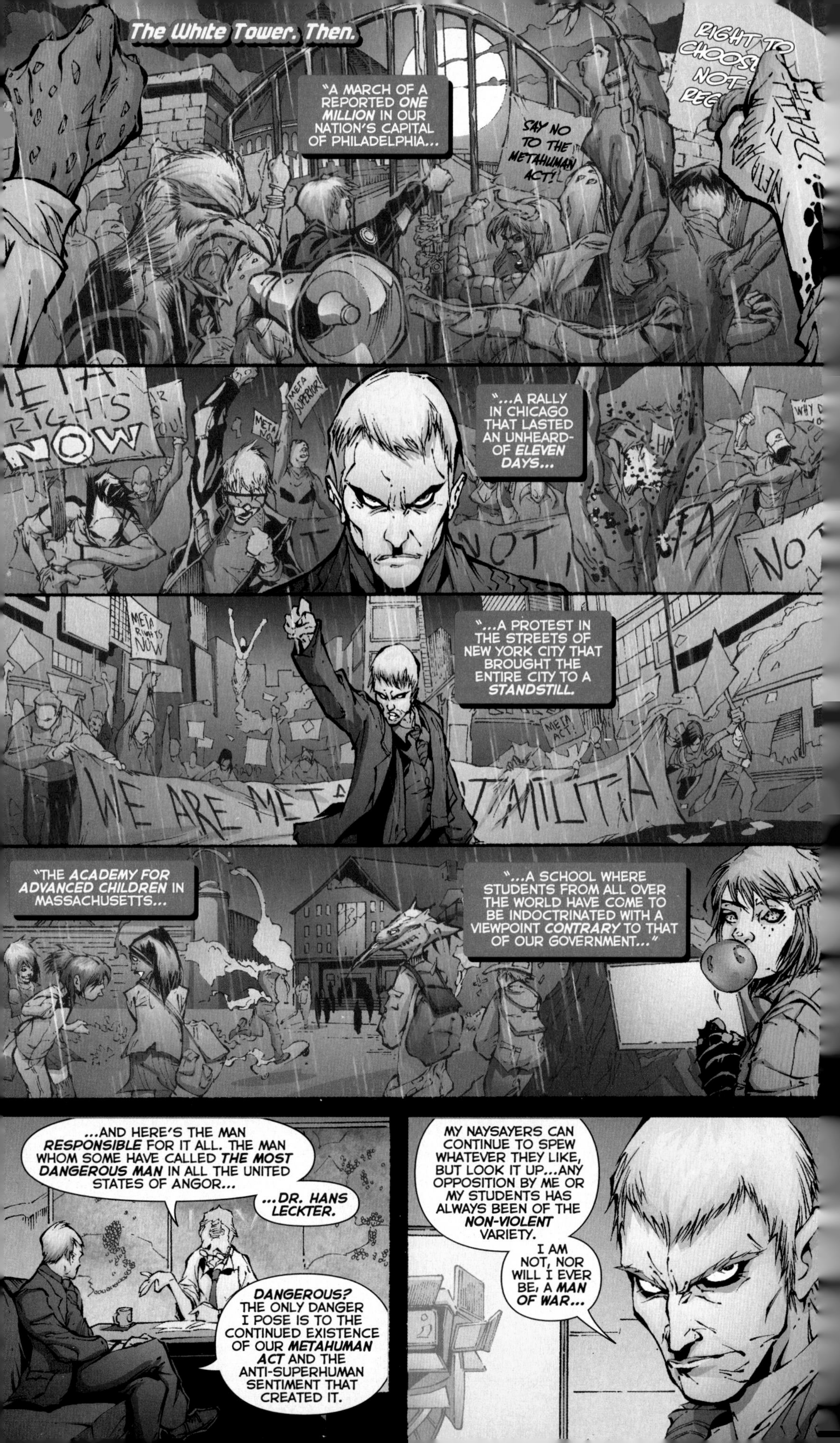
The White Tower. Then.
"A MARCH OF A REPORTED ONE MILLION IN OUR NATION'S CAPITAL OF PHILADELPHIA...
SAY NO TO THE METAHUMAN ACT!
RIGHT TO CHOOSE NOT REG
"...A RALLY IN CHICAGO THAT LASTED AN UNHEARD-OF ELEVEN DAYS...
META RIGHTS NOW
META SUPERIOR!
"...A PROTEST IN THE STREETS OF NEW YORK CITY THAT BROUGHT THE ENTIRE CITY TO A STANDSTILL.
META RIGHTS NOW
META ACT!
"THE ACADEMY FOR ADVANCED CHILDREN IN MASSACHUSETTS...
"...A SCHOOL WHERE STUDENTS FROM ALL OVER THE WORLD HAVE COME TO BE INDOCTRINATED WITH A VIEWPOINT CONTRARY TO THAT OF OUR GOVERNMENT..."
...AND HERE'S THE MAN RESPONSIBLE FOR IT ALL. THE MAN WHOM SOME HAVE CALLED THE MOST DANGEROUS MAN IN ALL THE UNITED STATES OF ANGOR...
...DR. HANS LECKTER.
DANGEROUS? THE ONLY DANGER I POSE IS TO THE CONTINUED EXISTENCE OF OUR METAHUMAN ACT AND THE ANTI-SUPERHUMAN SENTIMENT THAT CREATED IT.
MY NAYSAYERS CAN CONTINUE TO SPEW WHATEVER THEY LIKE, BUT LOOK IT UP...ANY OPPOSITION BY ME OR MY STUDENTS HAS ALWAYS BEEN OF THE NON-VIOLENT VARIETY.
I AM NOT, NOR WILL I EVER BE, A MAN OF WAR...

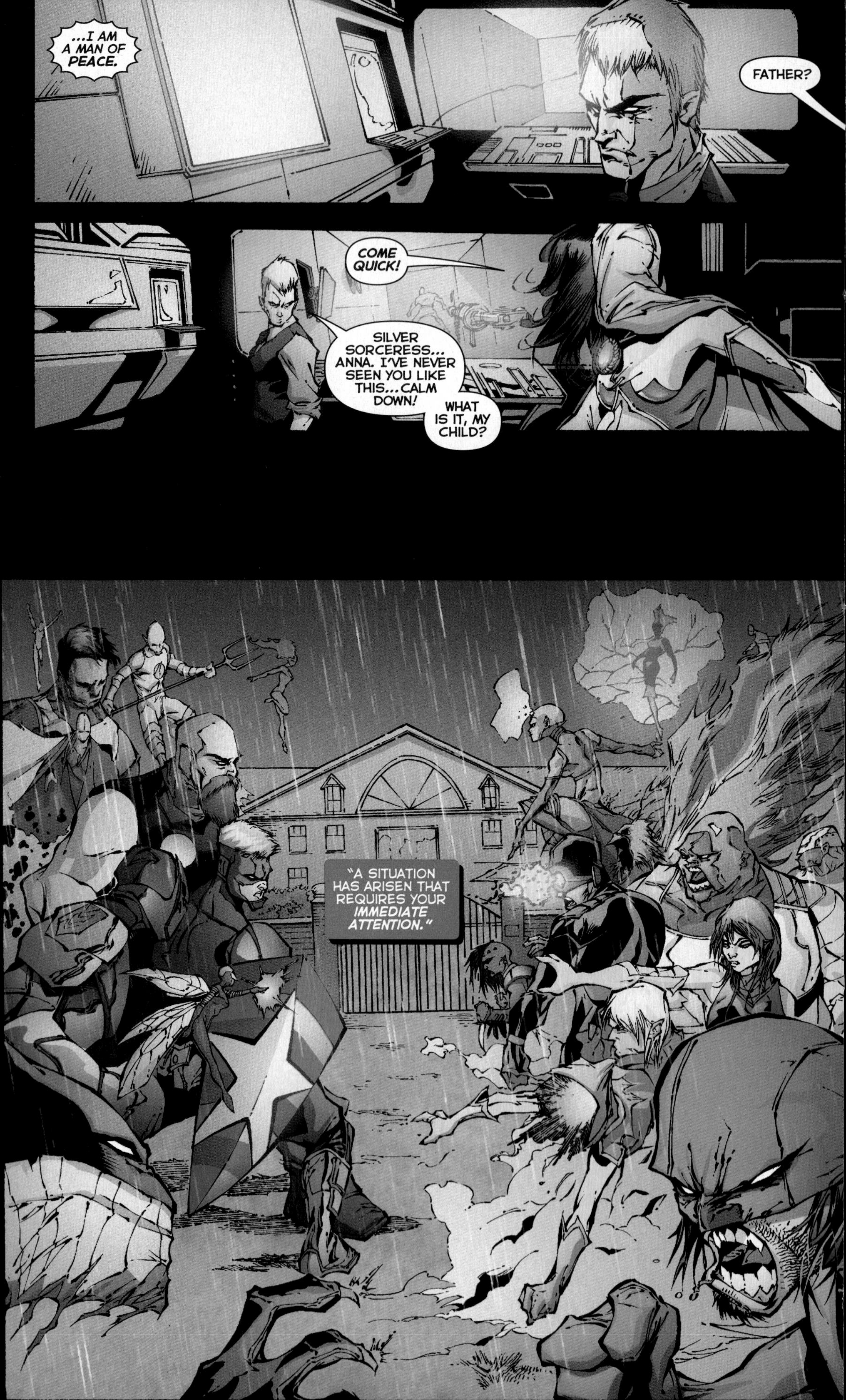
...I AM A MAN OF PEACE.
FATHER?
COME QUICK!
SILVER SORCERESS... ANNA. I'VE NEVER SEEN YOU LIKE THIS...CALM DOWN!
WHAT IS IT, MY CHILD?
"A SITUATION HAS ARISEN THAT REQUIRES YOUR IMMEDIATE ATTENTION."

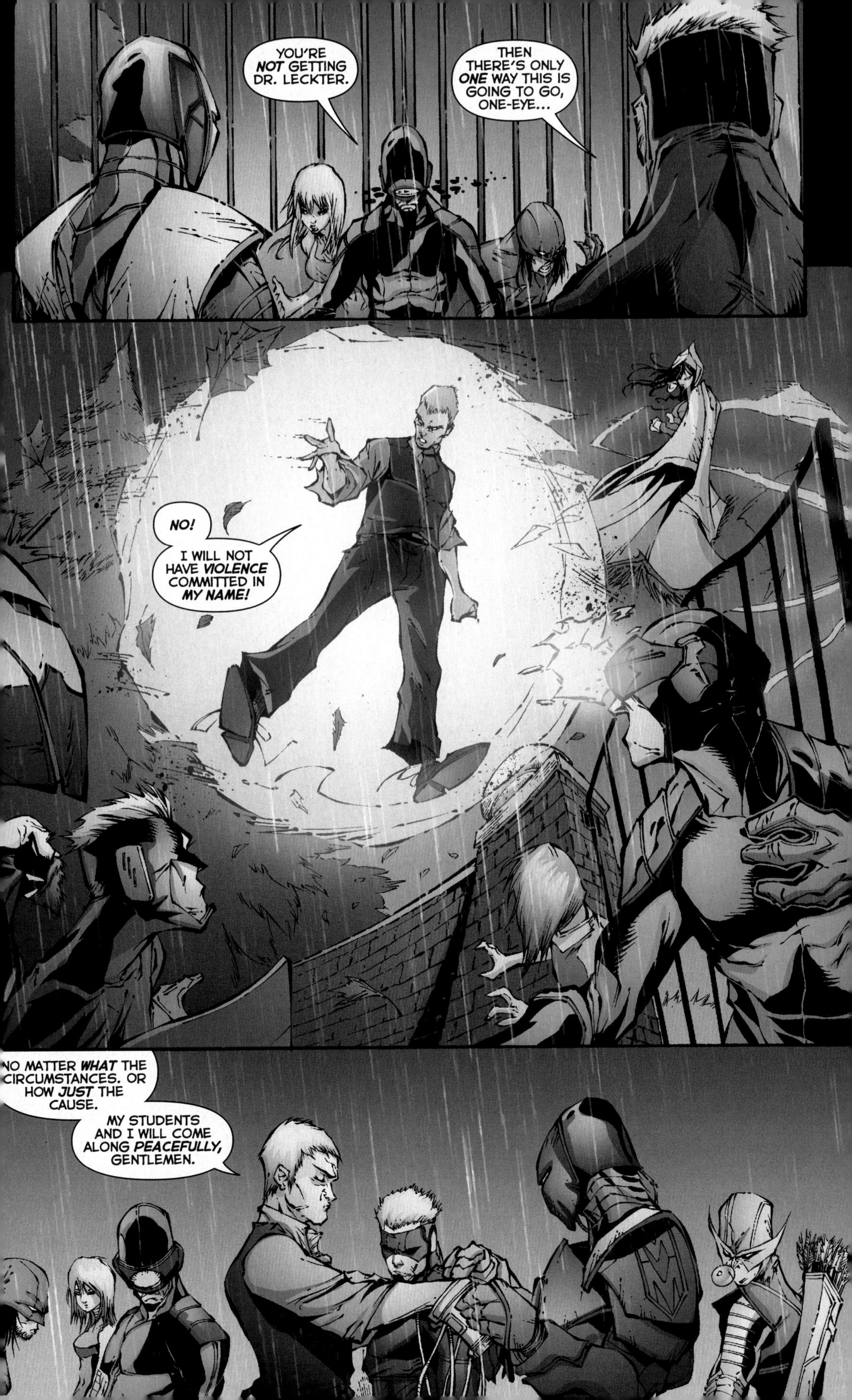

YOU'RE NOT GETTING DR. LECKTER.
THEN THERE'S ONLY ONE WAY THIS IS GOING TO GO, ONE-EYE...
NO!
I WILL NOT HAVE VIOLENCE COMMITTED IN MY NAME!
NO MATTER WHAT THE CIRCUMSTANCES. OR HOW JUST THE CAUSE.
MY STUDENTS AND I WILL COME ALONG PEACEFULLY, GENTLEMEN.

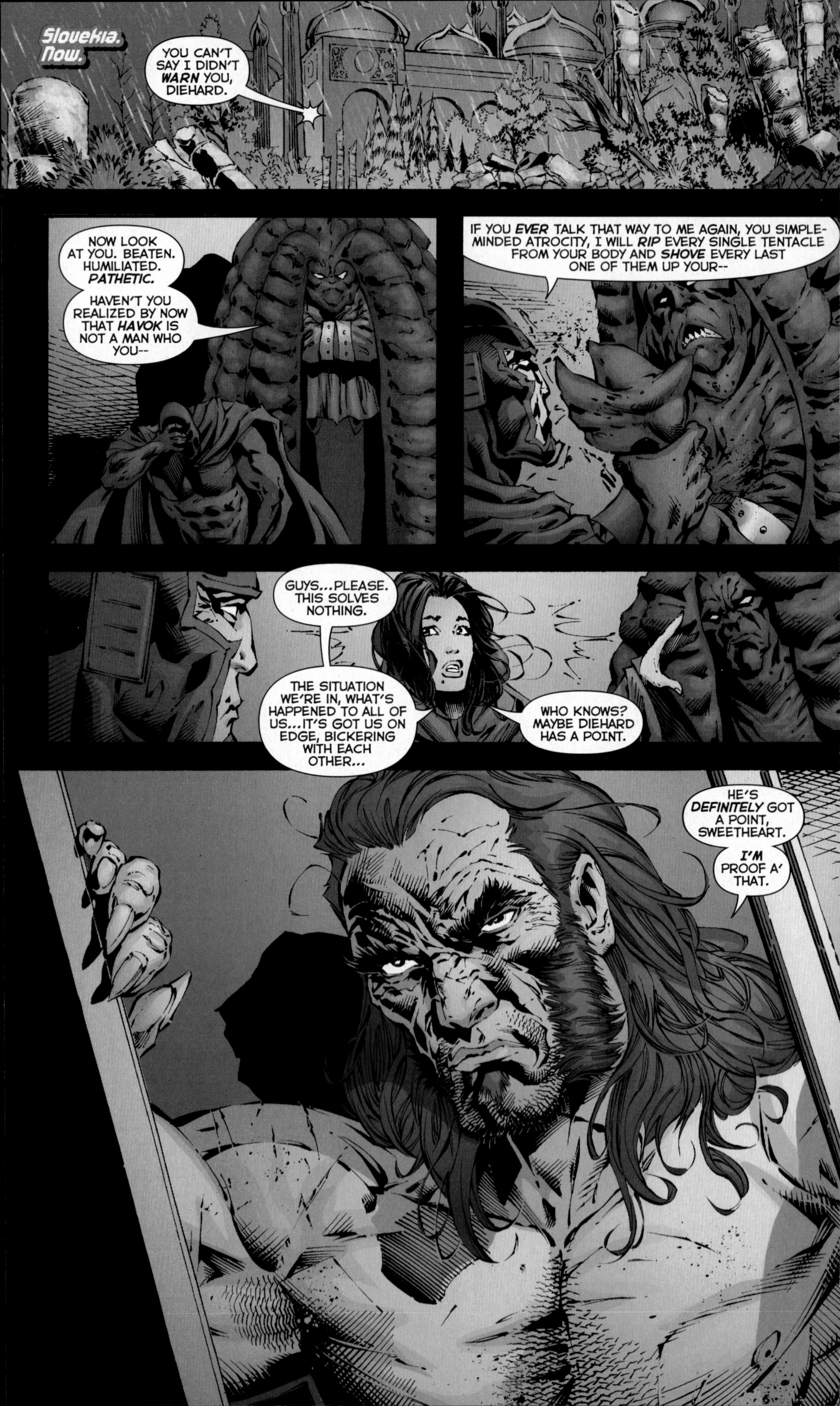
Slovekia. Now.
YOU CAN'T SAY I DIDN'T WARN YOU, DIEHARD.
NOW LOOK AT YOU. BEATEN. HUMILIATED. PATHETIC.
HAVEN'T YOU REALIZED BY NOW THAT HAVOK IS NOT A MAN WHO YOU--
IF YOU EVER TALK THAT WAY TO ME AGAIN, YOU SIMPLE-MINDED ATROCITY, I WILL RIP EVERY SINGLE TENTACLE FROM YOUR BODY AND SHOVE EVERY LAST ONE OF THEM UP YOUR--
GUYS...PLEASE. THIS SOLVES NOTHING.
THE SITUATION WE'RE IN, WHAT'S HAPPENED TO ALL OF US...IT'S GOT US ON EDGE, BICKERING WITH EACH OTHER...
WHO KNOWS? MAYBE DIEHARD HAS A POINT.
HE'S DEFINITELY GOT A POINT, SWEETHEART.
I'M PROOF A' THAT.

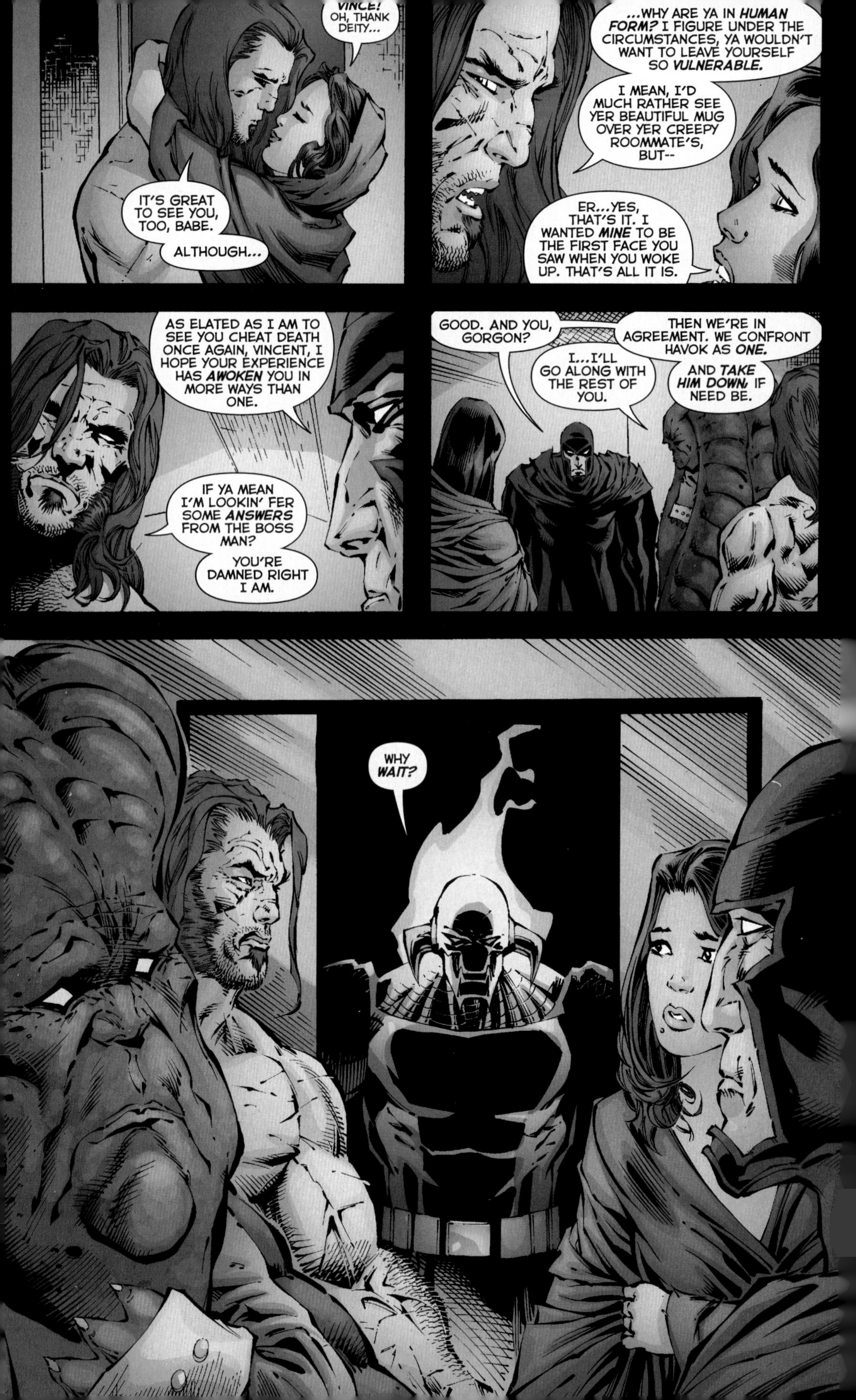
VINCE! OH, THANK DEITY...
IT'S GREAT TO SEE YOU, TOO, BABE.
ALTHOUGH...
...WHY ARE YA IN HUMAN FORM? I FIGURE UNDER THE CIRCUMSTANCES, YA WOULDN'T WANT TO LEAVE YOURSELF SO VULNERABLE.
I MEAN, I'D MUCH RATHER SEE YER BEAUTIFUL MUG OVER YER CREEPY ROOMMATE'S, BUT--
ER...YES, THAT'S IT. I WANTED MINE TO BE THE FIRST FACE YOU SAW WHEN YOU WOKE UP. THAT'S ALL IT IS.
AS ELATED AS I AM TO SEE YOU CHEAT DEATH ONCE AGAIN, VINCENT, I HOPE YOUR EXPERIENCE HAS AWOKEN YOU IN MORE WAYS THAN ONE.
IF YA MEAN I'M LOOKIN' FER SOME ANSWERS FROM THE BOSS MAN?
YOU'RE DAMNED RIGHT I AM.
THEN WE'RE IN AGREEMENT. WE CONFRONT HAVOK AS ONE.
AND TAKE HIM DOWN, IF NEED BE.
GOOD. AND YOU, GORGON?
I...I'LL GO ALONG WITH THE REST OF YOU.
WHY WAIT?

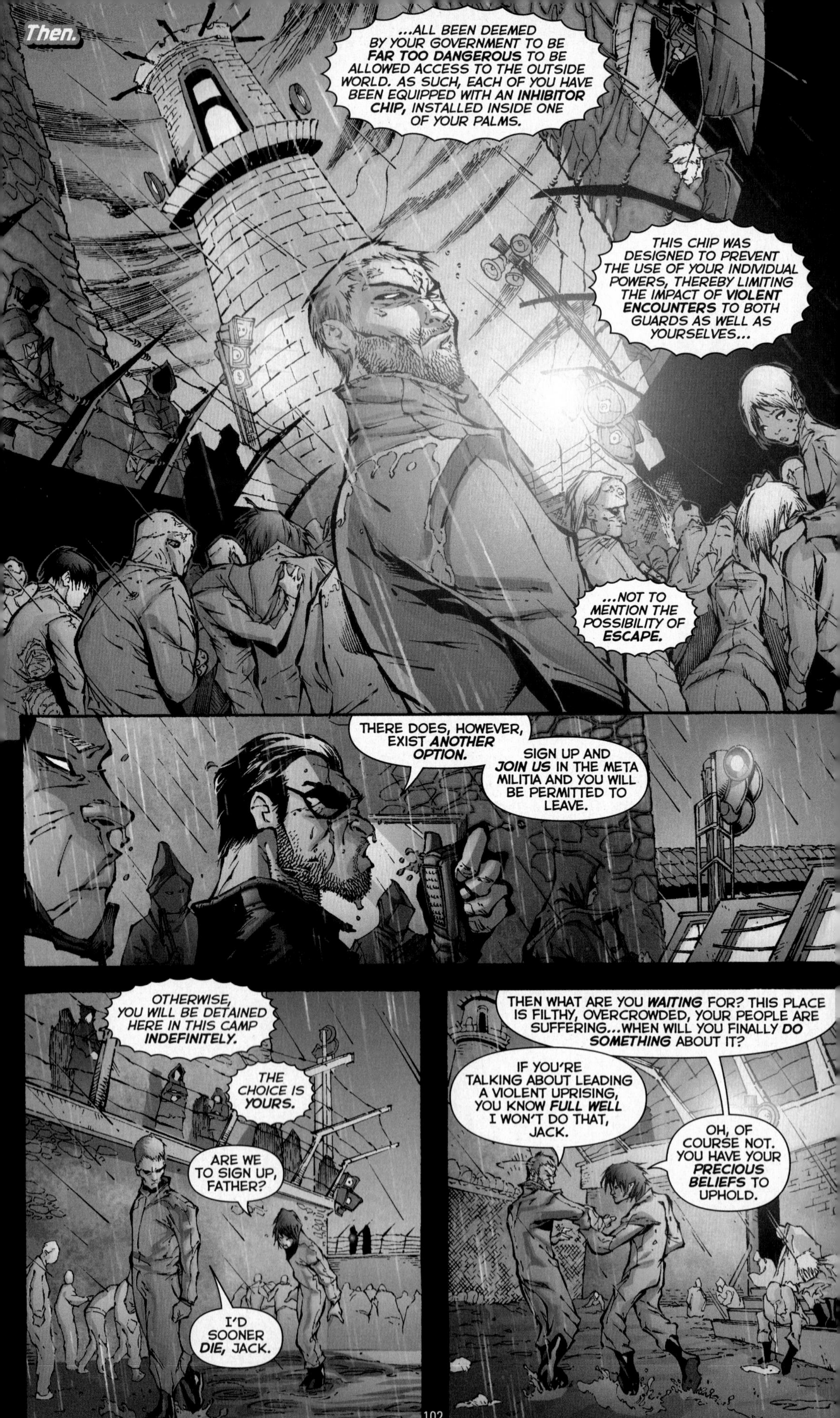

Then.
...ALL BEEN DEEMED BY YOUR GOVERNMENT TO BE FAR TOO DANGEROUS TO BE ALLOWED ACCESS TO THE OUTSIDE WORLD. AS SUCH, EACH OF YOU HAVE BEEN EQUIPPED WITH AN INHIBITOR CHIP, INSTALLED INSIDE ONE OF YOUR PALMS.
THIS CHIP WAS DESIGNED TO PREVENT THE USE OF YOUR INDIVIDUAL POWERS, THEREBY LIMITING THE IMPACT OF VIOLENT ENCOUNTERS TO BOTH GUARDS AS WELL AS YOURSELVES...
...NOT TO MENTION THE POSSIBILITY OF ESCAPE.
THERE DOES, HOWEVER, EXIST ANOTHER OPTION.
SIGN UP AND JOIN US IN THE META MILITIA AND YOU WILL BE PERMITTED TO LEAVE.
OTHERWISE, YOU WILL BE DETAINED HERE IN THIS CAMP INDEFINITELY.
THE CHOICE IS YOURS.
ARE WE TO SIGN UP, FATHER?
I'D SOONER DIE, JACK.
THEN WHAT ARE YOU WAITING FOR? THIS PLACE IS FILTHY, OVERCROWDED, YOUR PEOPLE ARE SUFFERING...WHEN WILL YOU FINALLY DO SOMETHING ABOUT IT?
IF YOU'RE TALKING ABOUT LEADING A VIOLENT UPRISING, YOU KNOW FULL WELL I WON'T DO THAT, JACK.
OH, OF COURSE NOT. YOU HAVE YOUR PRECIOUS BELIEFS TO UPHOLD.

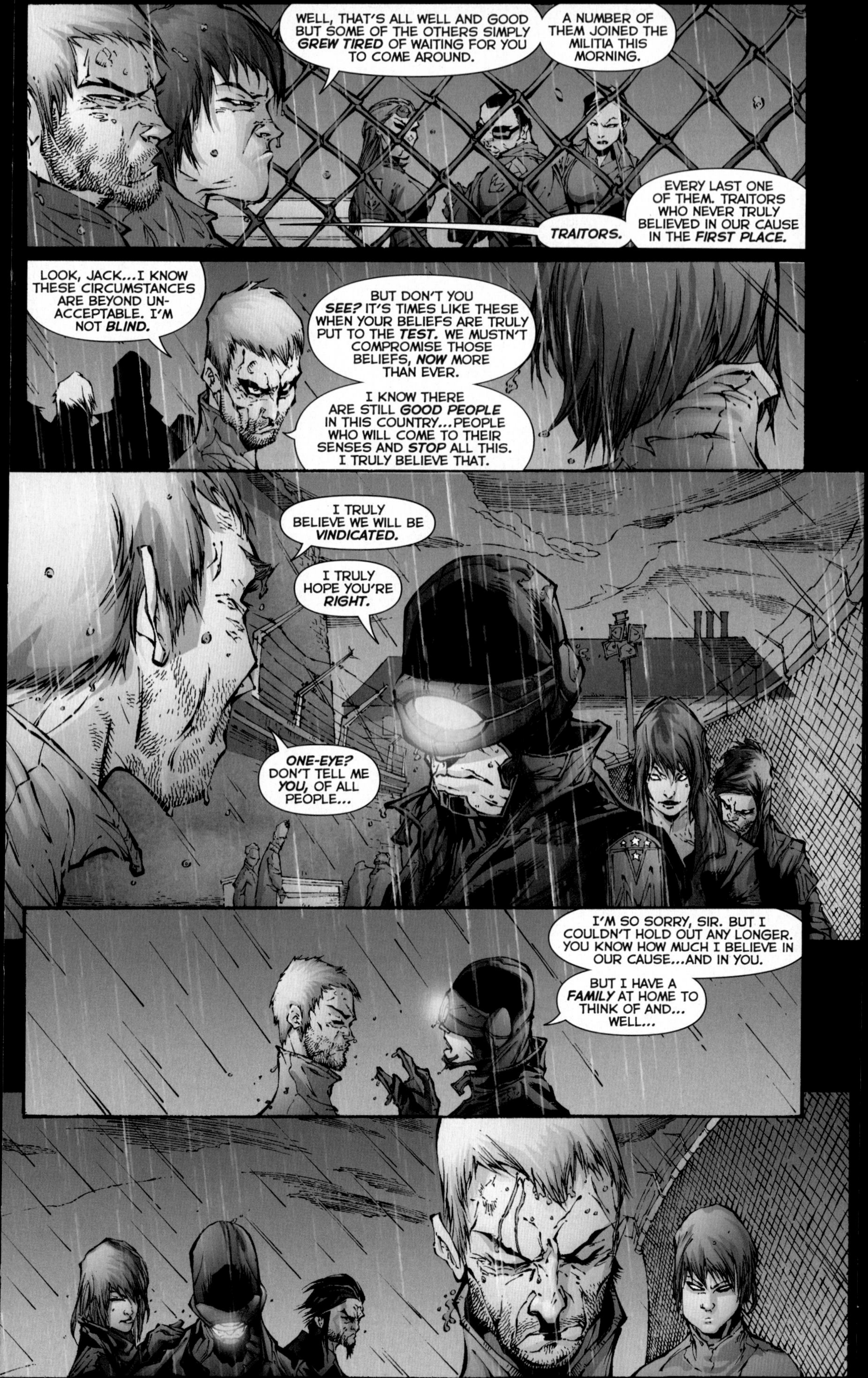

WELL, THAT'S ALL WELL AND GOOD BUT SOME OF THE OTHERS SIMPLY GREW TIRED OF WAITING FOR YOU TO COME AROUND.
A NUMBER OF THEM JOINED THE MILITIA THIS MORNING.
TRAITORS.
EVERY LAST ONE OF THEM. TRAITORS WHO NEVER TRULY BELIEVED IN OUR CAUSE IN THE FIRST PLACE.
LOOK, JACK...I KNOW THESE CIRCUMSTANCES ARE BEYOND UN-ACCEPTABLE. I'M NOT BLIND.
BUT DON'T YOU SEE? IT'S TIMES LIKE THESE WHEN YOUR BELIEFS ARE TRULY PUT TO THE TEST. WE MUSTN'T COMPROMISE THOSE BELIEFS, NOW MORE THAN EVER.
I KNOW THERE ARE STILL GOOD PEOPLE IN THIS COUNTRY...PEOPLE WHO WILL COME TO THEIR SENSES AND STOP ALL THIS. I TRULY BELIEVE THAT.
I TRULY BELIEVE WE WILL BE VINDICATED.
I TRULY HOPE YOU'RE RIGHT.
ONE-EYE? DON'T TELL ME YOU, OF ALL PEOPLE...
I'M SO SORRY, SIR. BUT I COULDN'T HOLD OUT ANY LONGER. YOU KNOW HOW MUCH I BELIEVE IN OUR CAUSE...AND IN YOU.
BUT I HAVE A FAMILY AT HOME TO THINK OF AND... WELL...

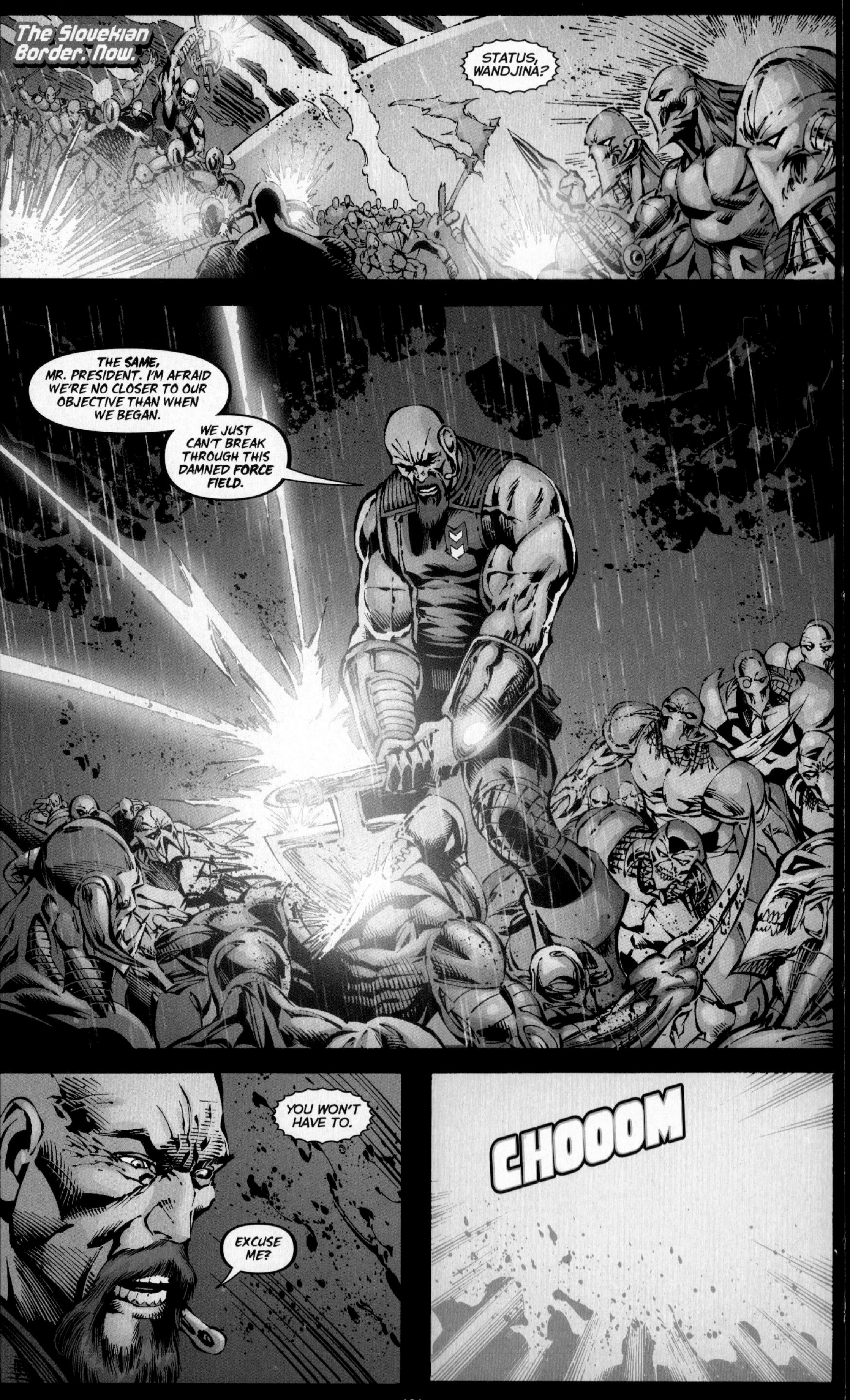
The Slovekian Border: Now.
STATUS, WANDJINA?
THE SAME, MR. PRESIDENT. I'M AFRAID WE'RE NO CLOSER TO OUR OBJECTIVE THAN WHEN WE BEGAN.
WE JUST CAN'T BREAK THROUGH THIS DAMNED FORCE FIELD.
YOU WON'T HAVE TO.
EXCUSE ME?
CHOOOM

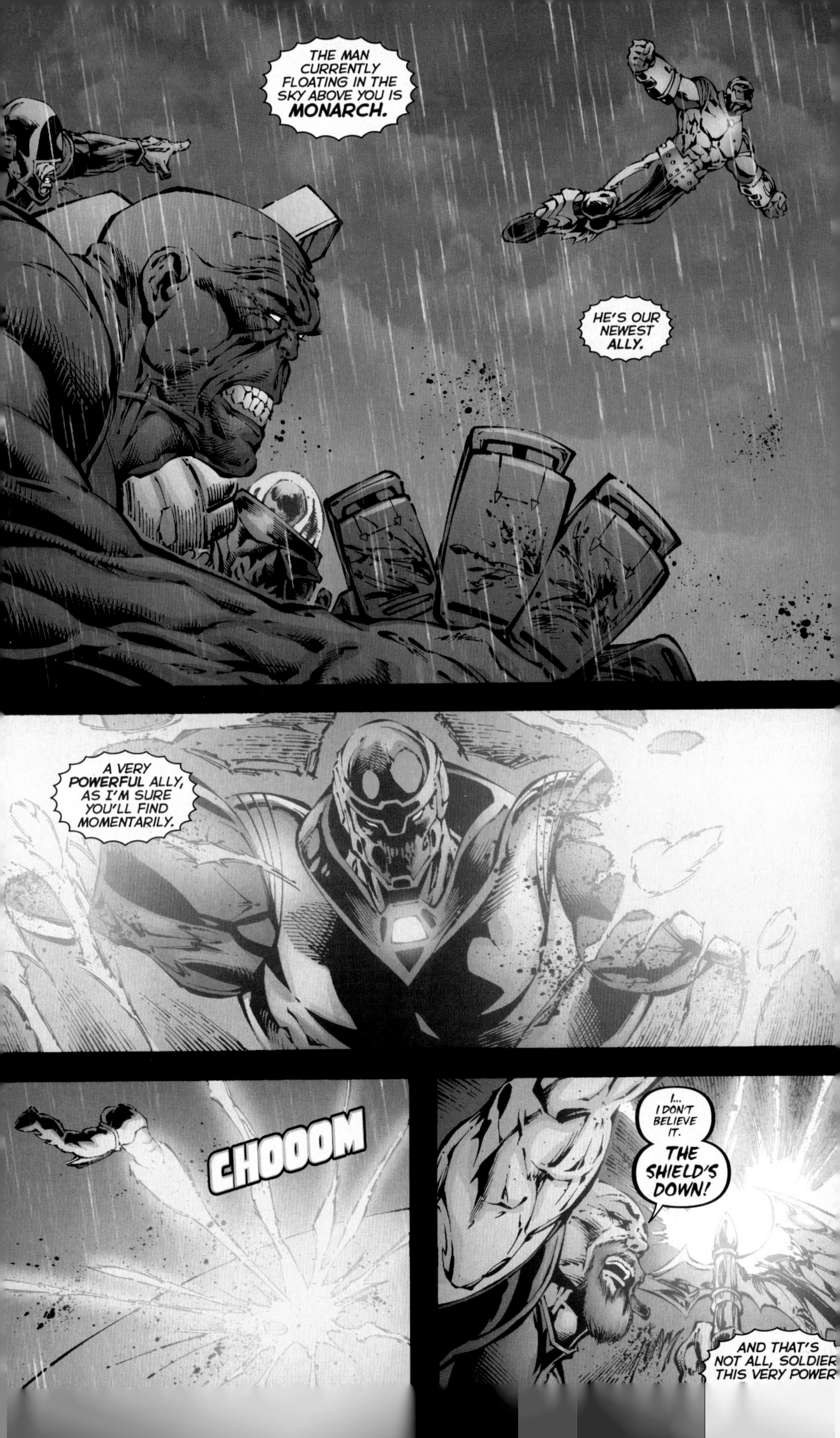
THE MAN CURRENTLY FLOATING IN THE SKY ABOVE YOU IS **MONARCH.**
HE'S OUR NEWEST **ALLY.**
A VERY **POWERFUL** ALLY, AS I'M SURE YOU'LL FIND MOMENTARILY.
CHOOOM
I... I DON'T BELIEVE IT.
THE SHIELD'S DOWN!
AND THAT'S NOT ALL, SOLDIER THIS VERY POWER

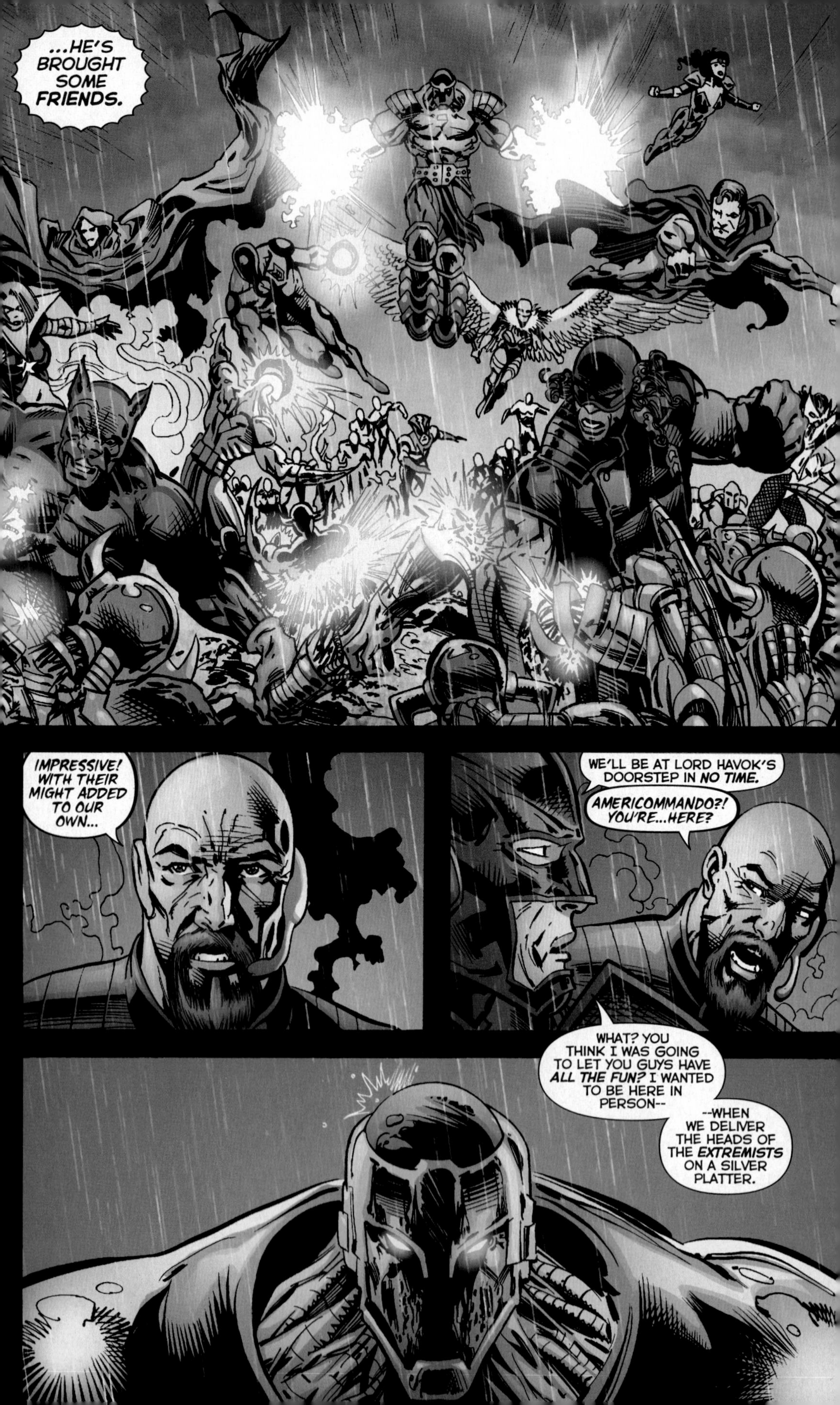
...HE'S BROUGHT SOME FRIENDS.
IMPRESSIVE! WITH THEIR MIGHT ADDED TO OUR OWN...
WE'LL BE AT LORD HAVOK'S DOORSTEP IN NO TIME.
AMERICOMMANDO?! YOU'RE...HERE?
WHAT? YOU THINK I WAS GOING TO LET YOU GUYS HAVE ALL THE FUN? I WANTED TO BE HERE IN PERSON--
--WHEN WE DELIVER THE HEADS OF THE EXTREMISTS ON A SILVER PLATTER.

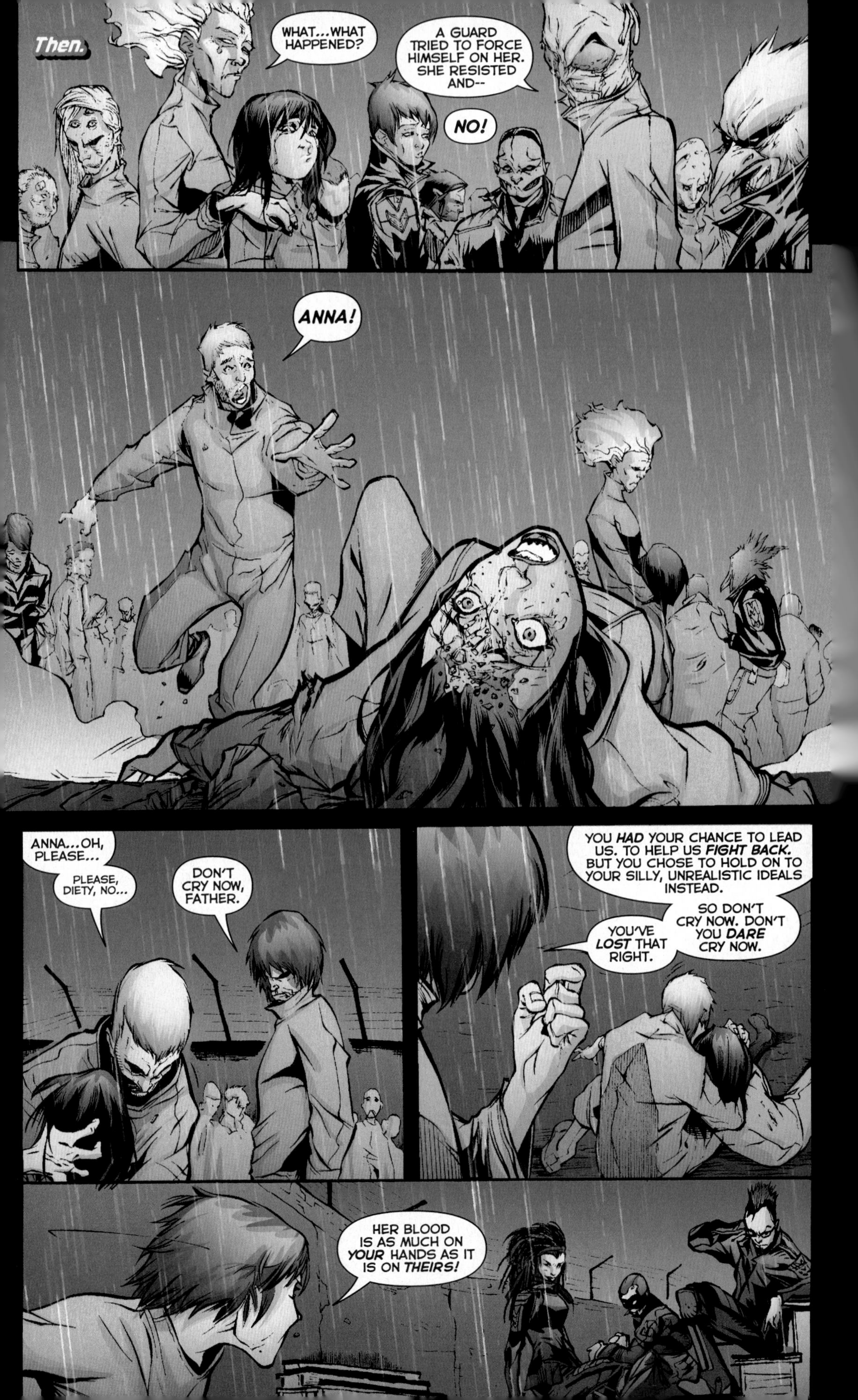
Then.
WHAT...WHAT HAPPENED?
A GUARD TRIED TO FORCE HIMSELF ON HER. SHE RESISTED AND--
NO!
ANNA!
ANNA...OH, PLEASE...
PLEASE, DIETY, NO...
DON'T CRY NOW, FATHER.
YOU HAD YOUR CHANCE TO LEAD US. TO HELP US FIGHT BACK. BUT YOU CHOSE TO HOLD ON TO YOUR SILLY, UNREALISTIC IDEALS INSTEAD.
SO DON'T CRY NOW. DON'T YOU DARE CRY NOW.
YOU'VE LOST THAT RIGHT.
HER BLOOD IS AS MUCH ON YOUR HANDS AS IT IS ON THEIRS!

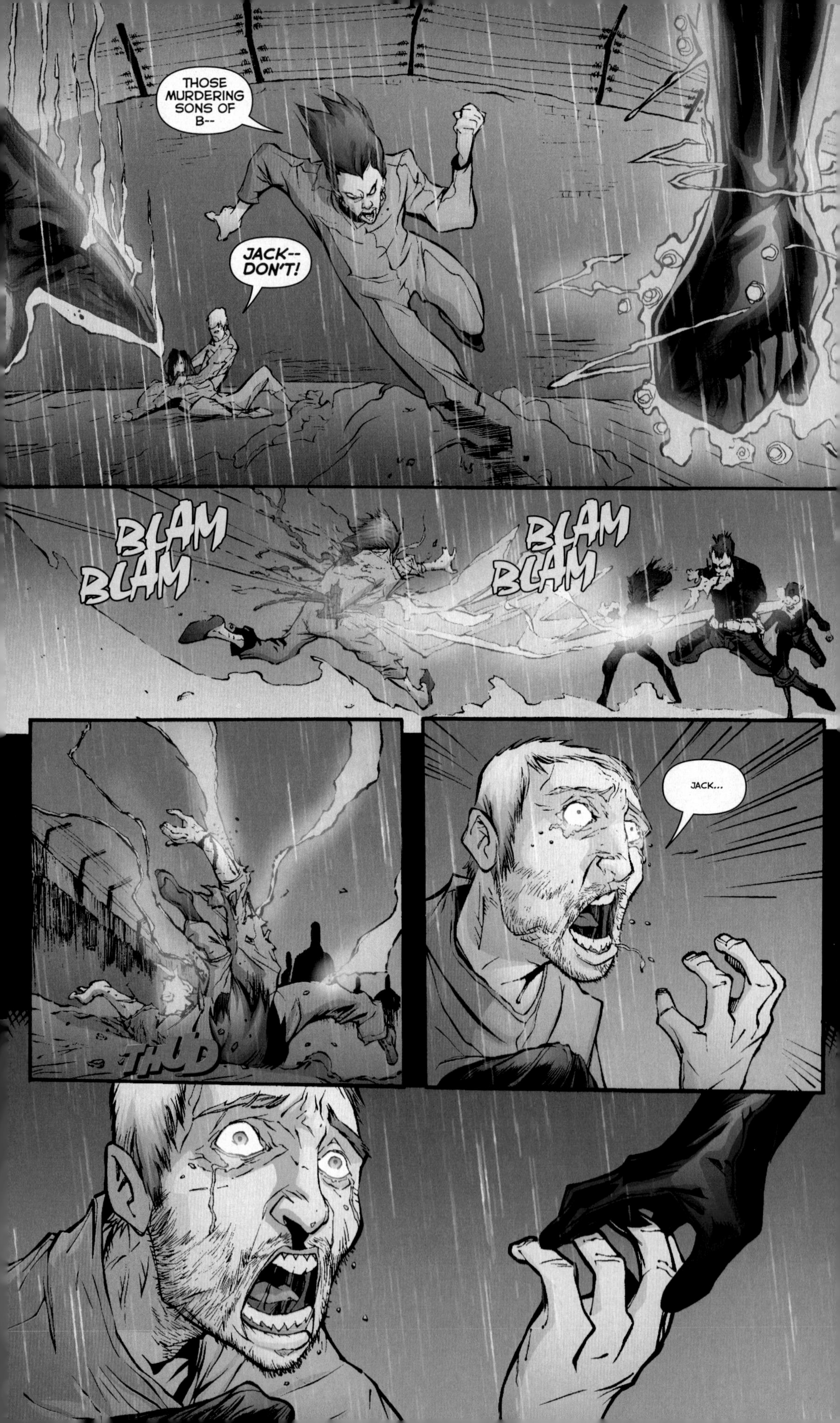
THOSE MURDERING SONS OF B--
JACK-- DON'T!
BLAM BLAM
BLAM BLAM
THUD
JACK...

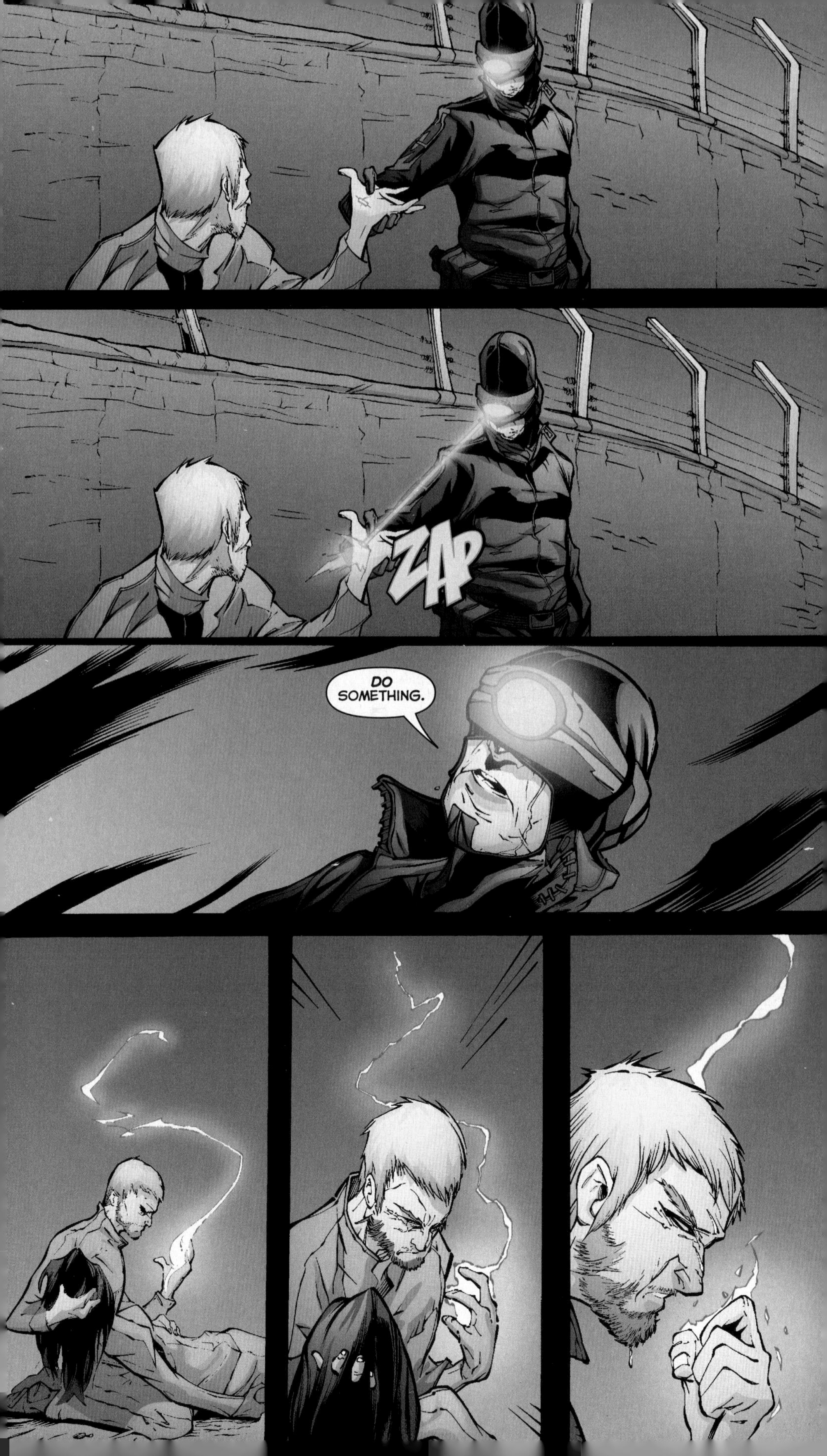
ZAP
DO SOMETHING.

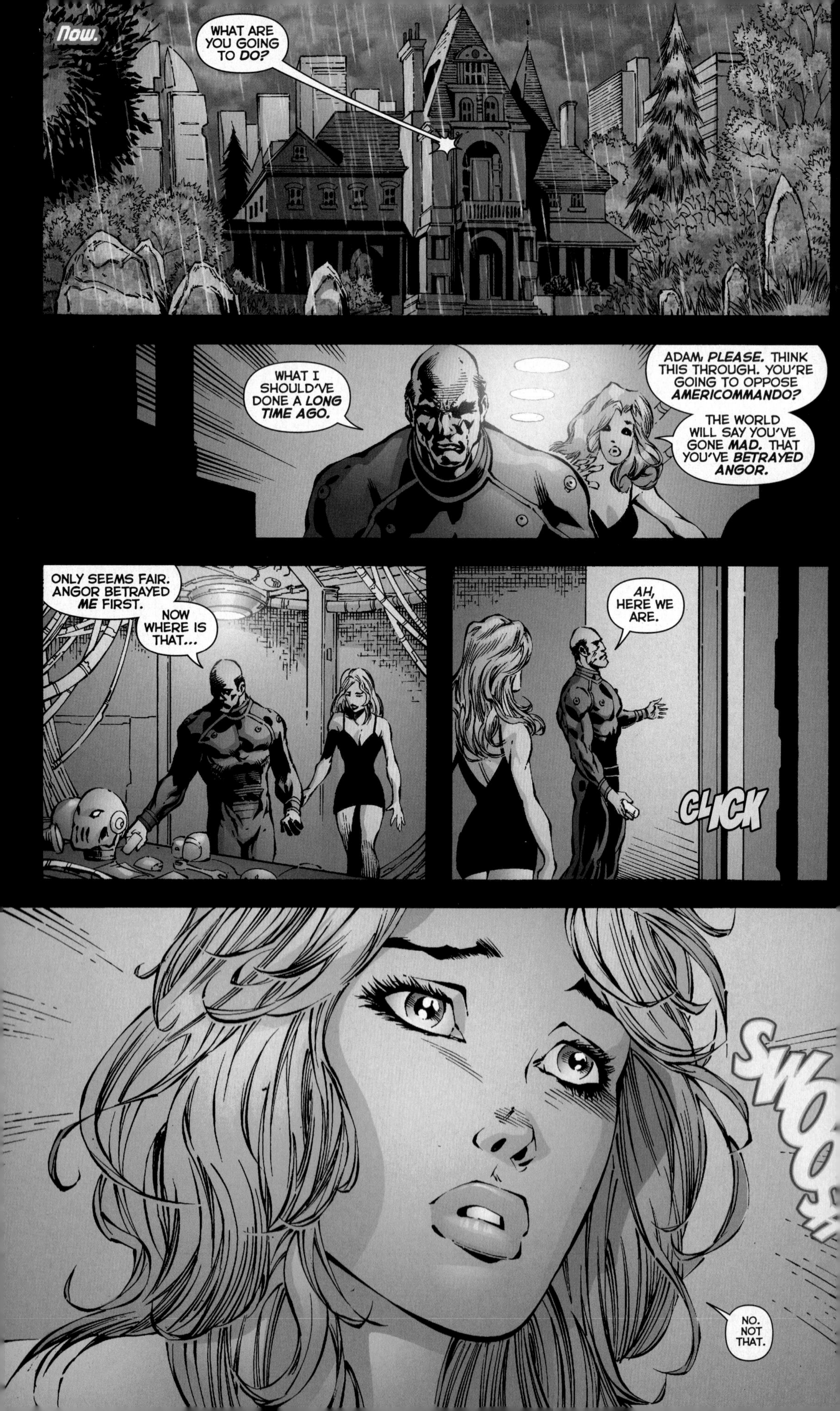
Now.
WHAT ARE YOU GOING TO DO?
WHAT I SHOULD'VE DONE A LONG TIME AGO.
ADAM, PLEASE. THINK THIS THROUGH. YOU'RE GOING TO OPPOSE AMERICOMMANDO?
THE WORLD WILL SAY YOU'VE GONE MAD. THAT YOU'VE BETRAYED ANGOR.
ONLY SEEMS FAIR. ANGOR BETRAYED ME FIRST.
NOW WHERE IS THAT...
AH, HERE WE ARE.
CLICK
NO. NOT THAT.

NOT THE DAMNED *RAVEN* ARMOR.

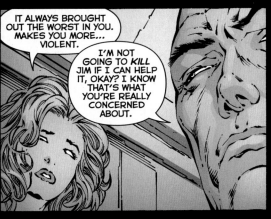

IT ALWAYS BROUGHT OUT THE WORST IN YOU. MAKES YOU MORE... VIOLENT.

I'M NOT GOING TO *KILL* JIM IF I CAN HELP IT, OKAY? I KNOW THAT'S WHAT YOU'RE REALLY CONCERNED ABOUT.

WHAT? NO...I MEAN *YES*...YOU SHOULDN'T. I MEAN--

PLEASE, DIANE. LET'S NOT *PLAY GAMES*, SHALL WE?

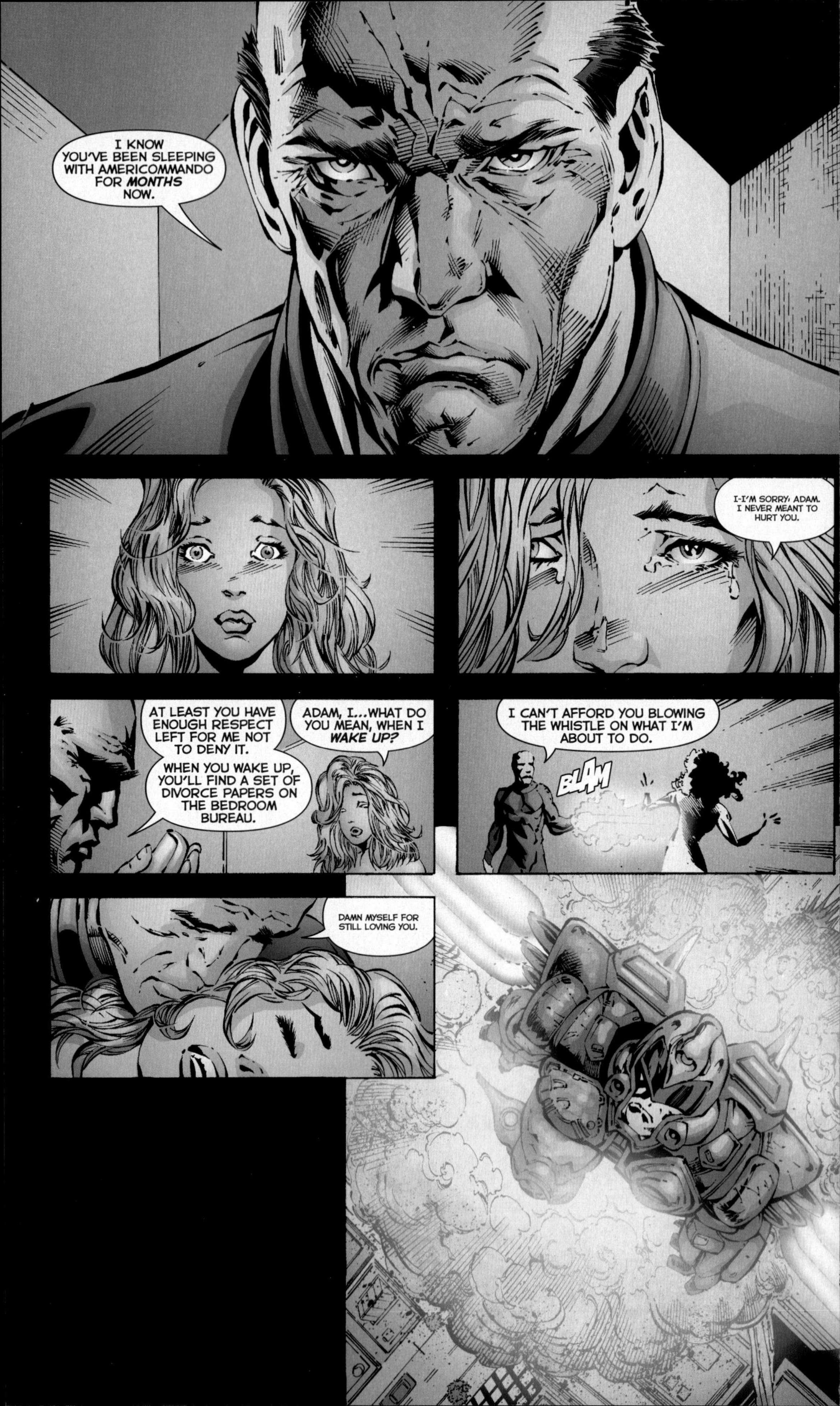
I KNOW YOU'VE BEEN SLEEPING WITH AMERICOMMANDO FOR *MONTHS* NOW.
I-I'M SORRY, ADAM. I NEVER MEANT TO HURT YOU.
AT LEAST YOU HAVE ENOUGH RESPECT LEFT FOR ME NOT TO DENY IT.
WHEN YOU WAKE UP, YOU'LL FIND A SET OF DIVORCE PAPERS ON THE BEDROOM BUREAU.
ADAM, I...WHAT DO YOU MEAN, WHEN I *WAKE UP?*
I CAN'T AFFORD YOU BLOWING THE WHISTLE ON WHAT I'M ABOUT TO DO.
BLAM
DAMN MYSELF FOR STILL LOVING YOU.

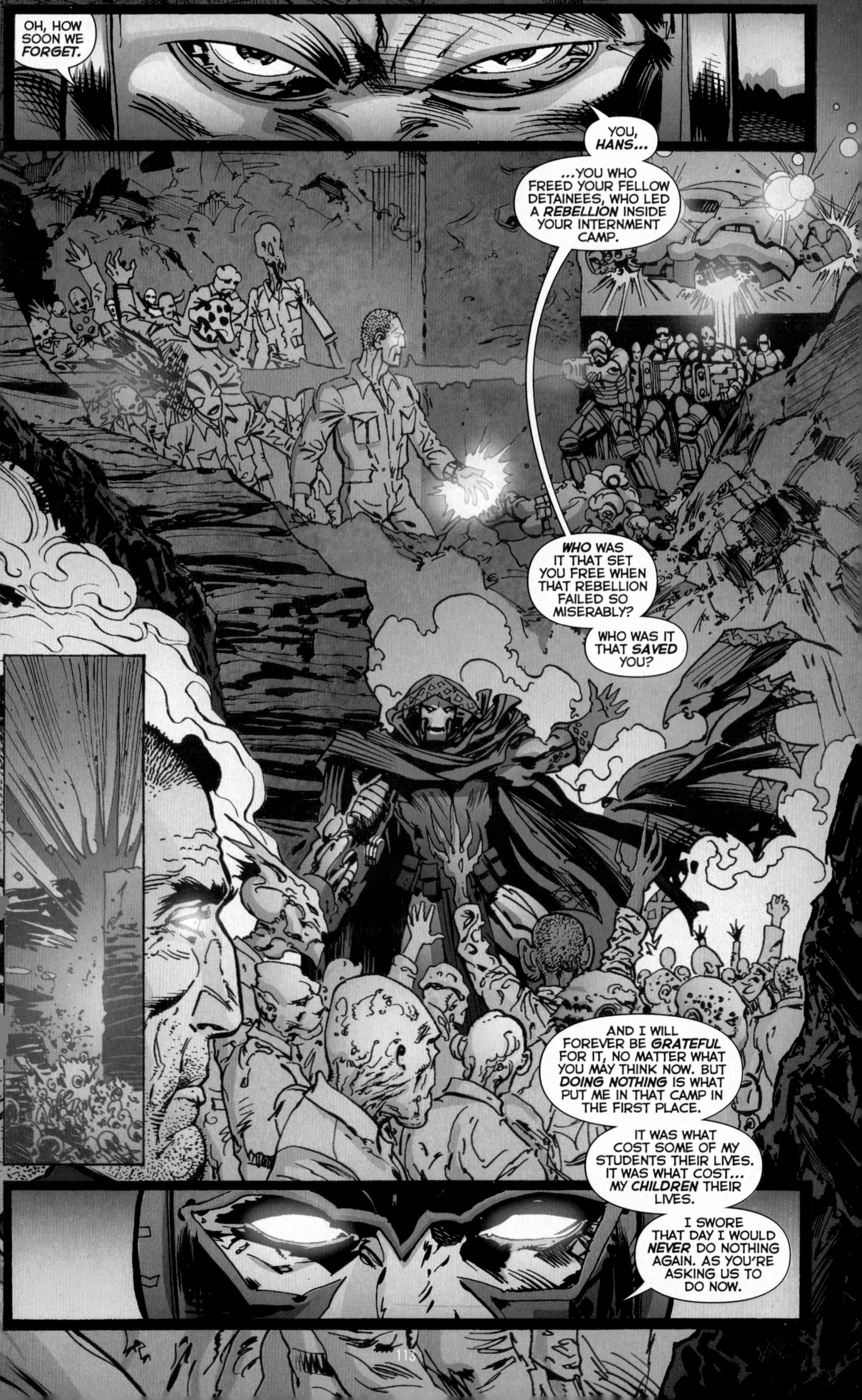
OH, HOW SOON WE FORGET.
YOU, HANS...
...YOU WHO FREED YOUR FELLOW DETAINEES, WHO LED A REBELLION INSIDE YOUR INTERNMENT CAMP.
WHO WAS IT THAT SET YOU FREE WHEN THAT REBELLION FAILED SO MISERABLY?
WHO WAS IT THAT SAVED YOU?
AND I WILL FOREVER BE GRATEFUL FOR IT, NO MATTER WHAT YOU MAY THINK NOW. BUT DOING NOTHING IS WHAT PUT ME IN THAT CAMP IN THE FIRST PLACE.
IT WAS WHAT COST SOME OF MY STUDENTS THEIR LIVES. IT WAS WHAT COST... MY CHILDREN THEIR LIVES.
I SWORE THAT DAY I WOULD NEVER DO NOTHING AGAIN. AS YOU'RE ASKING US TO DO NOW.

"I SEE.

"AND WHATABOUT THE *REST* OF YOU?

"WHAT ABOUT YOU, *MORTIMER*...

"YOU WHOSE *MIND* WAS LIKE SO MUCH *BROKEN GLASS* WHEN I FOUND YOU.

"*WHO* WAS IT THAT AGONIZINGLY HELPED YOU PUT THOSE *SHATTERED PIECES* BACK TOGETHER?

"AND YOU, *VINCENT.*

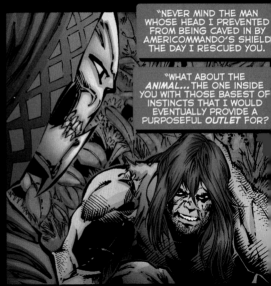

"NEVER MIND THE MAN WHOSE HEAD I PREVENTED FROM BEING CAVED IN BY AMERICOMMANDO'S SHIELD THE DAY I RESCUED YOU.

"WHAT ABOUT THE *ANIMAL...* THE ONE INSIDE YOU WITH THOSE BASEST OF INSTINCTS THAT I WOULD EVENTUALLY PROVIDE A PURPOSEFUL *OUTLET* FOR?

"OR YOU, *LOUISE.*

"HOW COULD YOU FORGET WHAT I DID FOR YOUR *BROTHER?* OR HOW I PROVIDED YOU WITH THE TRAINING TO OVERCOME THE *DEMON* INSIDE OF YOU?

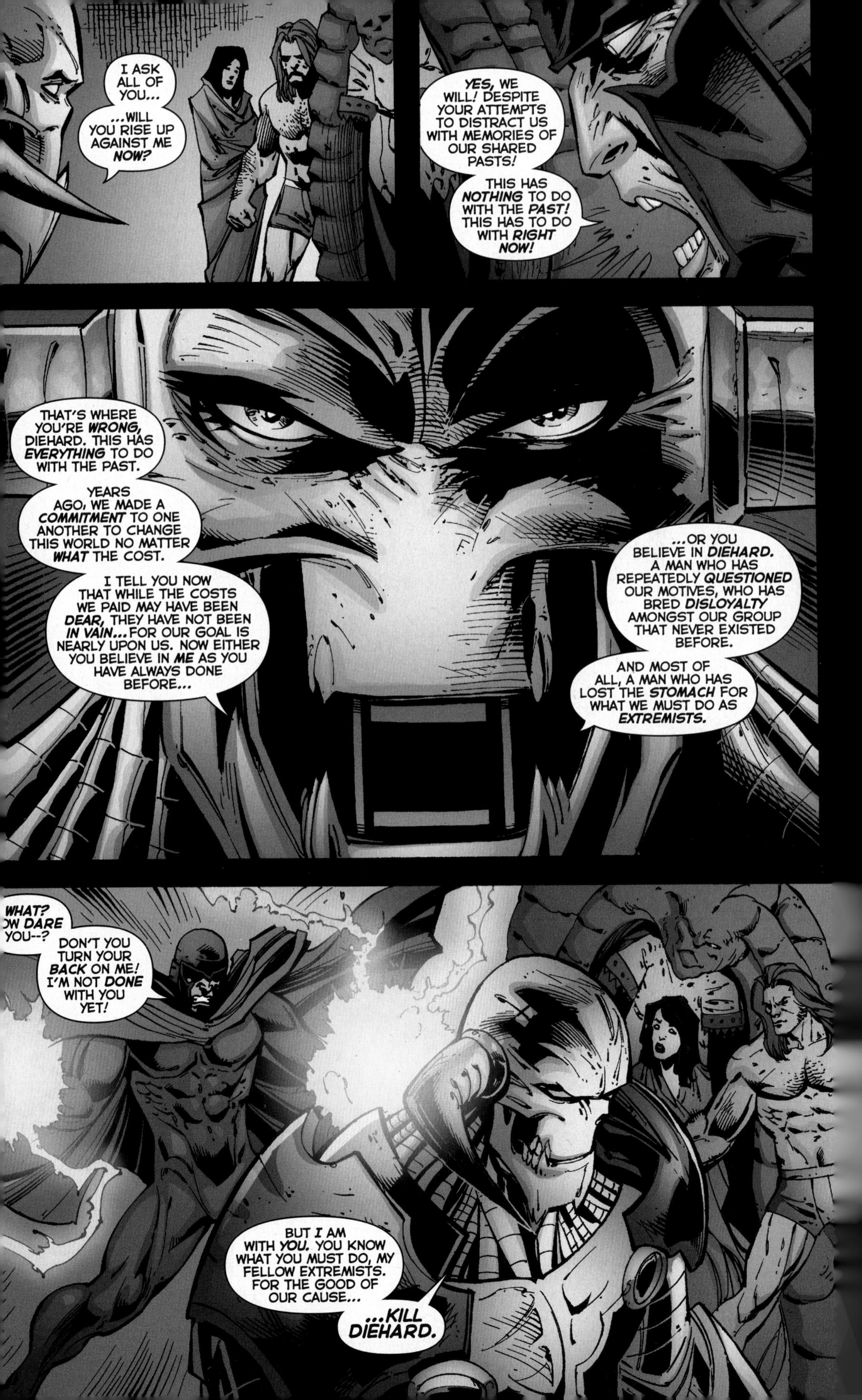
I ASK ALL OF YOU...
...WILL YOU RISE UP AGAINST ME NOW?
YES, WE WILL! DESPITE YOUR ATTEMPTS TO DISTRACT US WITH MEMORIES OF OUR SHARED PASTS!
THIS HAS NOTHING TO DO WITH THE PAST! THIS HAS TO DO WITH RIGHT NOW!
THAT'S WHERE YOU'RE WRONG, DIEHARD. THIS HAS EVERYTHING TO DO WITH THE PAST.
YEARS AGO, WE MADE A COMMITMENT TO ONE ANOTHER TO CHANGE THIS WORLD NO MATTER WHAT THE COST.
I TELL YOU NOW THAT WHILE THE COSTS WE PAID MAY HAVE BEEN DEAR, THEY HAVE NOT BEEN IN VAIN... FOR OUR GOAL IS NEARLY UPON US. NOW EITHER YOU BELIEVE IN ME AS YOU HAVE ALWAYS DONE BEFORE...
...OR YOU BELIEVE IN DIEHARD. A MAN WHO HAS REPEATEDLY QUESTIONED OUR MOTIVES, WHO HAS BRED DISLOYALTY AMONGST OUR GROUP THAT NEVER EXISTED BEFORE.
AND MOST OF ALL, A MAN WHO HAS LOST THE STOMACH FOR WHAT WE MUST DO AS EXTREMISTS.
WHAT? OW DARE YOU--?
DON'T YOU TURN YOUR BACK ON ME! I'M NOT DONE WITH YOU YET!
BUT I AM WITH YOU. YOU KNOW WHAT YOU MUST DO, MY FELLOW EXTREMISTS. FOR THE GOOD OF OUR CAUSE...
...KILL DIEHARD.

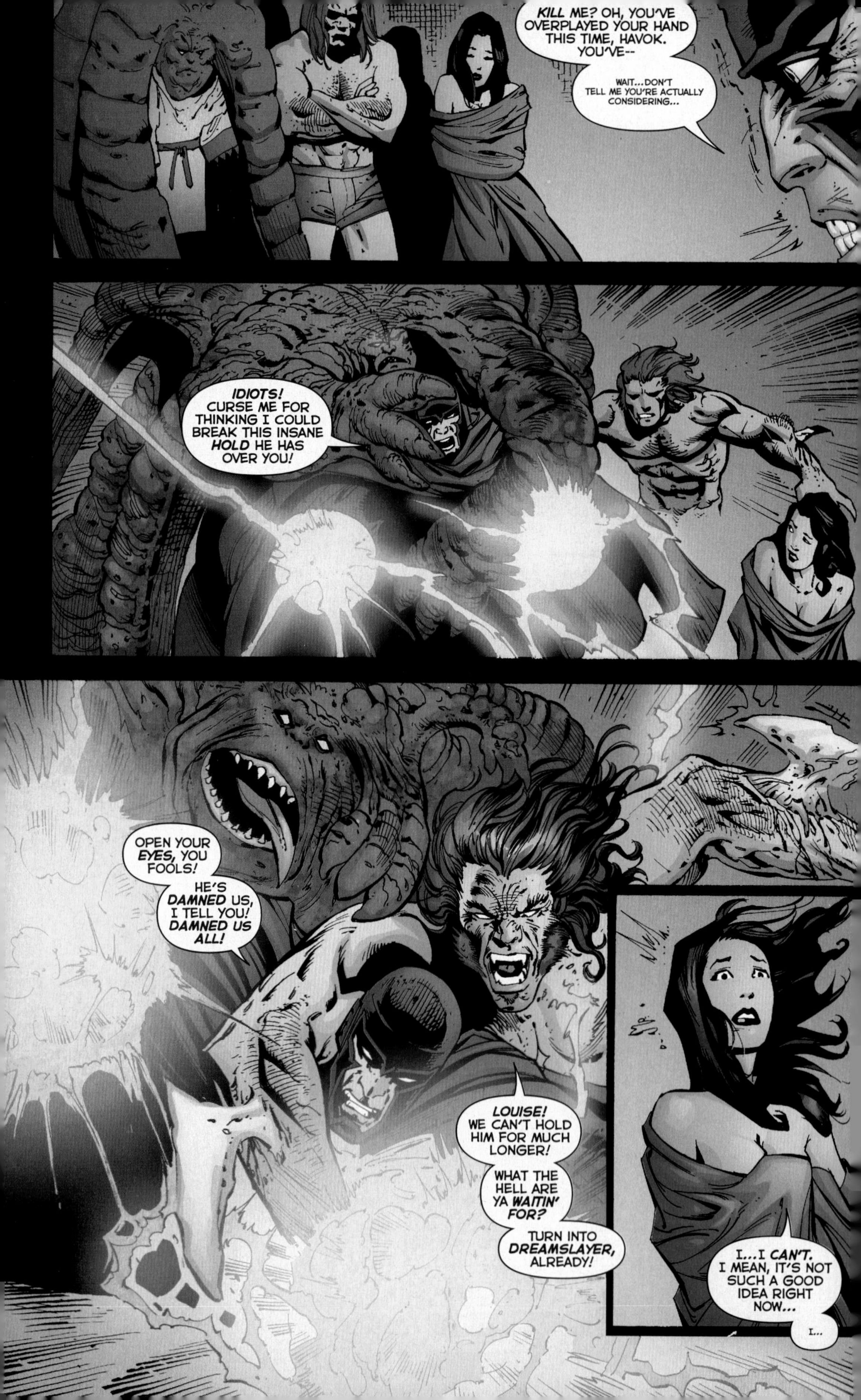

KILL ME? OH, YOU'VE OVERPLAYED YOUR HAND THIS TIME, HAVOK. YOU'VE--
WAIT...DON'T TELL ME YOU'RE ACTUALLY CONSIDERING...
IDIOTS! CURSE ME FOR THINKING I COULD BREAK THIS INSANE HOLD HE HAS OVER YOU!
OPEN YOUR EYES, YOU FOOLS!
HE'S DAMNED US, I TELL YOU! DAMNED US ALL!
LOUISE! WE CAN'T HOLD HIM FOR MUCH LONGER!
WHAT THE HELL ARE YA WAITIN' FOR?
TURN INTO DREAMSLAYER, ALREADY!
I...I CAN'T. I MEAN, IT'S NOT SUCH A GOOD IDEA RIGHT NOW...
I...

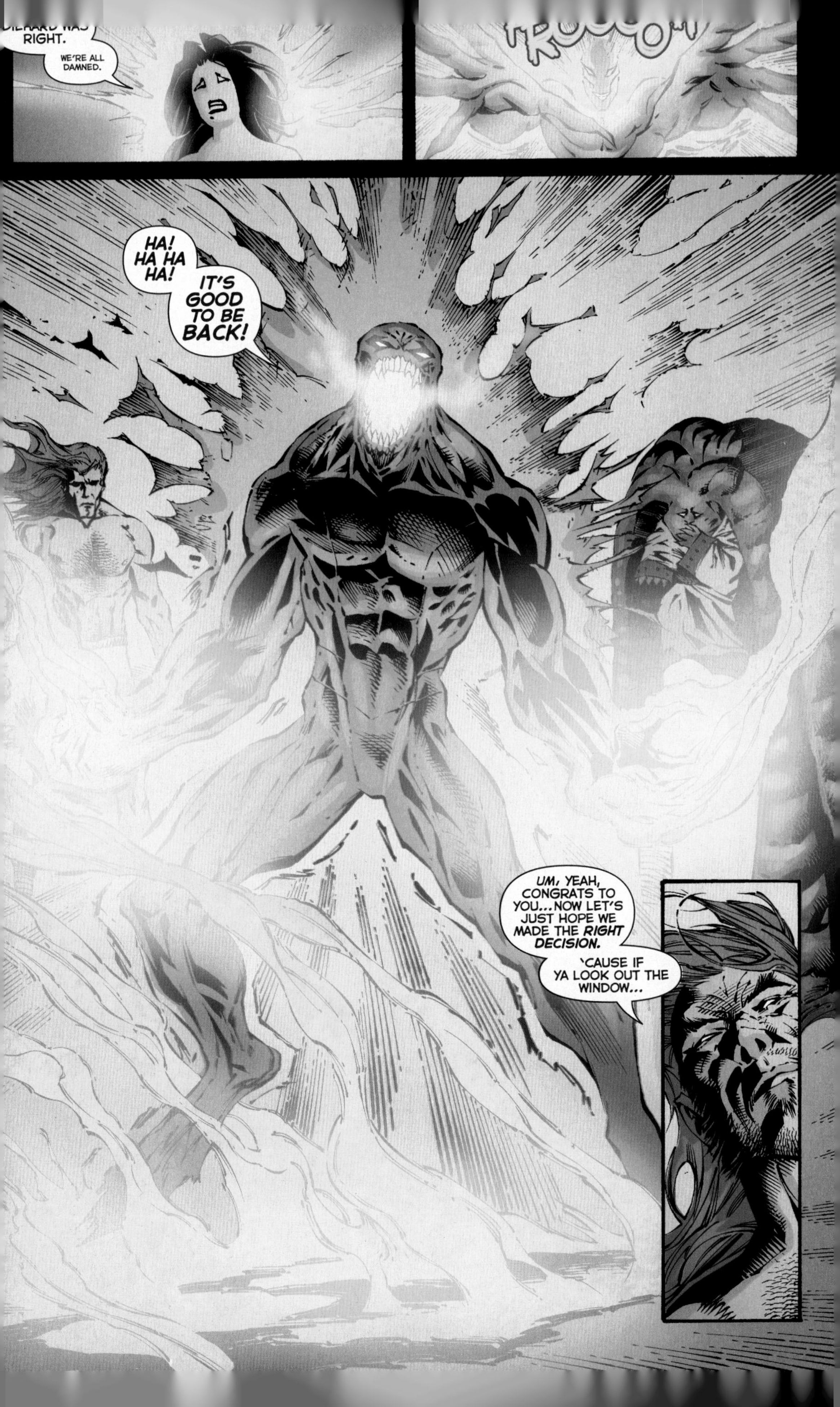
DILHARD WAS RIGHT.
WE'RE ALL DAMNED.
HA! HA HA HA!
IT'S GOOD TO BE BACK!
UM, YEAH, CONGRATS TO YOU...NOW LET'S JUST HOPE WE MADE THE *RIGHT* *DECISION.*
`CAUSE IF YA LOOK OUT THE WINDOW...

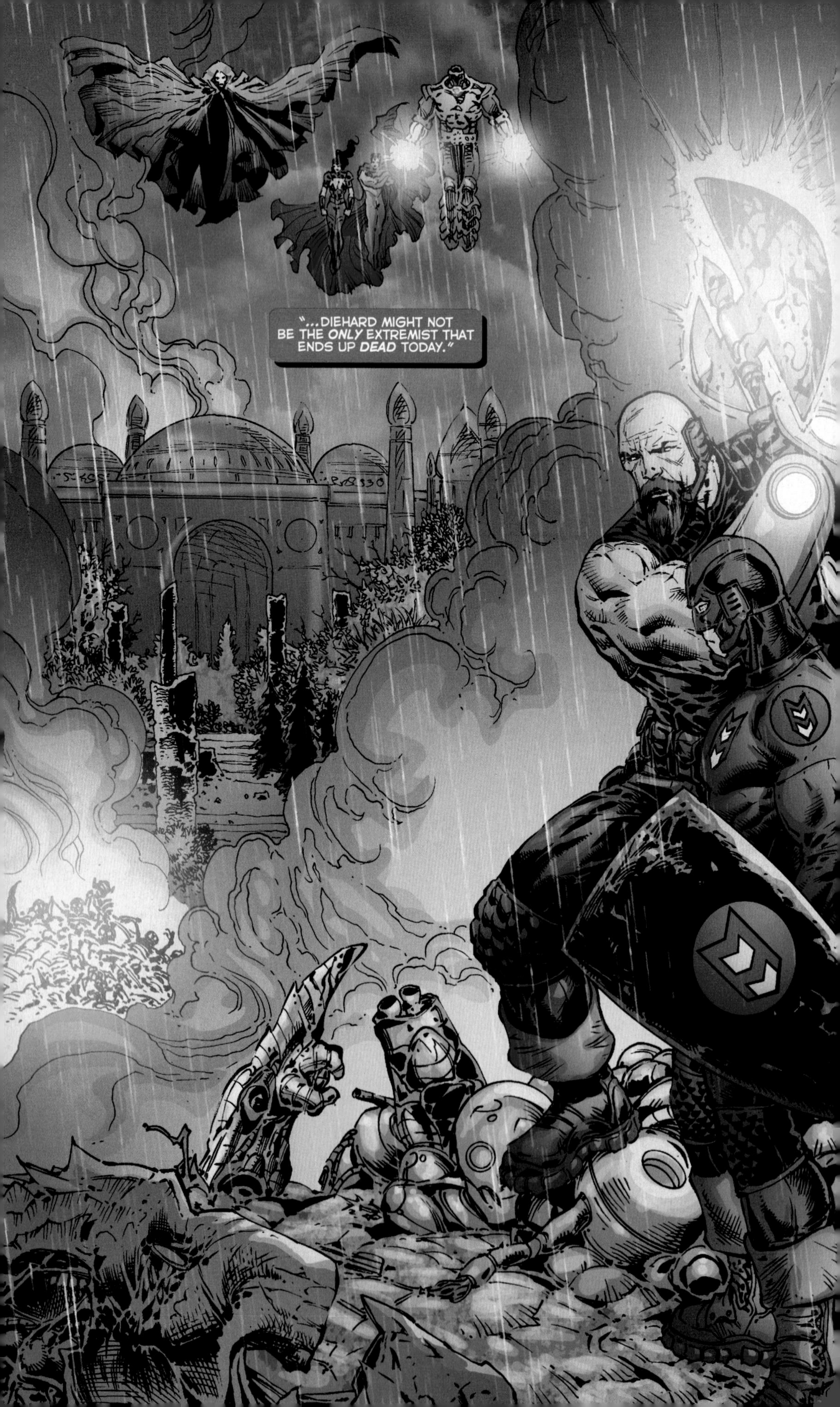
"...DIEHARD MIGHT NOT BE THE ONLY EXTREMIST THAT ENDS UP DEAD TODAY."

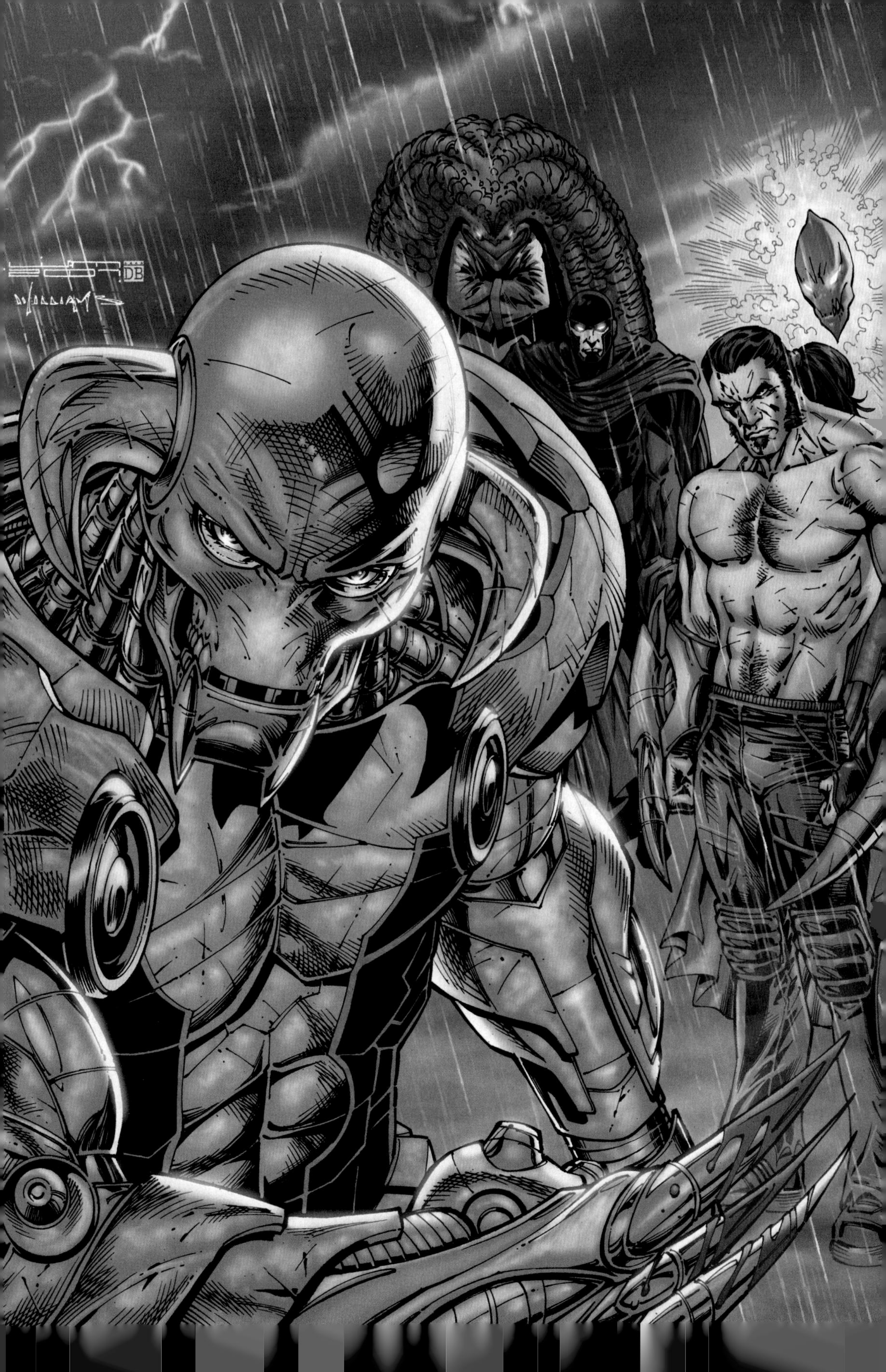

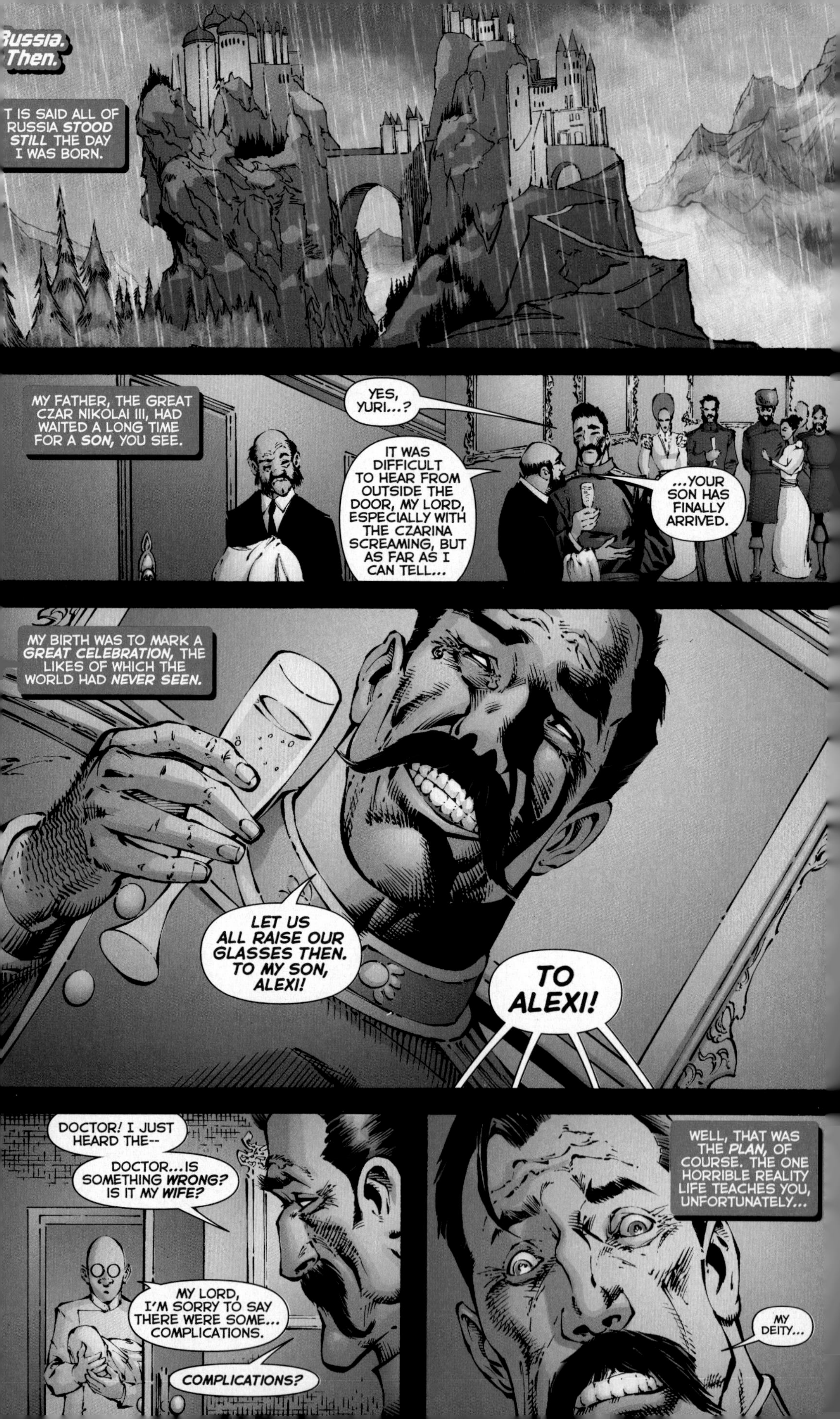
Russia. Then.
IT IS SAID ALL OF RUSSIA STOOD STILL THE DAY I WAS BORN.
MY FATHER, THE GREAT CZAR NIKOLAI III, HAD WAITED A LONG TIME FOR A SON, YOU SEE.
YES, YURI...?
IT WAS DIFFICULT TO HEAR FROM OUTSIDE THE DOOR, MY LORD, ESPECIALLY WITH THE CZARINA SCREAMING, BUT AS FAR AS I CAN TELL...
...YOUR SON HAS FINALLY ARRIVED.
MY BIRTH WAS TO MARK A GREAT CELEBRATION, THE LIKES OF WHICH THE WORLD HAD NEVER SEEN.
LET US ALL RAISE OUR GLASSES THEN. TO MY SON, ALEXI!
TO ALEXI!
DOCTOR! I JUST HEARD THE--
DOCTOR...IS SOMETHING WRONG? IS IT MY WIFE?
MY LORD, I'M SORRY TO SAY THERE WERE SOME... COMPLICATIONS.
COMPLICATIONS?
WELL, THAT WAS THE PLAN, OF COURSE. THE ONE HORRIBLE REALITY LIFE TEACHES YOU, UNFORTUNATELY...
MY DEITY...

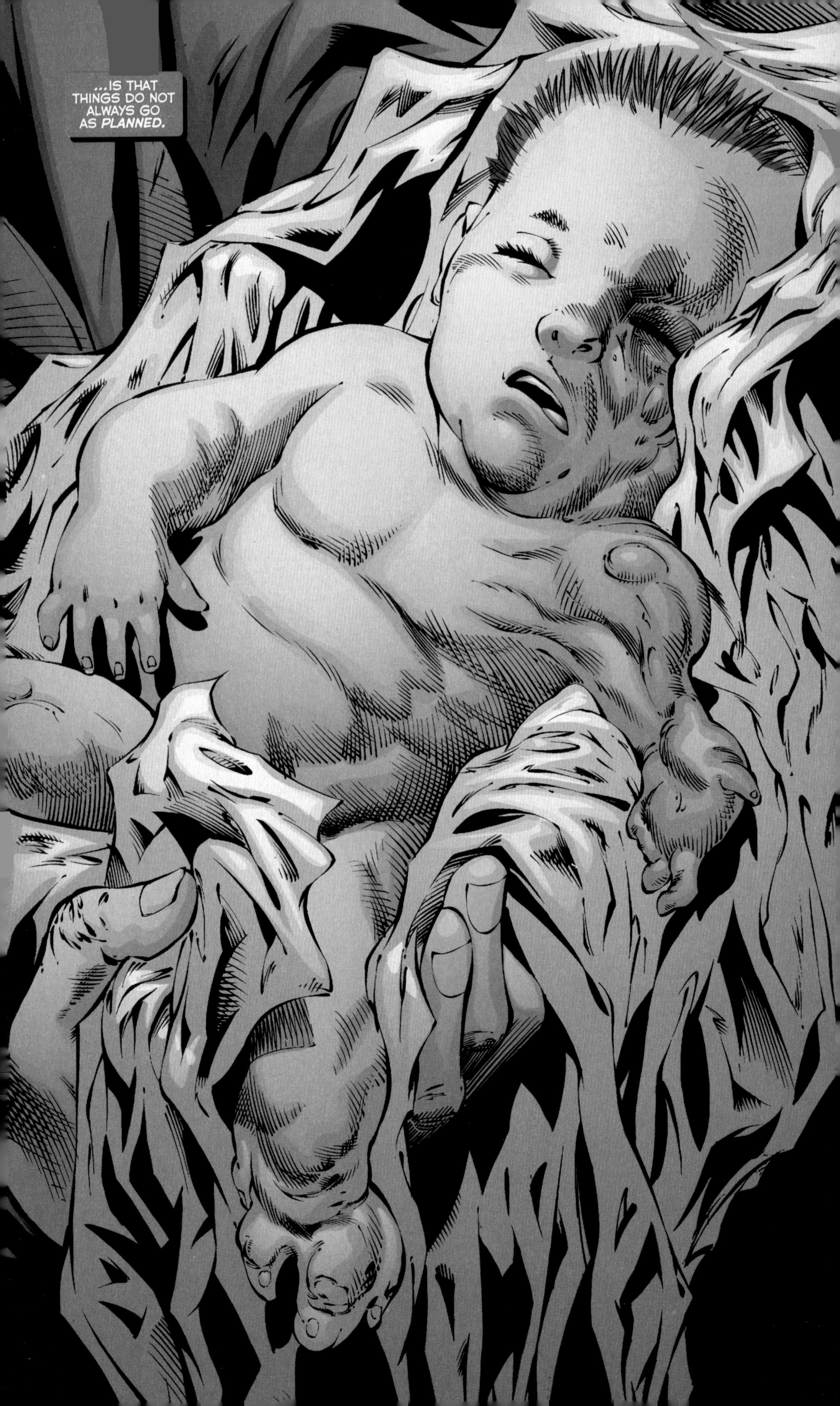
...IS THAT THINGS DO NOT ALWAYS GO AS *PLANNED.*

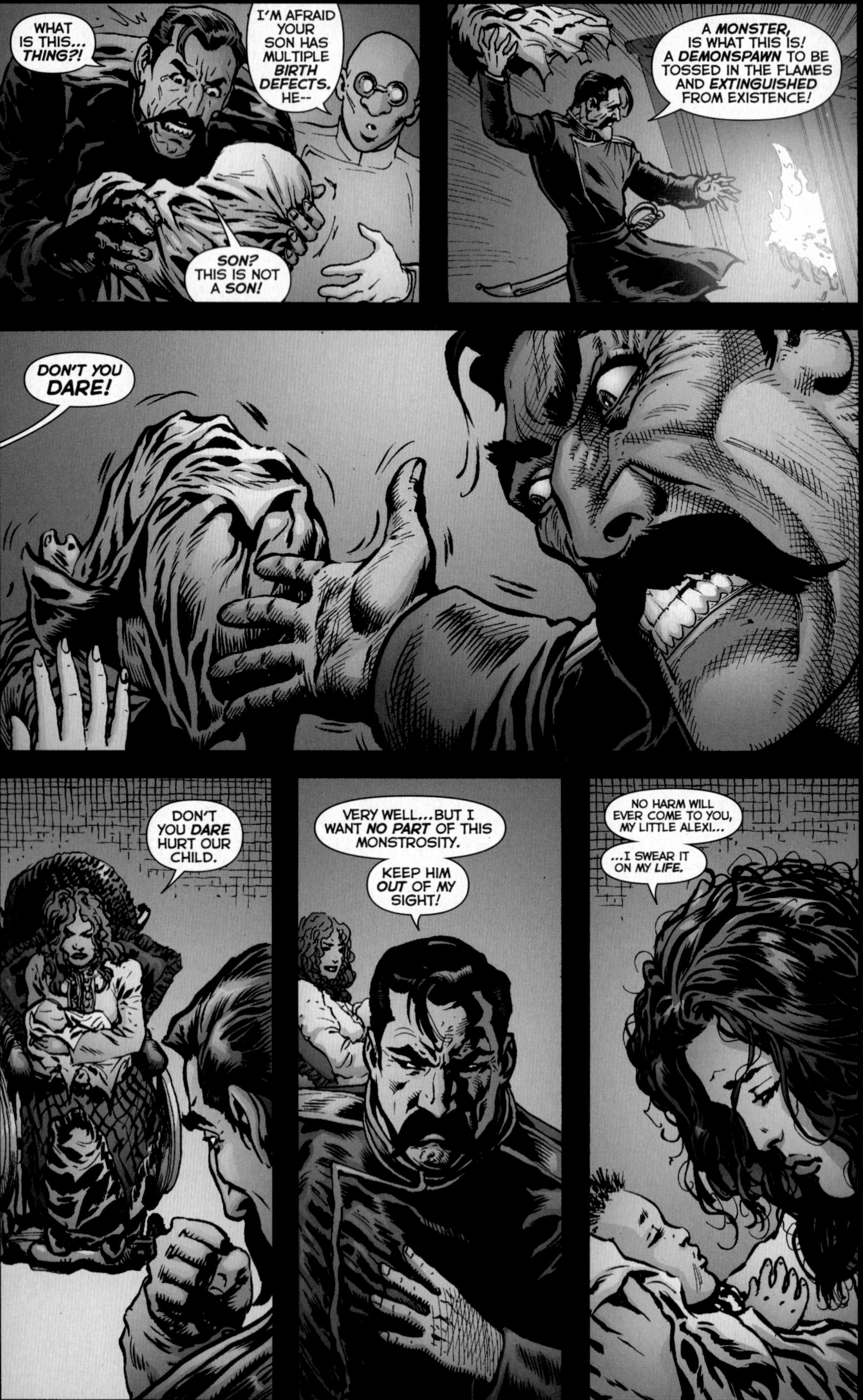
WHAT IS THIS... THING?!
I'M AFRAID YOUR SON HAS MULTIPLE BIRTH DEFECTS. HE--
SON? THIS IS NOT A SON!
A MONSTER, IS WHAT THIS IS! A DEMONSPAWN TO BE TOSSED IN THE FLAMES AND EXTINGUISHED FROM EXISTENCE!
DON'T YOU DARE!
DON'T YOU DARE HURT OUR CHILD.
VERY WELL...BUT I WANT NO PART OF THIS MONSTROSITY.
KEEP HIM OUT OF MY SIGHT!
NO HARM WILL EVER COME TO YOU, MY LITTLE ALEXI...
...I SWEAR IT ON MY LIFE.

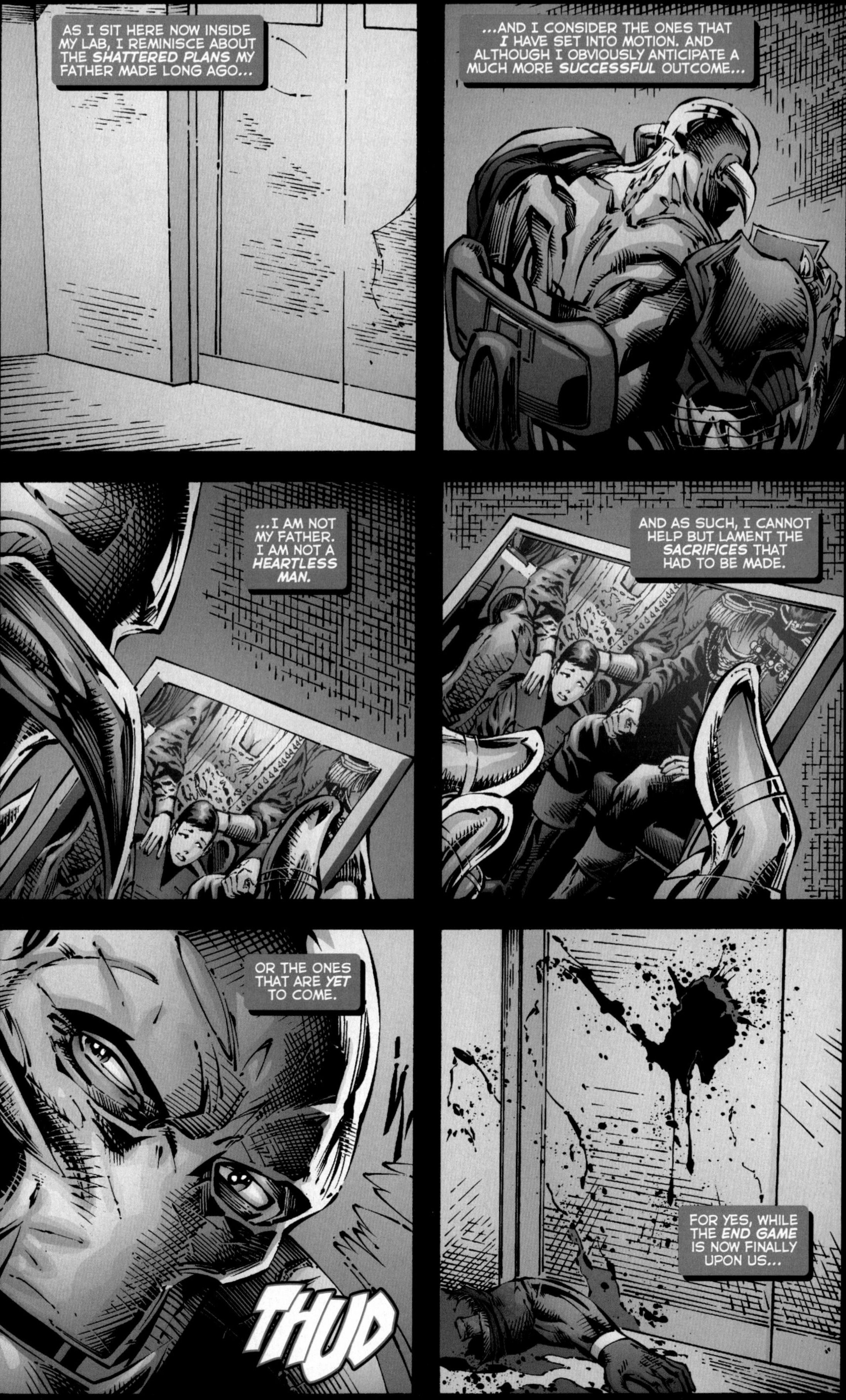
AS I SIT HERE NOW INSIDE MY LAB, I REMINISCE ABOUT THE SHATTERED PLANS MY FATHER MADE LONG AGO...
...AND I CONSIDER THE ONES THAT I HAVE SET INTO MOTION. AND ALTHOUGH I OBVIOUSLY ANTICIPATE A MUCH MORE SUCCESSFUL OUTCOME...
...I AM NOT MY FATHER. I AM NOT A HEARTLESS MAN.
AND AS SUCH, I CANNOT HELP BUT LAMENT THE SACRIFICES THAT HAD TO BE MADE.
OR THE ONES THAT ARE YET TO COME.
THUD
FOR YES, WHILE THE END GAME IS NOW FINALLY UPON US...

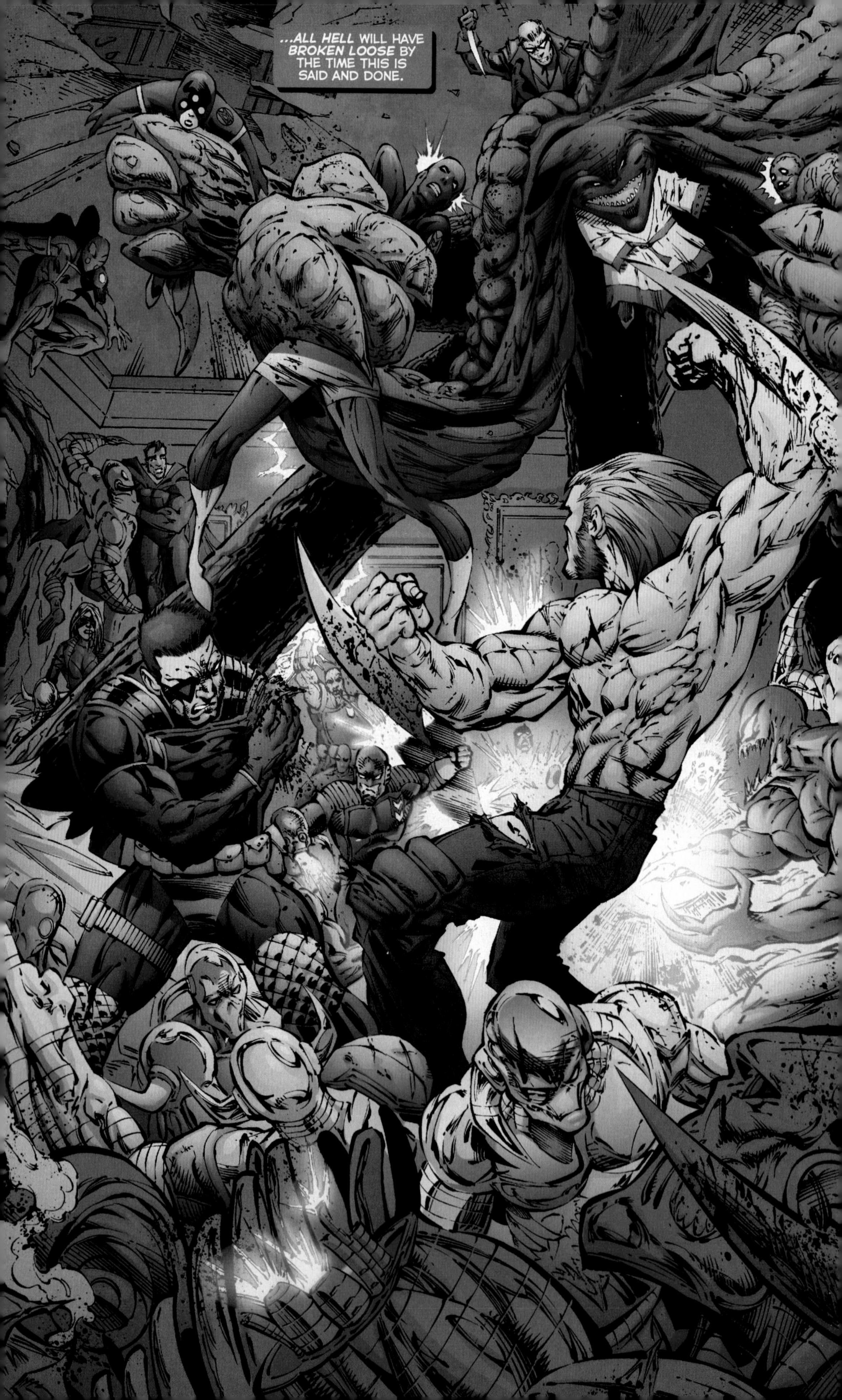
...ALL HELL WILL HAVE BROKEN LOOSE BY THE TIME THIS IS SAID AND DONE.

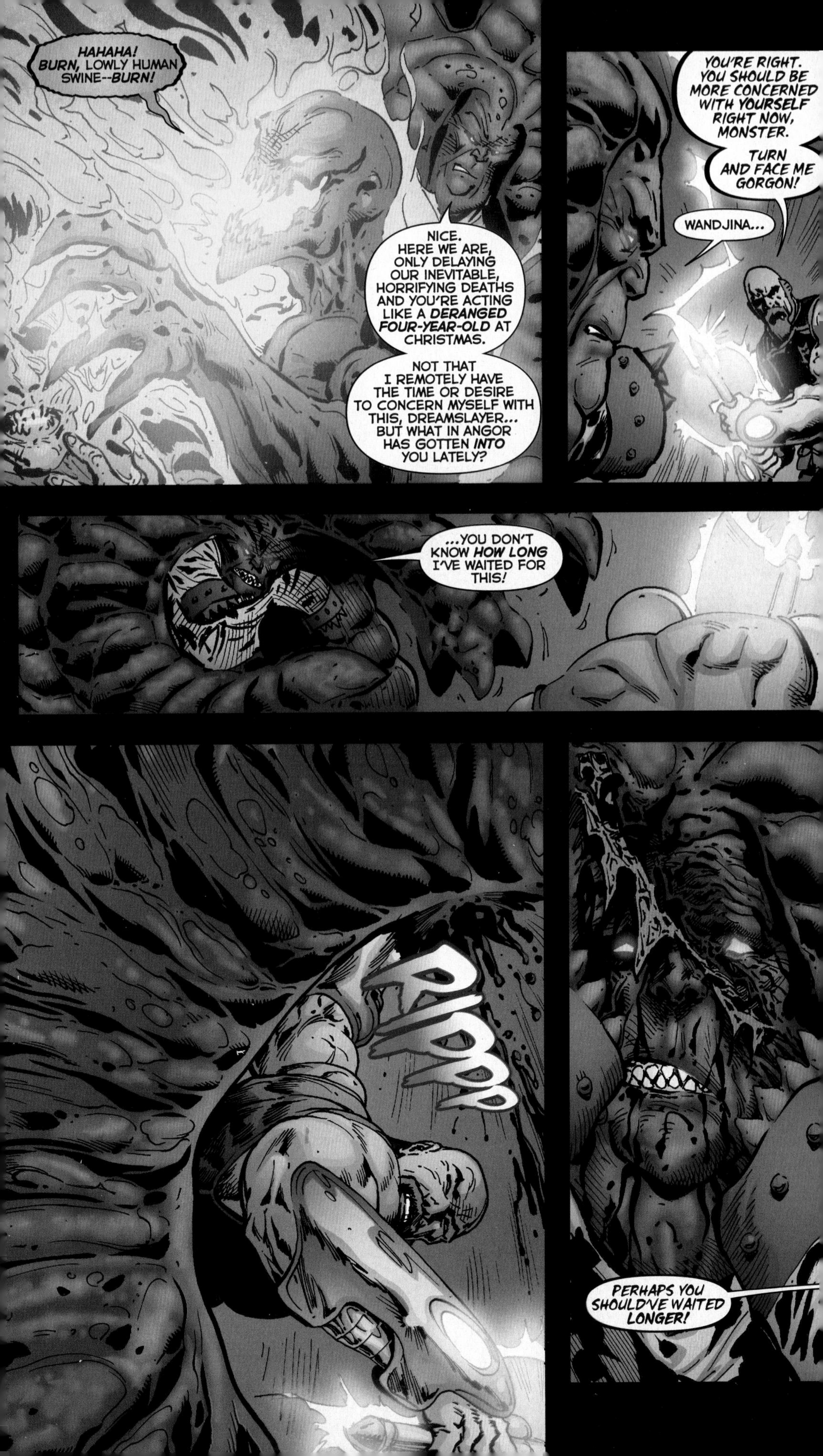
HAHAHA! BURN, LOWLY HUMAN SWINE--BURN!
NICE. HERE WE ARE, ONLY DELAYING OUR INEVITABLE, HORRIFYING DEATHS AND YOU'RE ACTING LIKE A DERANGED FOUR-YEAR-OLD AT CHRISTMAS.
NOT THAT I REMOTELY HAVE THE TIME OR DESIRE TO CONCERN MYSELF WITH THIS, DREAMSLAYER... BUT WHAT IN ANGOR HAS GOTTEN INTO YOU LATELY?
YOU'RE RIGHT. YOU SHOULD BE MORE CONCERNED WITH YOURSELF RIGHT NOW, MONSTER.
TURN AND FACE ME GORGON!
WANDJINA...
...YOU DON'T KNOW HOW LONG I'VE WAITED FOR THIS!
RIPPP
PERHAPS YOU SHOULD'VE WAITED LONGER!

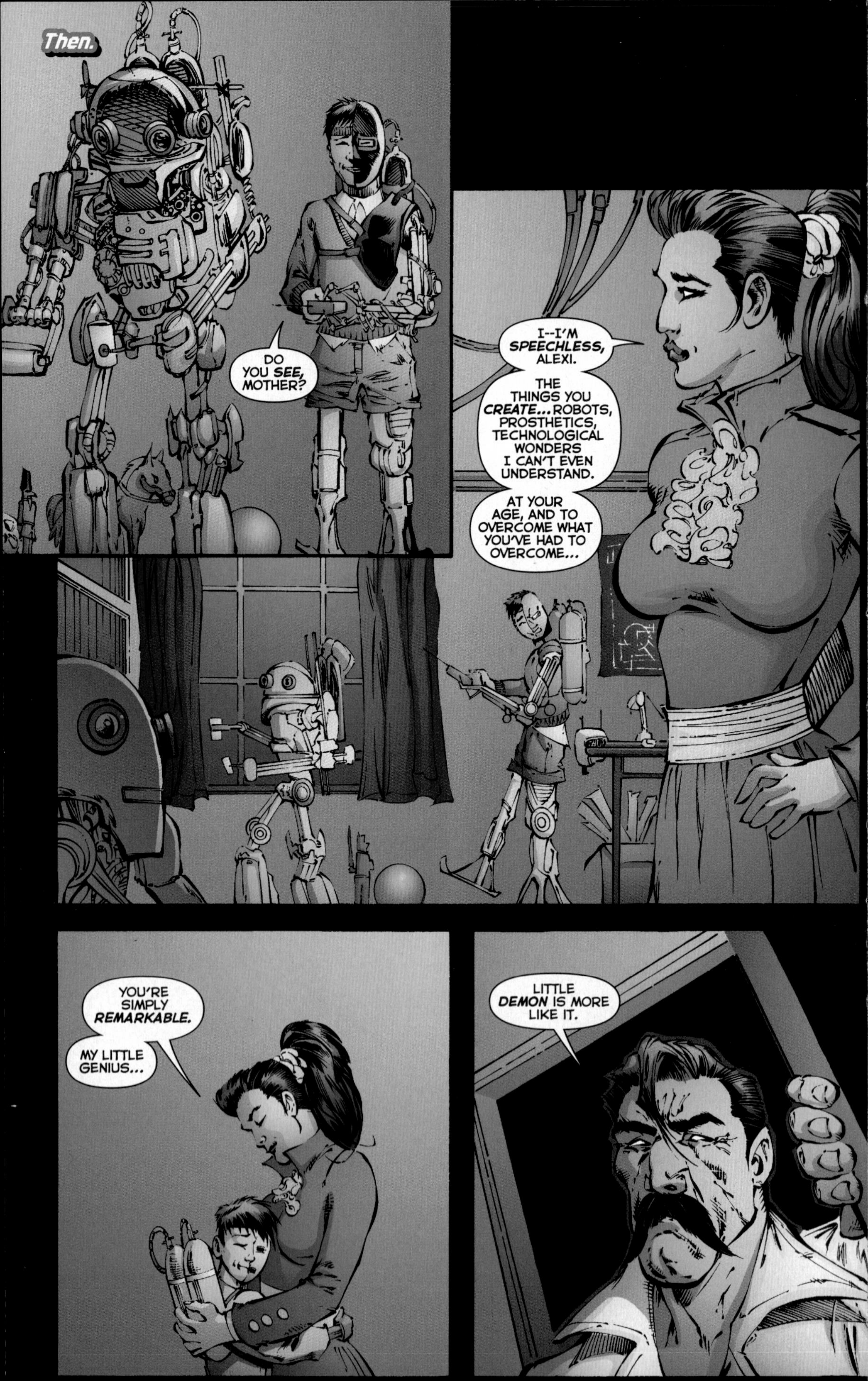

Then.
DO YOU SEE, MOTHER?
I--I'M SPEECHLESS, ALEXI.
THE THINGS YOU CREATE... ROBOTS, PROSTHETICS, TECHNOLOGICAL WONDERS I CAN'T EVEN UNDERSTAND.
AT YOUR AGE, AND TO OVERCOME WHAT YOU'VE HAD TO OVERCOME...
YOU'RE SIMPLY REMARKABLE.
MY LITTLE GENIUS...
LITTLE DEMON IS MORE LIKE IT.

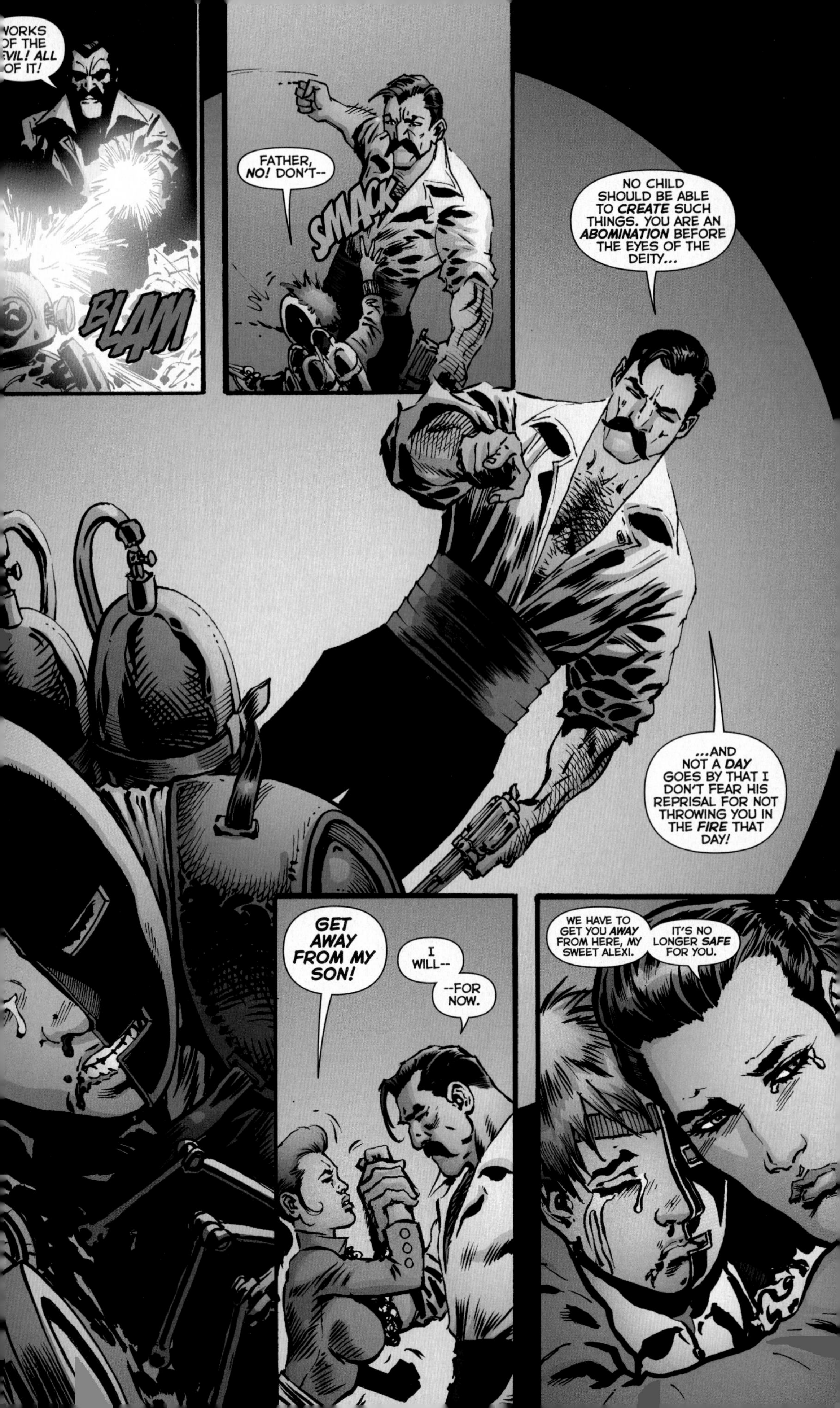
WORKS OF THE EVIL! ALL OF IT!
BLAM
FATHER, NO! DON'T--
SMACK
NO CHILD SHOULD BE ABLE TO CREATE SUCH THINGS. YOU ARE AN ABOMINATION BEFORE THE EYES OF THE DEITY...
...AND NOT A DAY GOES BY THAT I DON'T FEAR HIS REPRISAL FOR NOT THROWING YOU IN THE FIRE THAT DAY!
GET AWAY FROM MY SON!
I WILL--
--FOR NOW.
WE HAVE TO GET YOU AWAY FROM HERE, MY SWEET ALEXI.
IT'S NO LONGER SAFE FOR YOU.

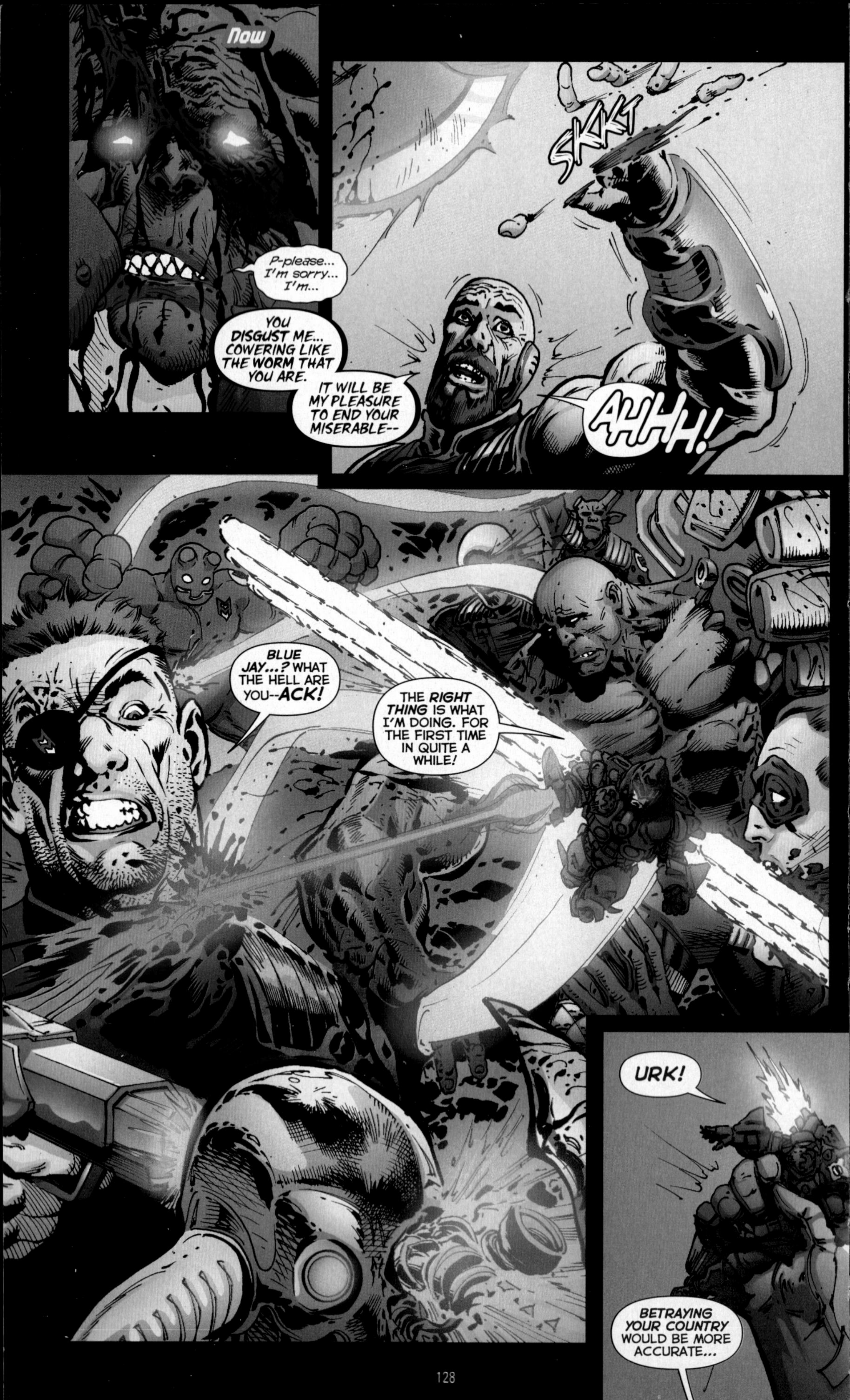
Now
SKKT
P-please... I'm sorry... I'm...
YOU DISGUST ME... COWERING LIKE THE WORM THAT YOU ARE.
IT WILL BE MY PLEASURE TO END YOUR MISERABLE--
AHHH!
BLUE JAY...? WHAT THE HELL ARE YOU--ACK!
THE RIGHT THING IS WHAT I'M DOING. FOR THE FIRST TIME IN QUITE A WHILE!
URK!
BETRAYING YOUR COUNTRY WOULD BE MORE ACCURATE...

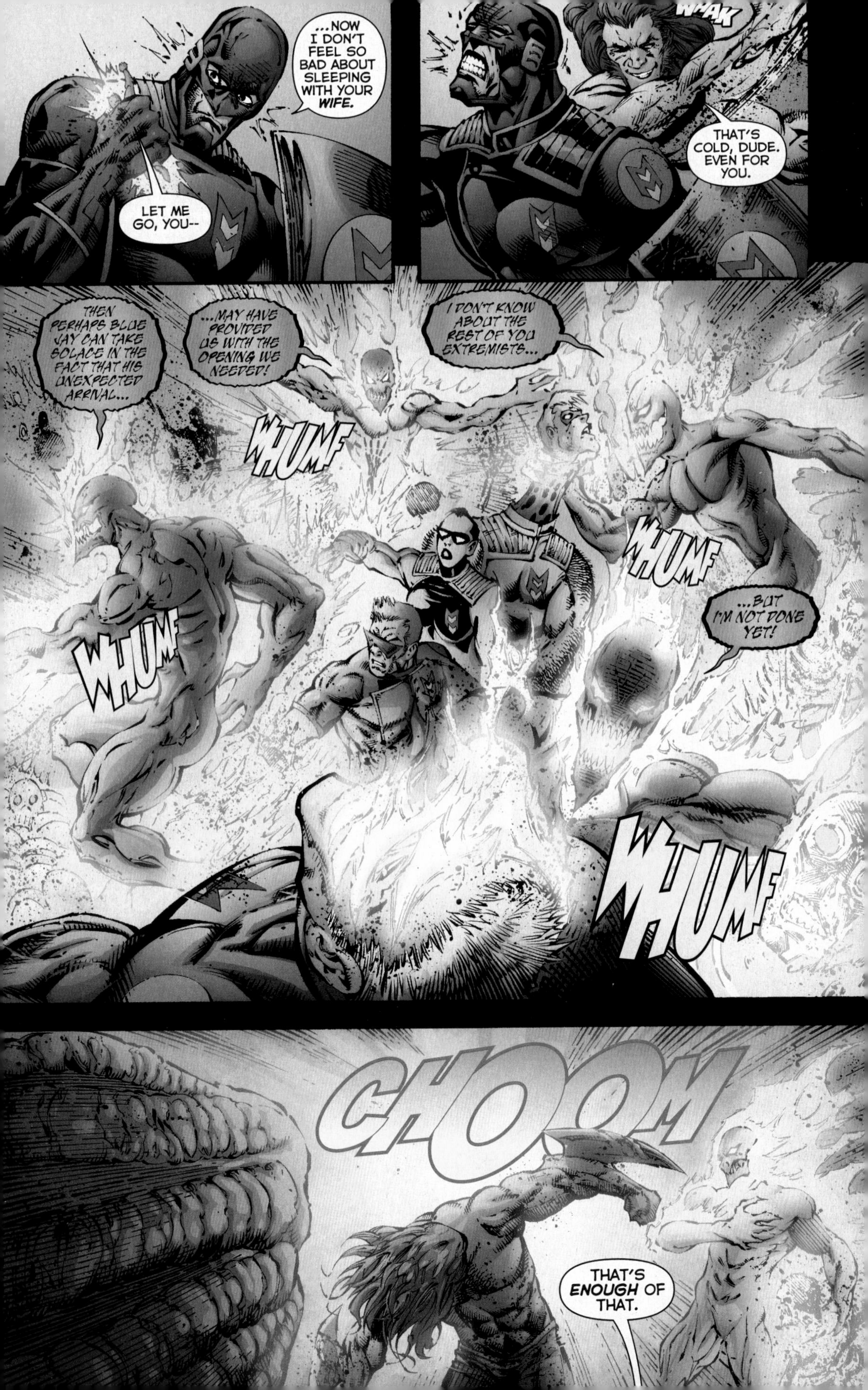
...NOW I DON'T FEEL SO BAD ABOUT SLEEPING WITH YOUR WIFE.
LET ME GO, YOU--
WHAK
THAT'S COLD, DUDE. EVEN FOR YOU.
THEN PERHAPS BLUE JAY CAN TAKE SOLACE IN THE FACT THAT HIS UNEXPECTED ARRIVAL...
...MAY HAVE PROVIDED US WITH THE OPENING WE NEEDED!
I DON'T KNOW ABOUT THE REST OF YOU EXTREMISTS...
WHUMF
WHUMF
...BUT I'M NOT DONE YET!
WHUMF
WHUMF
CHOOM
THAT'S ENOUGH OF THAT.

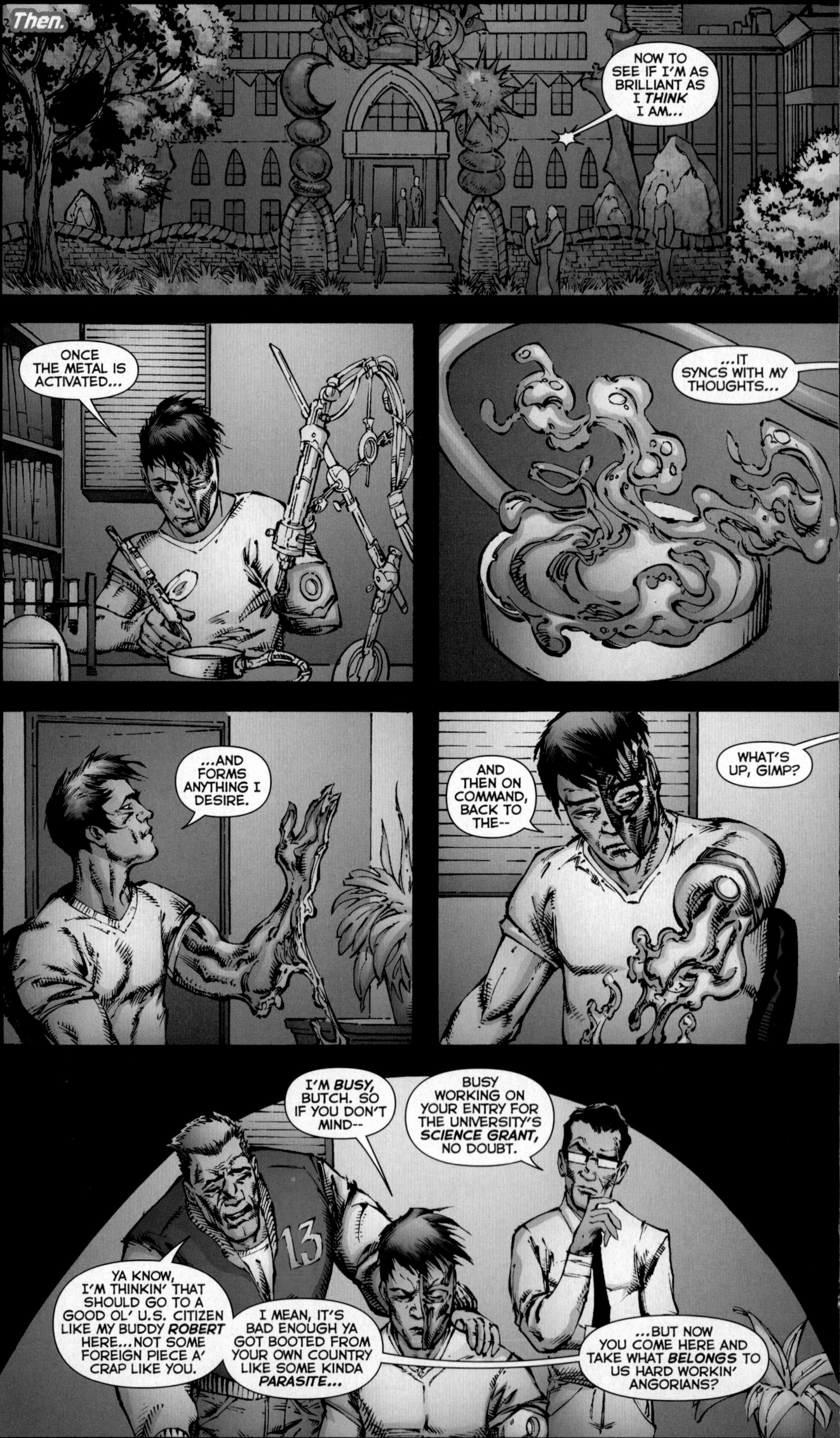
Then.
NOW TO SEE IF I'M AS BRILLIANT AS I THINK I AM...
ONCE THE METAL IS ACTIVATED...
...IT SYNCS WITH MY THOUGHTS...
...AND FORMS ANYTHING I DESIRE.
AND THEN ON COMMAND, BACK TO THE--
WHAT'S UP, GIMP?
I'M BUSY, BUTCH. SO IF YOU DON'T MIND--
BUSY WORKING ON YOUR ENTRY FOR THE UNIVERSITY'S SCIENCE GRANT, NO DOUBT.
YA KNOW, I'M THINKIN' THAT SHOULD GO TO A GOOD OL' U.S. CITIZEN LIKE MY BUDDY ROBERT HERE...NOT SOME FOREIGN PIECE A' CRAP LIKE YOU.
I MEAN, IT'S BAD ENOUGH YA GOT BOOTED FROM YOUR OWN COUNTRY LIKE SOME KINDA PARASITE...
...BUT NOW YOU COME HERE AND TAKE WHAT BELONGS TO US HARD WORKIN' ANGORIANS?

NO WAY, PHANTOM A' THE OPERA. NOT ON BUTCH GANNON'S WATCH!
I'D BE CAREFUL IF I WERE YOU, BUTCH...
WHOOPS! MY BAD...GUESS I WASN'T CAREFUL ENOUGH.
WHAT IS THIS GUNK ANY--
WHOA! WHAT'S IT DOIN'?! WHAT THE--
MMPPPHHH!
FOR DEITY'S SAKE, ALEXI--GET IT OFF HIM! IT'S CRUSHING HIS HEAD!
I WARNED HIM TO BE CAREFUL, DIDN'T I? HE HAS NO ONE TO BLAME BUT HIMSELF.
BRNNNG
NOW IF YOU DON'T MIND, I HAVE A CALL TO TAKE...
ALEXI... IT'S YURI.
YURI... YOU'LL HAVE TO EXCUSE ME, BUT I'M IN THE MIDDLE OF SOMETHING--
I HAVE SOME BAD NEWS, ALEXI. YOUR FATHER...HE FOUND OUT YOUR MOTHER WAS SECRETLY FINANCING YOUR LIFE IN THE STATES, AND...WELL, HE LOST HIS TEMPER AND...
...SHE'S DEAD, ALEXI.

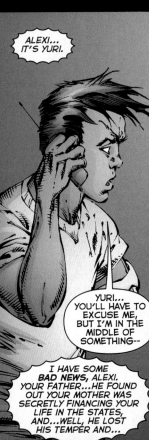

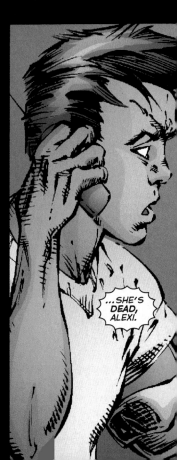

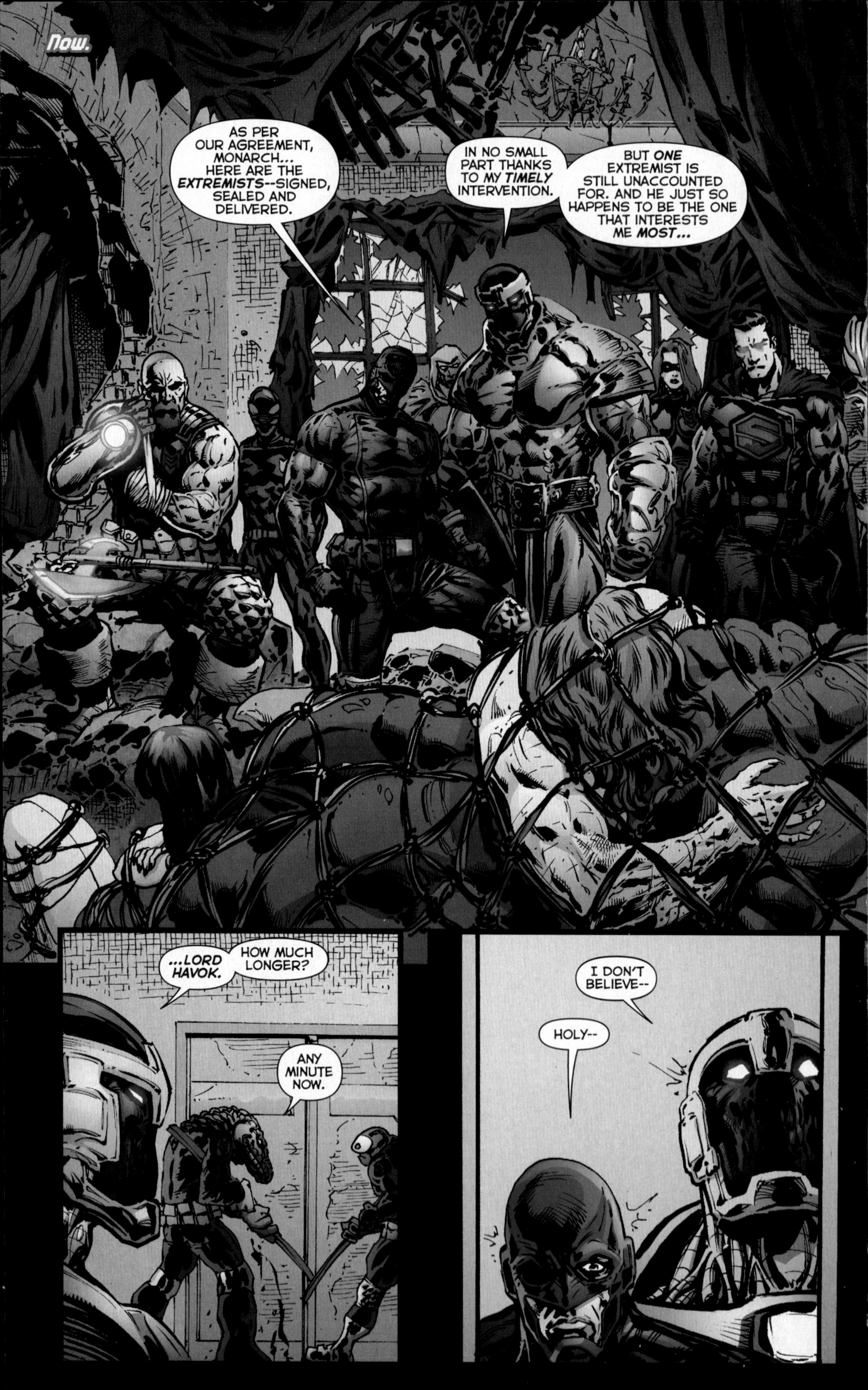
Now.
AS PER OUR AGREEMENT, MONARCH... HERE ARE THE EXTREMISTS--SIGNED, SEALED AND DELIVERED.
IN NO SMALL PART THANKS TO MY TIMELY INTERVENTION.
BUT ONE EXTREMIST IS STILL UNACCOUNTED FOR. AND HE JUST SO HAPPENS TO BE THE ONE THAT INTERESTS ME MOST...
...LORD HAVOK.
HOW MUCH LONGER?
ANY MINUTE NOW.
I DON'T BELIEVE--
HOLY--

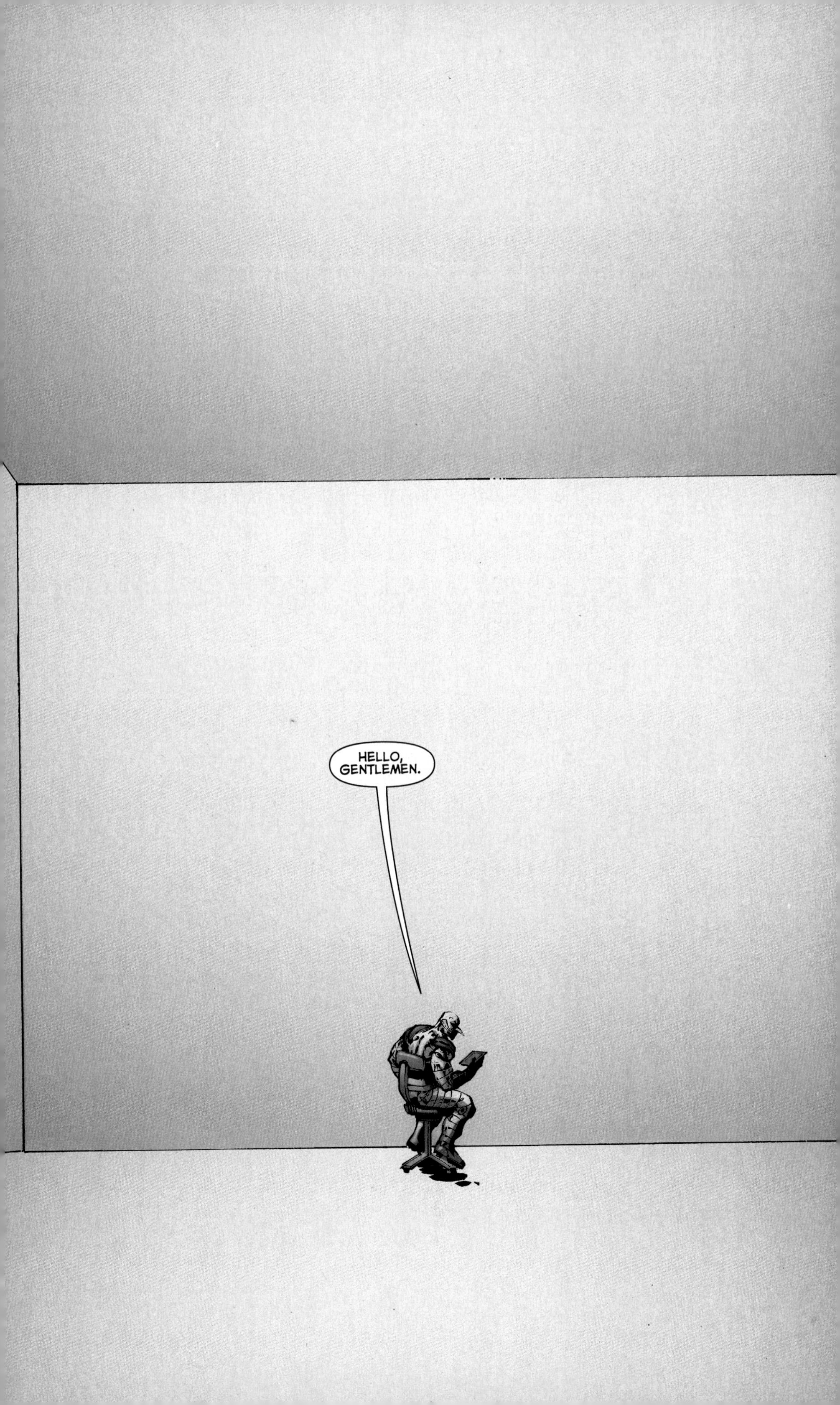
HELLO, GENTLEMEN.

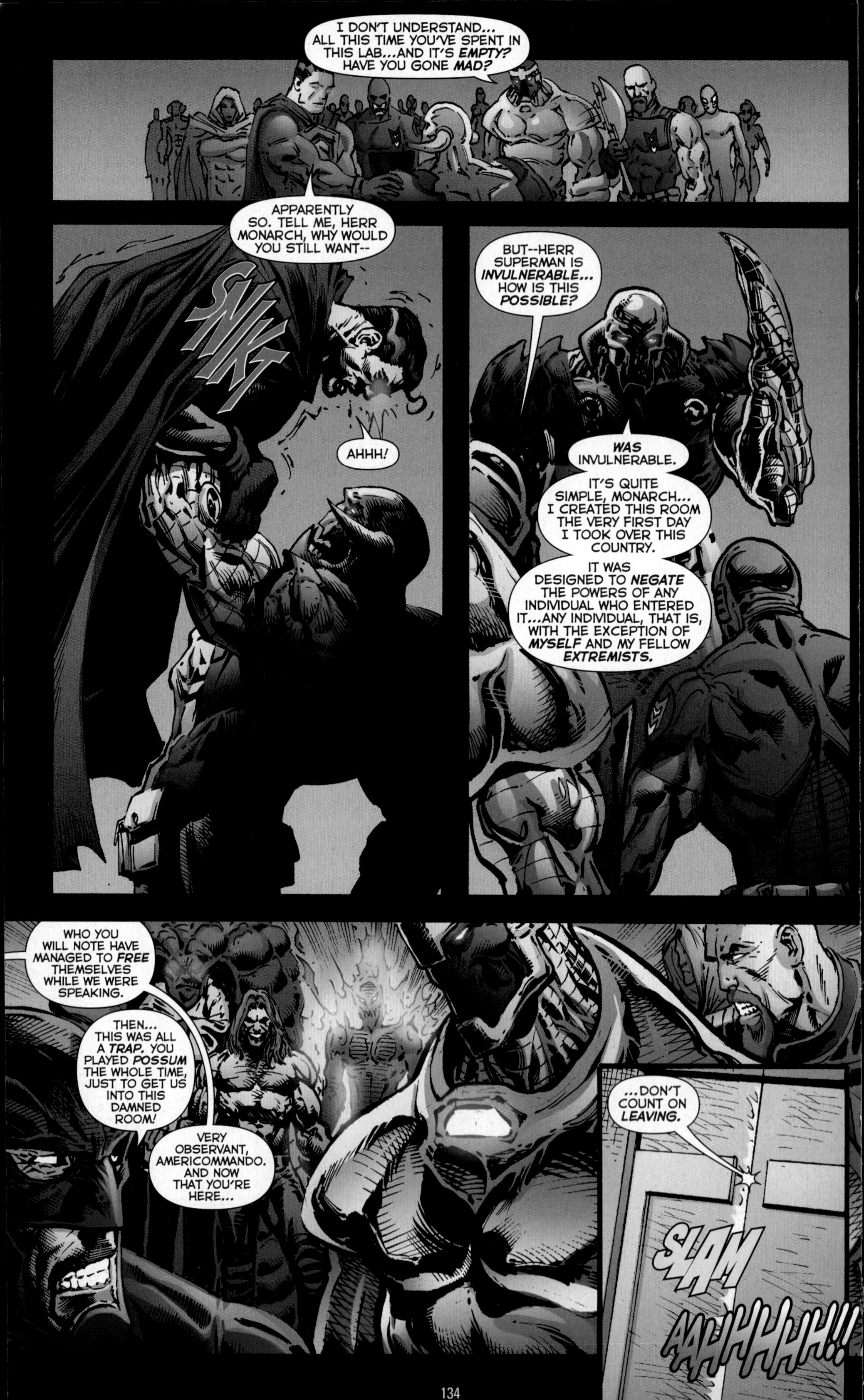

I DON'T UNDERSTAND... ALL THIS TIME YOU'VE SPENT IN THIS LAB...AND IT'S EMPTY? HAVE YOU GONE MAD?
APPARENTLY SO. TELL ME, HERR MONARCH, WHY WOULD YOU STILL WANT--
SNIKT
AHHH!
BUT--HERR SUPERMAN IS INVULNERABLE... HOW IS THIS POSSIBLE?
WAS INVULNERABLE.
IT'S QUITE SIMPLE, MONARCH... I CREATED THIS ROOM THE VERY FIRST DAY I TOOK OVER THIS COUNTRY.
IT WAS DESIGNED TO NEGATE THE POWERS OF ANY INDIVIDUAL WHO ENTERED IT...ANY INDIVIDUAL, THAT IS, WITH THE EXCEPTION OF MYSELF AND MY FELLOW EXTREMISTS.
WHO YOU WILL NOTE HAVE MANAGED TO FREE THEMSELVES WHILE WE WERE SPEAKING.
THEN... THIS WAS ALL A TRAP. YOU PLAYED POSSUM THE WHOLE TIME, JUST TO GET US INTO THIS DAMNED ROOM!
VERY OBSERVANT, AMERICOMMANDO. AND NOW THAT YOU'RE HERE...
...DON'T COUNT ON LEAVING.
SLAM
AAHHHHH!!

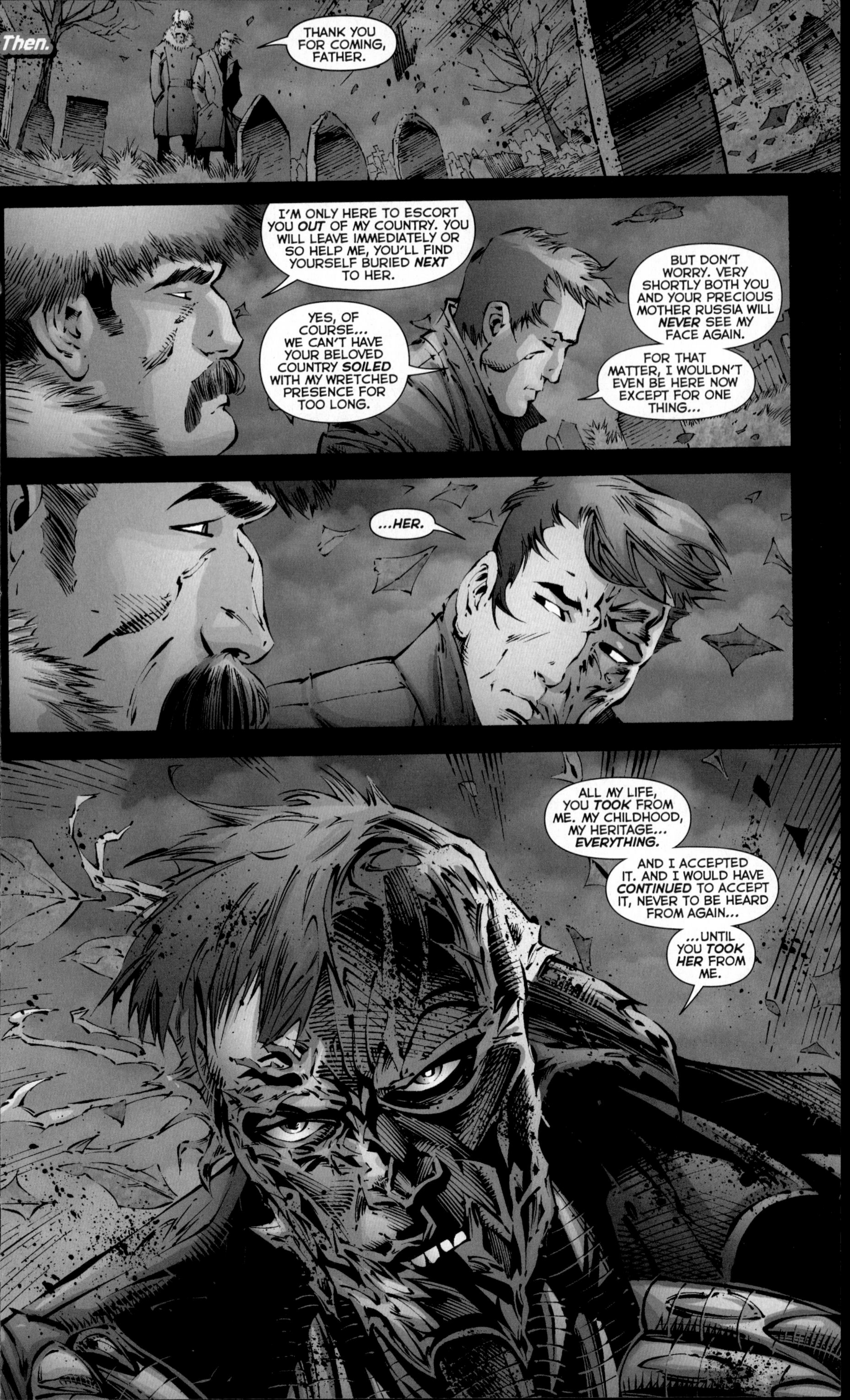
Then.
THANK YOU FOR COMING, FATHER.
I'M ONLY HERE TO ESCORT YOU OUT OF MY COUNTRY. YOU WILL LEAVE IMMEDIATELY OR SO HELP ME, YOU'LL FIND YOURSELF BURIED NEXT TO HER.
YES, OF COURSE... WE CAN'T HAVE YOUR BELOVED COUNTRY SOILED WITH MY WRETCHED PRESENCE FOR TOO LONG.
BUT DON'T WORRY. VERY SHORTLY BOTH YOU AND YOUR PRECIOUS MOTHER RUSSIA WILL NEVER SEE MY FACE AGAIN.
FOR THAT MATTER, I WOULDN'T EVEN BE HERE NOW EXCEPT FOR ONE THING...
...HER.
ALL MY LIFE, YOU TOOK FROM ME. MY CHILDHOOD, MY HERITAGE... EVERYTHING.
AND I ACCEPTED IT. AND I WOULD HAVE CONTINUED TO ACCEPT IT, NEVER TO BE HEARD FROM AGAIN...
...UNTIL YOU TOOK HER FROM ME.

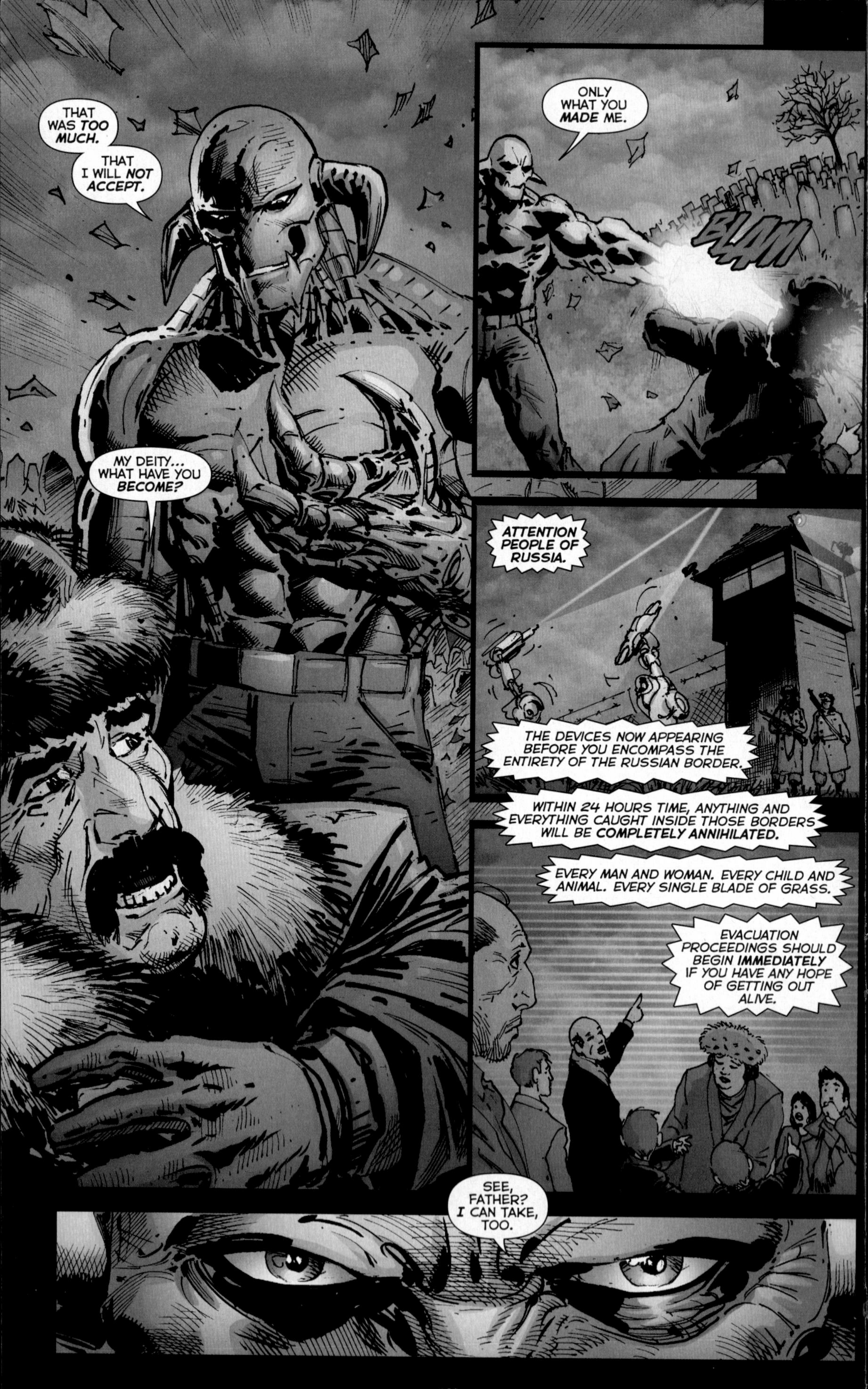
THAT WAS TOO MUCH.
THAT I WILL NOT ACCEPT.
MY DEITY... WHAT HAVE YOU BECOME?
ONLY WHAT YOU MADE ME.
BLAM
ATTENTION PEOPLE OF RUSSIA.
THE DEVICES NOW APPEARING BEFORE YOU ENCOMPASS THE ENTIRETY OF THE RUSSIAN BORDER.
WITHIN 24 HOURS TIME, ANYTHING AND EVERYTHING CAUGHT INSIDE THOSE BORDERS WILL BE COMPLETELY ANNIHILATED.
EVERY MAN AND WOMAN. EVERY CHILD AND ANIMAL. EVERY SINGLE BLADE OF GRASS.
EVACUATION PROCEEDINGS SHOULD BEGIN IMMEDIATELY IF YOU HAVE ANY HOPE OF GETTING OUT ALIVE.
SEE, FATHER? I CAN TAKE, TOO.

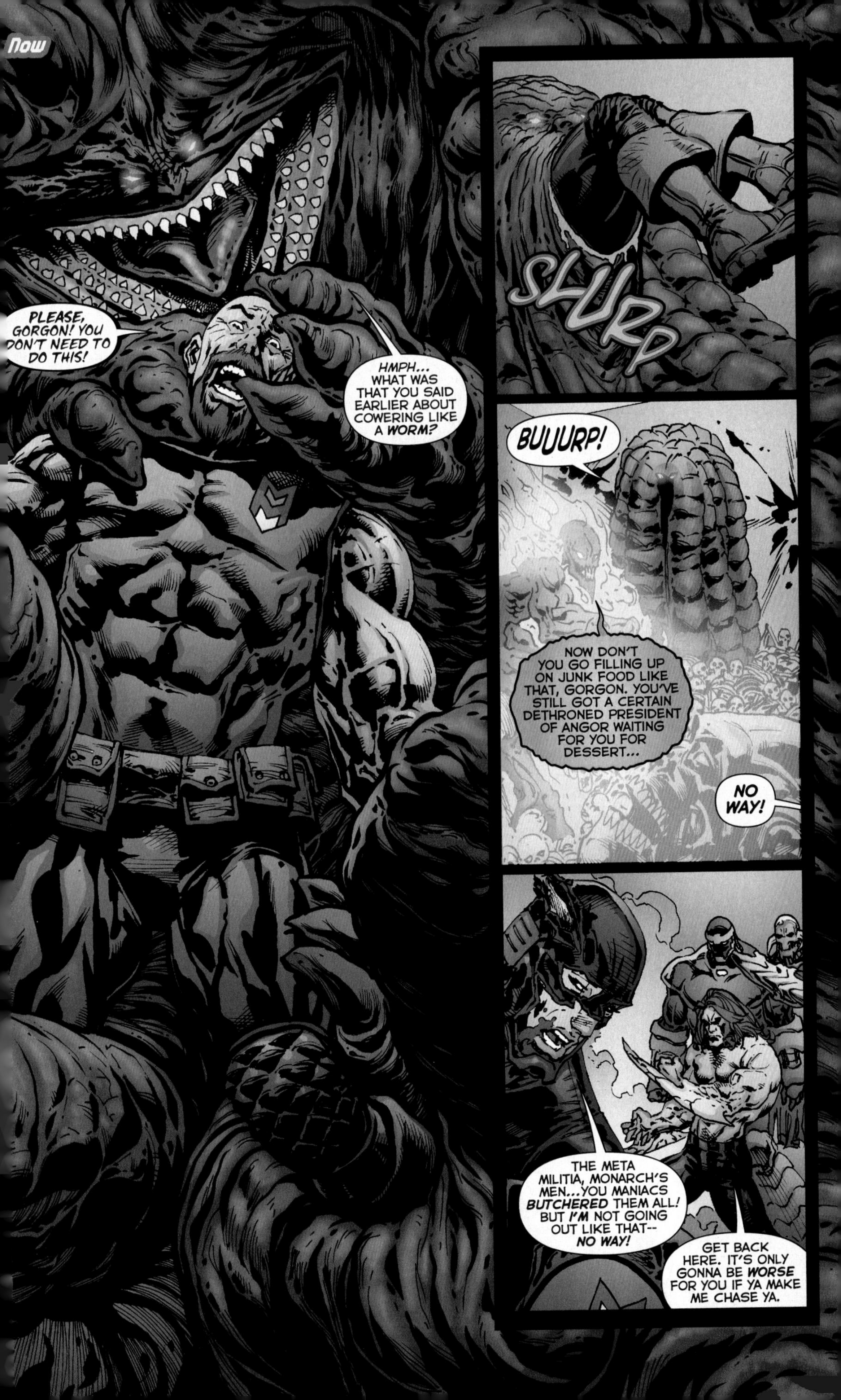
Now
PLEASE, GORGON! YOU DON'T NEED TO DO THIS!
HMPH... WHAT WAS THAT YOU SAID EARLIER ABOUT COWERING LIKE A WORM?
SLURP
BUUURP!
NOW DON'T YOU GO FILLING UP ON JUNK FOOD LIKE THAT, GORGON. YOU'VE STILL GOT A CERTAIN DETHRONED PRESIDENT OF ANGOR WAITING FOR YOU FOR DESSERT...
NO WAY!
THE META MILITIA, MONARCH'S MEN...YOU MANIACS BUTCHERED THEM ALL! BUT I'M NOT GOING OUT LIKE THAT-- NO WAY!
GET BACK HERE. IT'S ONLY GONNA BE WORSE FOR YOU IF YA MAKE ME CHASE YA.

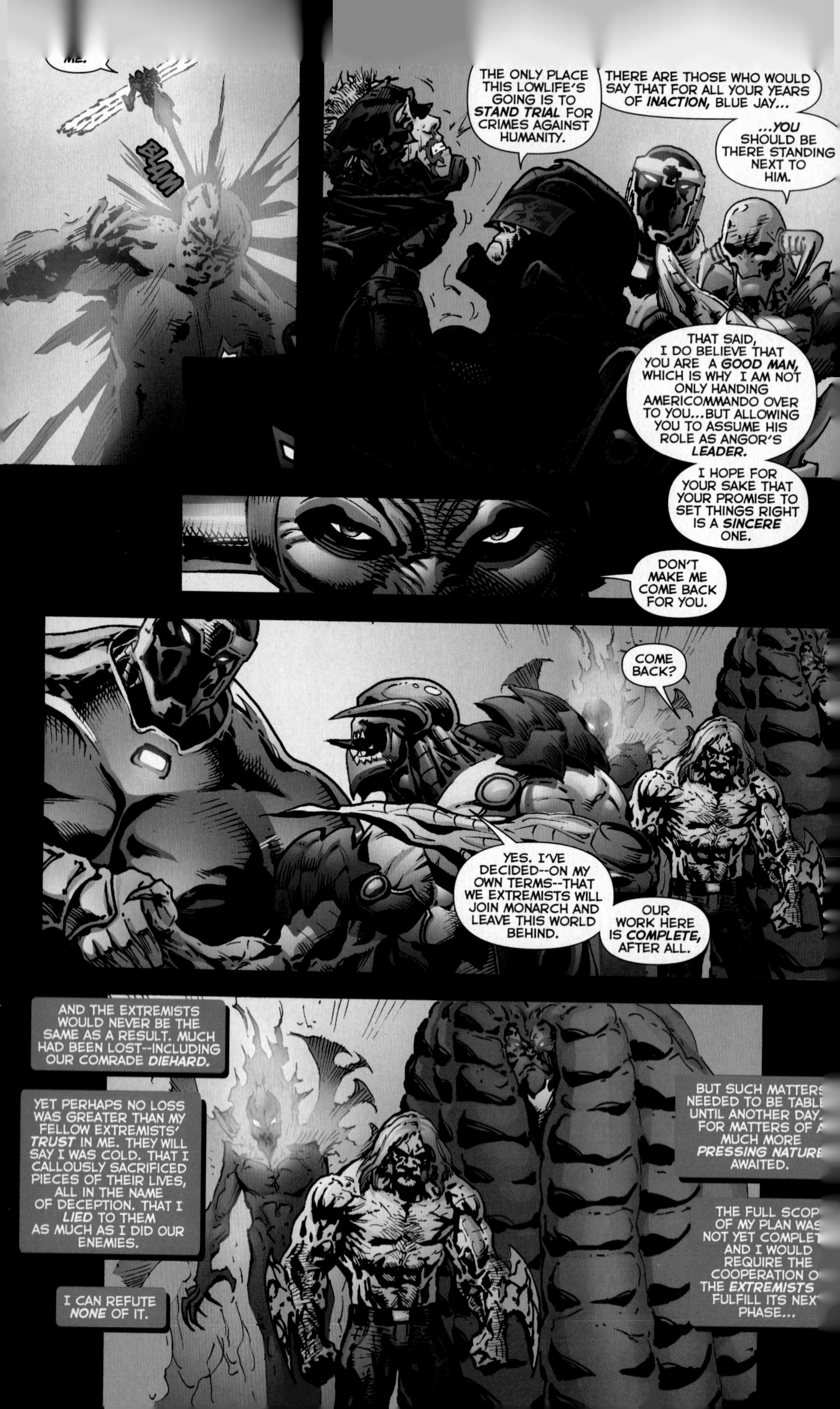
ME.
BLAM
THE ONLY PLACE THIS LOWLIFE'S GOING IS TO **STAND TRIAL** FOR CRIMES AGAINST HUMANITY.
THERE ARE THOSE WHO WOULD SAY THAT FOR ALL YOUR YEARS OF **INACTION,** BLUE JAY...
...**YOU** SHOULD BE THERE STANDING NEXT TO HIM.
THAT SAID, I DO BELIEVE THAT YOU ARE A **GOOD MAN,** WHICH IS WHY I AM NOT ONLY HANDING AMERICOMMANDO OVER TO YOU...BUT ALLOWING YOU TO ASSUME HIS ROLE AS ANGOR'S **LEADER.**
I HOPE FOR YOUR SAKE THAT YOUR PROMISE TO SET THINGS RIGHT IS A **SINCERE** ONE.
DON'T MAKE ME COME BACK FOR YOU.
COME BACK?
YES. I'VE DECIDED--ON MY OWN TERMS--THAT WE EXTREMISTS WILL JOIN MONARCH AND LEAVE THIS WORLD BEHIND.
OUR WORK HERE IS **COMPLETE,** AFTER ALL.
AND THE EXTREMISTS WOULD NEVER BE THE SAME AS A RESULT. MUCH HAD BEEN LOST--INCLUDING OUR COMRADE **DIEHARD.**
YET PERHAPS NO LOSS WAS GREATER THAN MY FELLOW EXTREMISTS' **TRUST** IN ME. THEY WILL SAY I WAS COLD. THAT I CALLOUSLY SACRIFICED PIECES OF THEIR LIVES, ALL IN THE NAME OF DECEPTION. THAT I **LIED** TO THEM AS MUCH AS I DID OUR ENEMIES.
I CAN REFUTE **NONE** OF IT.
BUT SUCH MATTERS NEEDED TO BE TABLE UNTIL ANOTHER DAY. FOR MATTERS OF A MUCH MORE **PRESSING NATURE** AWAITED.
THE FULL SCOP OF MY PLAN WAS NOT YET COMPLET AND I WOULD REQUIRE THE COOPERATION O THE **EXTREMISTS** FULFILL ITS NEXT PHASE...

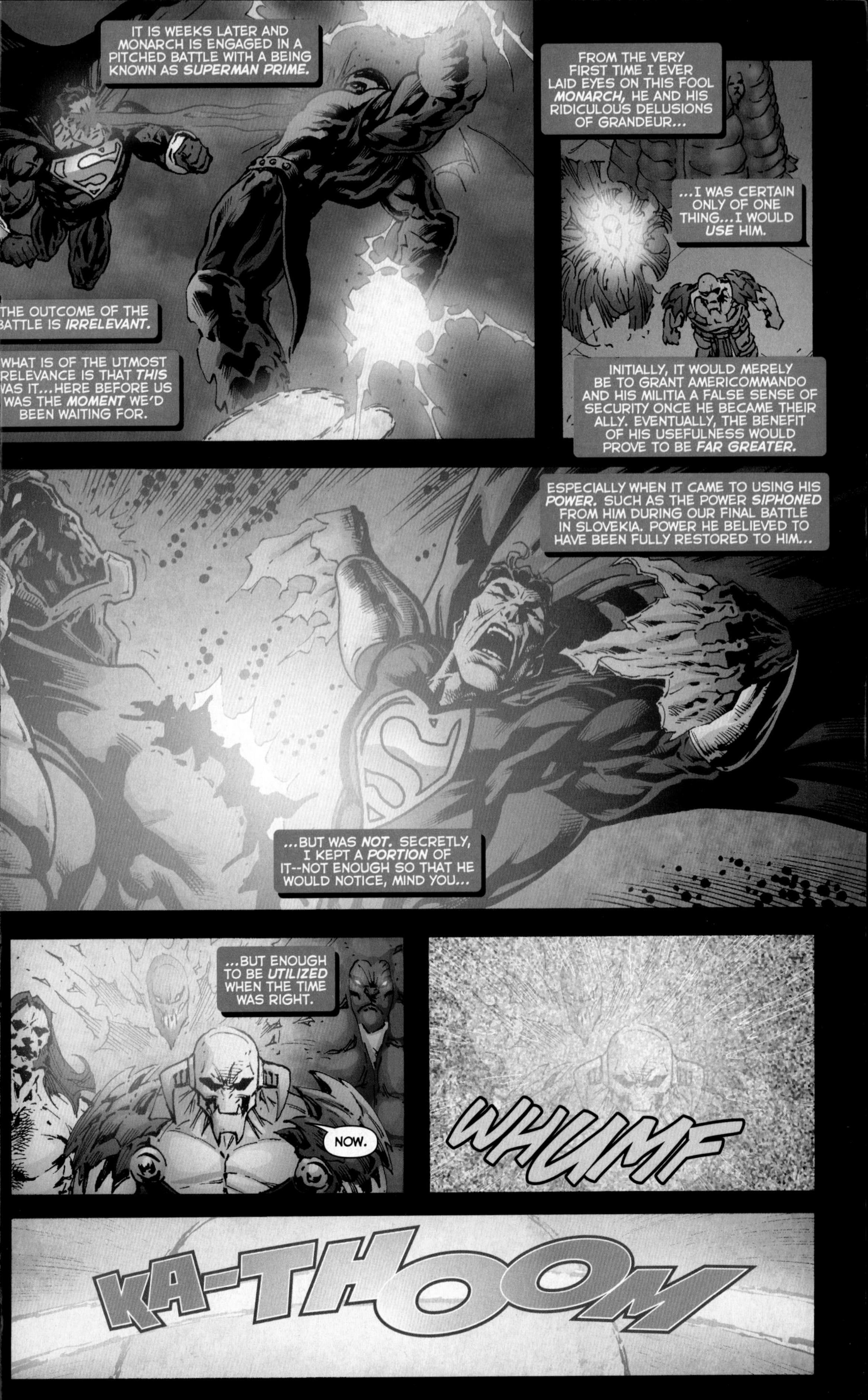

IT IS WEEKS LATER AND MONARCH IS ENGAGED IN A PITCHED BATTLE WITH A BEING KNOWN AS SUPERMAN PRIME.
THE OUTCOME OF THE BATTLE IS IRRELEVANT.
WHAT IS OF THE UTMOST RELEVANCE IS THAT THIS WAS IT...HERE BEFORE US WAS THE MOMENT WE'D BEEN WAITING FOR.
FROM THE VERY FIRST TIME I EVER LAID EYES ON THIS FOOL MONARCH, HE AND HIS RIDICULOUS DELUSIONS OF GRANDEUR...
...I WAS CERTAIN ONLY OF ONE THING...I WOULD USE HIM.
INITIALLY, IT WOULD MERELY BE TO GRANT AMERICOMMANDO AND HIS MILITIA A FALSE SENSE OF SECURITY ONCE HE BECAME THEIR ALLY. EVENTUALLY, THE BENEFIT OF HIS USEFULNESS WOULD PROVE TO BE FAR GREATER.
ESPECIALLY WHEN IT CAME TO USING HIS POWER. SUCH AS THE POWER SIPHONED FROM HIM DURING OUR FINAL BATTLE IN SLOVEKIA. POWER HE BELIEVED TO HAVE BEEN FULLY RESTORED TO HIM...
...BUT WAS NOT. SECRETLY, I KEPT A PORTION OF IT--NOT ENOUGH SO THAT HE WOULD NOTICE, MIND YOU...
...BUT ENOUGH TO BE UTILIZED WHEN THE TIME WAS RIGHT.
NOW.
WHUMF
KA-THOOM

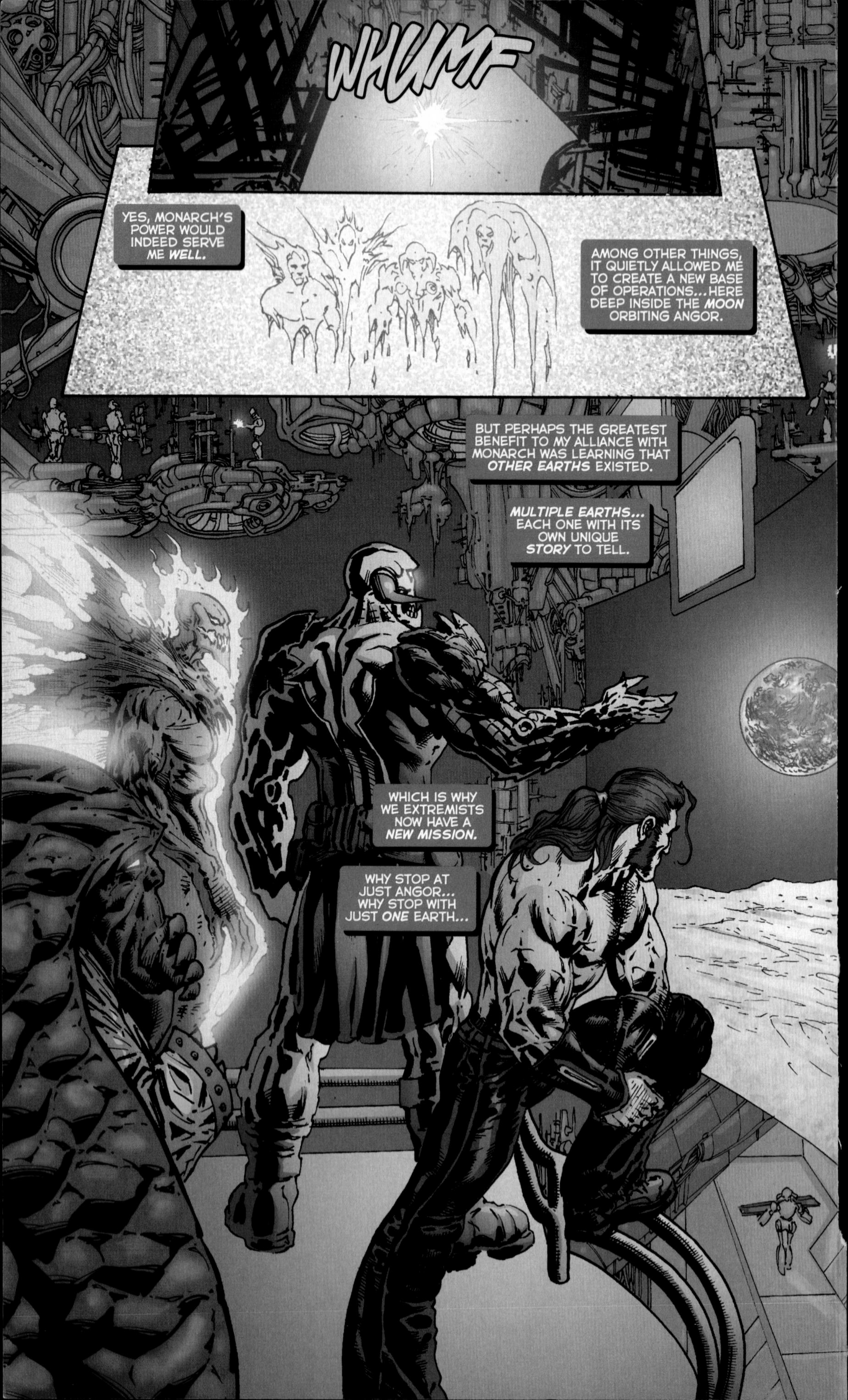
WHUMF
YES, MONARCH'S POWER WOULD INDEED SERVE ME WELL.
AMONG OTHER THINGS, IT QUIETLY ALLOWED ME TO CREATE A NEW BASE OF OPERATIONS...HERE DEEP INSIDE THE MOON ORBITING ANGOR.
BUT PERHAPS THE GREATEST BENEFIT TO MY ALLIANCE WITH MONARCH WAS LEARNING THAT OTHER EARTHS EXISTED.
MULTIPLE EARTHS... EACH ONE WITH ITS OWN UNIQUE STORY TO TELL.
WHICH IS WHY WE EXTREMISTS NOW HAVE A NEW MISSION.
WHY STOP AT JUST ANGOR... WHY STOP WITH JUST ONE EARTH...

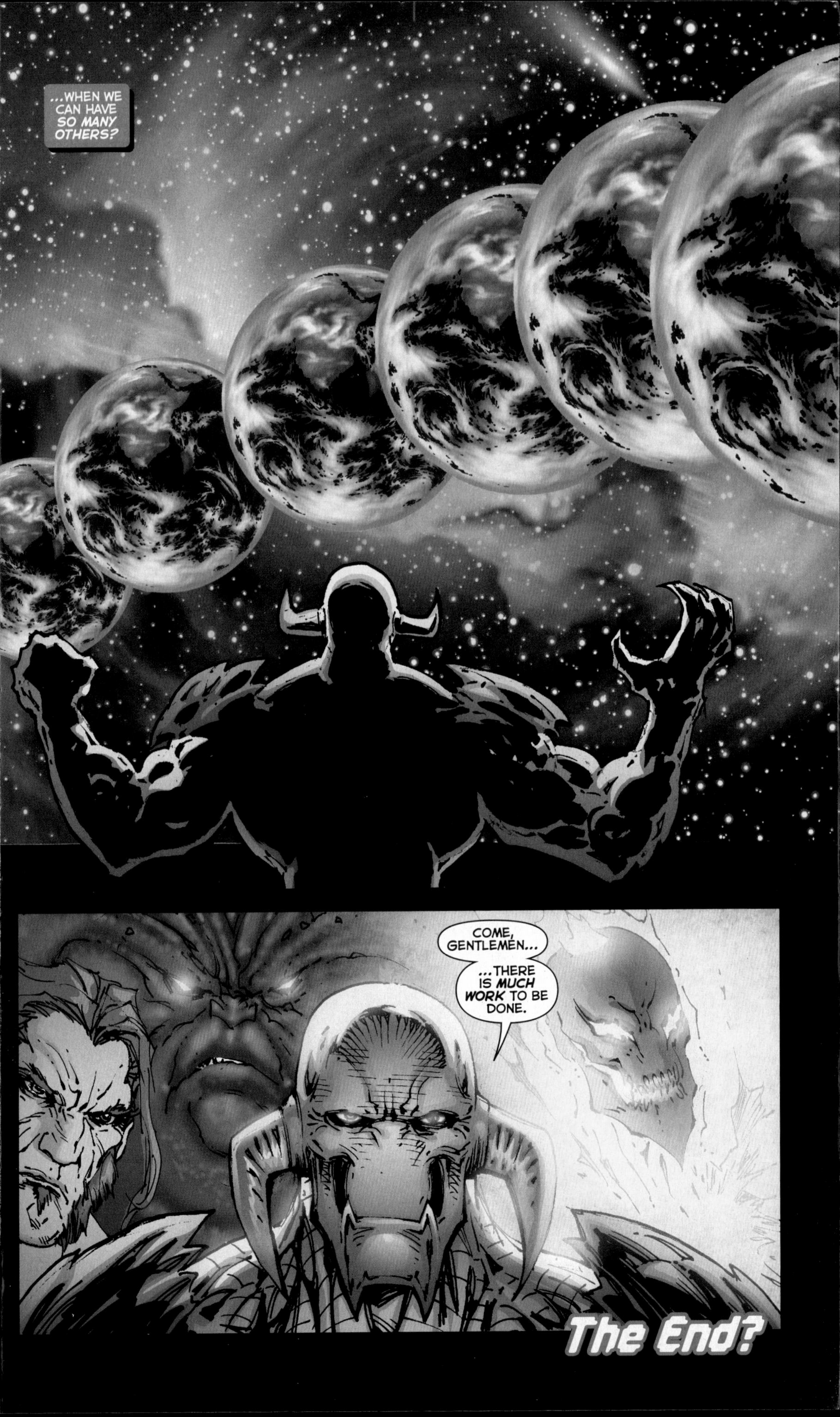
...WHEN WE CAN HAVE SO MANY OTHERS?
COME, GENTLEMEN...
...THERE IS MUCH WORK TO BE DONE.
The End?

READ MORE ADVENTURES OF YOUR FAVORITE HEROES IN THESE COLLECTIONS FROM DC COMICS:

KINGDOM COME

THE GREATEST SUPER-HERO EPIC OF TOMORROW!
KINGDOM COME
Mark WAID Alex ROSS

Mark Waid and **Alex Ross** deliver a grim tale of youth versus experience, tradition versus change and what defines a hero. KINGDOM COME is a riveting story pitting the old guard — Superman, Batman, Wonder Woman and their peers — against a new uncompromising generation.

WINNER OF FIVE EISNER AND HARVEY AWARDS, INCLUDING BEST LIMITED SERIES AND BEST ARTIST

IDENTITY CRISIS

NEW YORK TIMES BEST-SELLING AUTHOR OF THE ZERO GAME
BRAD MELTZER
RAGS MORALES MICHAEL BAIR
IDENTITY CRISIS
Introduction by JOSS WHEDON, creator of BUFFY THE VAMPIRE SLAYER and FIREFLY
"The IDENTITY CRISIS mystery involves the biggest DC heroes... and uses all of Mr. Meltzer's skills as a thriller novelist." — The New York Times

BRAD MELTZER
RAGS MORALES
MICHAEL BAIR

CRISIS ON INFINITE EARTHS

CRISIS ON INFINITE EARTHS
MARV WOLFMAN & GEORGE PÉREZ

MARV WOLFMAN
GEORGE PÉREZ

DC: THE NEW FRONTIER VOLUME 1

DC: The New Frontier
VOLUME ONE
BY DARWYN COOKE WITH DAVE STEWART

DARWYN COOKE
DAVE STEWART

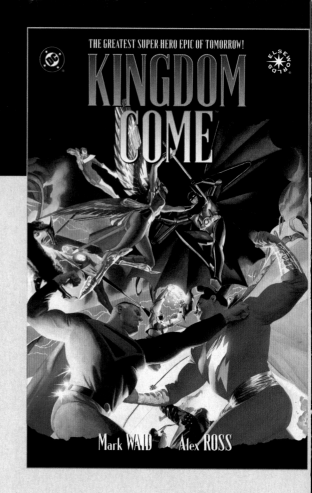

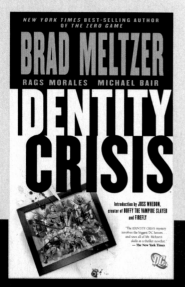

DON'T MISS THESE OTHER GREAT TITLES FROM AROUND THE DCU!

SUPERMAN:
BIRTHRIGHT

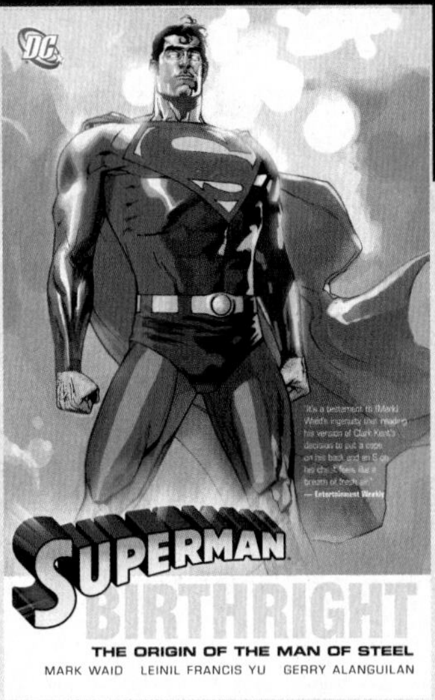
SUPERMAN
BIRTHRIGHT
THE ORIGIN OF THE MAN OF STEEL
MARK WAID LEINIL FRANCIS YU GERRY ALANGUILAN

MARK WAID
LEINIL FRANCIS YU
GERRY ALANGUILAN

BATMAN:
DARK VICTORY

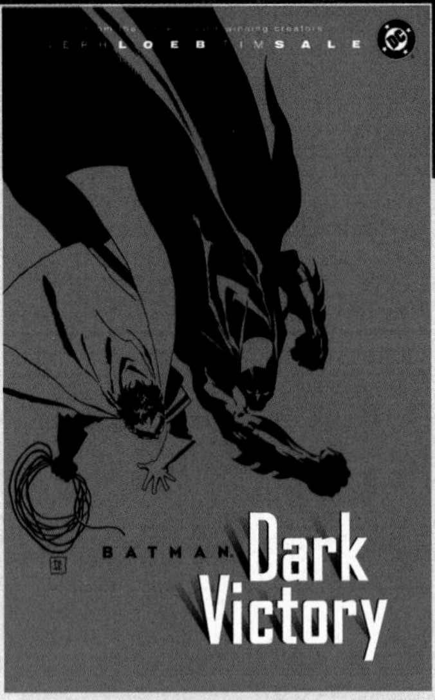
BATMAN
Dark
Victory

JEPH LOEB
TIM SALE

WONDER WOMAN:
GODS AND MORTALS

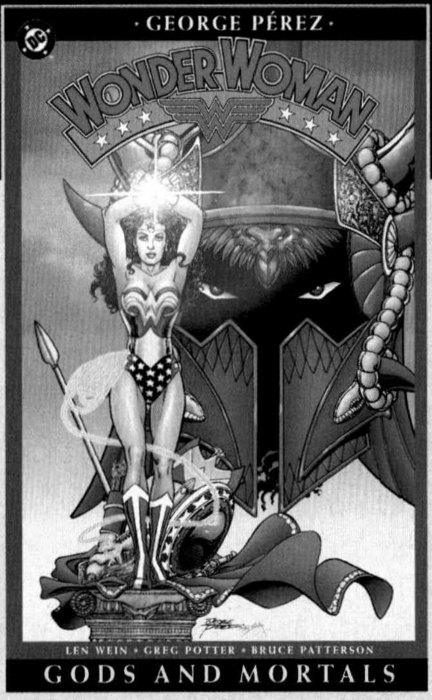
· GEORGE PÉREZ ·
WONDER WOMAN
LEN WEIN · GREG POTTER · BRUCE PATTERSON
GODS AND MORTALS

GEORGE PÉREZ
LEN WEIN/GREG POTTER
BRUCE PATTERSON

GREEN LANTERN:
NO FEAR

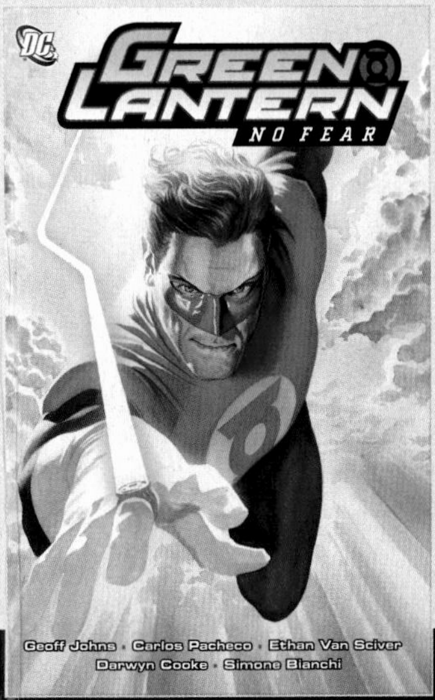
GREEN LANTERN
NO FEAR
Geoff Johns · Carlos Pacheco · Ethan Van Sciver
Darwyn Cooke · Simone Bianchi

GEOFF JOHNS
CARLOS PACHECO
ETHAN VAN SCIVER

GREEN ARROW:
QUIVER

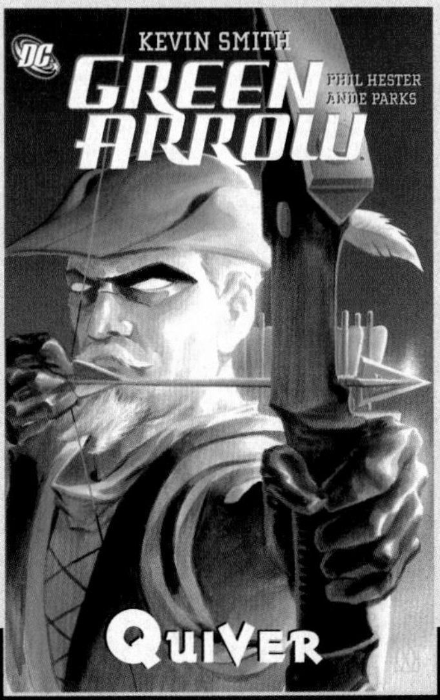
KEVIN SMITH
GREEN ARROW
PHIL HESTER
ANDE PARKS
QUIVER

KEVIN SMITH
PHIL HESTER
ANDE PARKS

TEEN TITANS:
A KID'S GAME

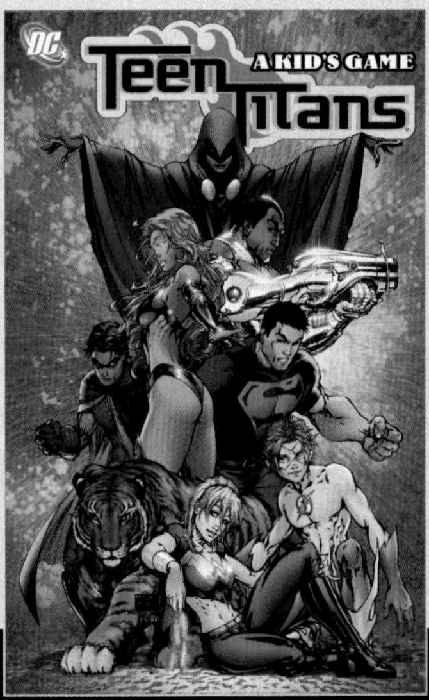
A KID'S GAME
Teen Titans

GEOFF JOHNS
MIKE McKONE

SEARCH THE GRAPHIC NOVELS SECTION OF
www.DCCOMICS.com
FOR ART AND INFORMATION ON ALL OF OUR BOOKS!

READ MORE EXPLOITS OF THE EMERALD WARRIOR
IN THESE COLLECTIONS FROM DC COMICS!

GREEN LANTERN

DC
GREEN LANTERN
REBIRTH
Introduction by Best-Selling Novelist and Author of Identity Crisis
BRAD MELTZER
MOOSE
Geoff Johns Ethan Van Sciver
Prentis Rollins

GREEN LANTERN: REBIRTH

He was the greatest Green Lantern of them all! Then Hal Jordan went mad and ultimately died in an attempt to redeem himself. But fate was not done with him.

Geoff Johns is joined by artists **Ethan Van Sciver** and **Prentis Rollins** in this epic story of a hero reborn!

GREEN LANTERN: EMERALD DAWN

DC
GREEN LANTERN
EMERALD DAWN

KEITH GIFFEN
GERARD JONES
M.D. BRIGHT

GREEN LANTERN: NO FEAR

DC
GREEN LANTERN
NO FEAR
Geoff Johns · Carlos Pacheco · Ethan Van Sciver
Darwyn Cooke · Simone Bianchi

GEOFF JOHNS
CARLOS PACHECO
ETHAN VAN SCIVER

GREEN LANTERN/ GREEN ARROW: VOLUME ONE

GREEN LANTERN GREEN ARROW volume one
DENNIS O'NEIL
NEAL ADAMS
DC

DENNIS O'NEIL
NEAL ADAMS

SEARCH THE GRAPHIC NOVELS SECTION OF
www.DCCOMICS.com

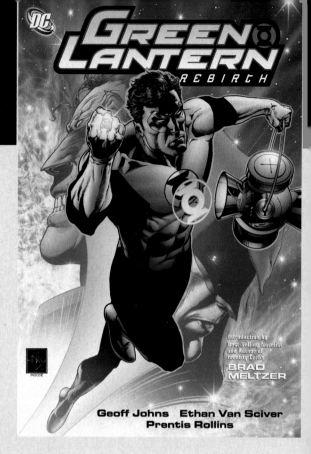